Dream! Hack! Build!

Unleash citizen-driven innovation with the power
of hackathons

Ann Molin

Love Dager | Mustafa Sherif

Carolina Emanuelson | Dr. Kristofer Vernmark

‹packt›

Dream! Hack! Build!

Group Product Manager: Aaron Tanna

Publishing Product Manager: Uzma Sheerin

Book Project Manager: Deeksha Thakkar

Senior Editor: Esha Banerjee

Copy Editor: Safis Editing

Indexer: Hemangini Bari

Production Designer: Vijay Kamble

DevRel Marketing Coordinator: Deepak Kumar and Mayank Singh

First published: April, 2024

Production reference: 2060524

Published by Packt Publishing Ltd.

Grosvenor House

11 St Paul's Square

Birmingham

B3 1RB, UK

ISBN 978-1-83508-533-2

www.packtpub.com

To my beloved mother Birgitta, whose courage taught me to live with conviction and who unwaveringly believed in my potential to achieve absolutely anything.

To my daughters Matilda and Lovisa, from whom I continue to learn the essence of genuine innovation and the immense joy of discovering uncharted territories in life.

To my esteemed co-authors, your commitment to excellence keeps fueling my inspiration to heights I never thought possible. This book would not be here without you.

– Ann Molin

Foreword

As the Executive Advisor to the CEO of Hitachi Energy and one of the recurring lecturers in the Build for Earth acceleration program on the topic of Business Planning, I am honored to introduce this remarkable book, *Dream! Hack! Build! – Unleash the Power of Citizen-Driven Innovation with Hackathons*. In today's rapidly evolving world, where the challenges we face are both complex and urgent, the role of innovation has never been more crucial. At Hitachi Energy, we recognize that addressing these challenges requires a next level of collaborative effort that harnesses the creativity and ingenuity of people from all walks of life around the globe.

The United Nations Sustainable Development Goals serve as the blueprint for a better and more sustainable future for all, and this is something we have taken to heart at Hitachi Energy. These goals provide an extensive framework for addressing pressing global issues such as climate change, poverty, and inequality. I believe it is our collective responsibility to work towards achieving these goals and securing a prosperous future for the generations to come.

One of the most pressing challenges we face today is the climate crisis. The need to transition to a low-carbon economy has never been more urgent, and the window of opportunity to take meaningful action is rapidly closing. However, addressing the climate crisis requires more than just technological innovation; it requires a fundamental shift, at a global level, in the way we think about and approach problem-solving.

This is where citizen-driven innovation comes in. Hackathons, with their collaborative and participatory nature, have emerged as powerful tools for driving innovation and solving complex problems. By leveraging the hackathon tool to a new standard with their unique methodology, the author Ann Molin and her co-authors Love Dager, Carolina Emanuelson, Mustafa Sherif, and Dr. Kristofer Vernmark, have managed to bring people from diverse backgrounds and skill sets together, to create solutions that we need for a better future. With the Dream! Hack! Build! method, hackathons enable us to tap into the collective intelligence of our communities and unleash the full potential of citizen-driven innovation.

This book is a testament to the power of citizen-driven innovation and the transformative impact it can have on our world. Through real-world examples and practical insights, the authors demonstrate how hackathons can be used to tackle some of the most pressing challenges facing society today and show you how you as a business leader can tap into this knowledge. From developing sustainable energy solutions to addressing social inequality, the possibilities are truly endless for the Hack for Earth approach to citizen-driven innovation.

Dream! Hack! Build! is an exceptionally inspiring and invaluable book, offering business leaders such as myself a firsthand glimpse into the transformative potential of hackathons and their profoundly positive impacts, spanning from large corporations to business professionals and representatives of broader society.

Ann Molin, alongside her esteemed co-authors Love Dager, Carolina Emanuelson, Mustafa Sherif, and Dr. Kristofer Vernmark, have skillfully woven together a systematic exploration of the unique methodology behind citizen-driven innovation through hackathons, complemented by vivid and illustrative examples. One such example is the monumental COP28 hackathon in Dubai, where over 1000 teams from 112 countries came together to engage in collaborative problem-solving.

Drawing from my extensive background in industry and global corporations and having had the privilege of participating in the Build for Earth acceleration program as a lecturer on business planning, I see immense potential for corporations, global companies, universities, schools, and various stakeholders to embrace the Dream! Hack! Build! methodology. This approach not only fosters impactful citizen-driven innovation but also provides crucial support towards achieving the United Nations' Sustainable Development Goals.

As we look to the future, it is clear that the path forward will not be easy, but rather full of obstacles. However, by harnessing the power of citizen-driven innovation, we can create a world that is more sustainable, equitable, and prosperous for all. I commend the authors for their dedication to this important cause and hope that their work will inspire others to join us in the journey towards a brighter future for humanity and the planet we call home.

This book is not only a must-read for innovators but also for visionary business leaders, CEOs, and C-level executives who aspire to be changemakers in their industries.

Sincerely,

Johan Söderström

Executive Advisor to the CEO, Hitachi Energy

Contributors

About the authors

Ann Molin

Ann is a trailblazer in global hackathons and citizen-driven innovation, celebrated for fostering sustainable solutions. Her work as an international speaker and recognized expert in innovation has graced platforms like the UN General Assembly and TEDx Stockholm. The unique Dream! Hack! Build! methodology is unmatched worldwide, and the recent Hack for Earth event at COP28 in Dubai – with 1000+ teams and 112 countries – highlights her capacity to unite diverse minds for change. As the founder of the Hack for Earth Foundation and co-founder of Hack for Earth AB, she channels her background as a psychologist into innovation and global sustainable development.

I want to thank the team at Packt Publishing for your dedicated support throughout this journey, especially Esha Banerjee and Uzma Sherin.

Love Dager

Love Dager is a serial entrepreneur, hackathon expert, and co-founder of Hack for Earth AB. Known for his outstanding achievements in creating tech communities, fostering innovation and impact, Love is well-versed with the tech industry and has worked for Norrsken, Microsoft and Hack for Earth. Pioneering the hackathon method for the government mission Hack for Sweden in 2019, Love adapted this previously tech-based format to tackle society's greatest challenges, laying the foundation to what would evolve into Hack for Earth and the Dream! Hack! Build! method. Back in his home country of Sweden he runs Stockholm Fintech, the nation's largest community within fintech, and invests in early-stage startups on the side. Love's passions are tech and empowering youth to become entrepreneurs.

Mustafa Sherif

Mustafa Sherif is an urban planner from Baghdad, and he now resides in Sweden. He is renowned for his people-focused city designs. Educated in Stockholm and Milan, his global insights drive his commitment to community-involved urban development. At Hack for Earth, as Community Manager, Sherif channels his passion for community and citizen-driven innovation into international hackathons. Additionally, Sherif's Urbanistica Podcast reaches over 140 countries globally. The podcast has become a vital platform for urban dialogue, emphasizing human-centric city planning. His multifaceted contributions underscore his influence in shaping the future of urban spaces globally.

Carolina Emanuelson

Carolina Emanuelson stands out as a dynamic force in talent management, notably shaping the future of Hack for Earth as Partner Manager with her innovative approach to partner community development and value-driven partner packages. Now at Apoteket AB, she leads Talent Acquisition and Employer Branding, masterfully steering strategies to attract top-notch candidates, fulfilling hiring needs, and propelling business growth. Her impressive career spans key roles, including at the Swedish Public Employment Service as Talent Manager in IT and Talent Acquisition and Employer Branding Lead GOALS. Carolina's expertise in enhancing employer branding and optimizing talent acquisition processes marks her as an influential figure in driving organizational success, underscoring her profound impact across various sectors.

Dr. Kristofer Vernmark

Kristofer Vernmark (PhD, MSc) is a researcher at Linköping University and the creator of the Build for Earth program. With 17 years of experience as a psychologist, manager, consultant, author, and researcher in digital mental health, Kristofer is a pioneer in integrating internet-based treatments into Swedish primary care. His efforts were recognized with the 2022 eMHIC award for Leadership in eMental Health Implementation. At the Hack for Earth Foundation, he guides global teams to develop sustainable solutions, showcasing his commitment to enhancing mental health care and promoting sustainability.

About the reviewer

Olle Lundin has a demonstrated history of working in the staffing and recruiting industry. He graduated from Linköping University and his career ranges from leading roles in IT companies to senior positions in governmental agencies. His leadership style combines his expertise in both business development and project management, enabling him to effectively drive success and achieve desired outcomes.. He is currently working as a social entrepreneur and founder of Swedish JobTech.

He can be reached at `olle.l.lundin@gmail.com`

Table of Contents

Part 2: Introduction to How to Hack

5

How to Organize an Impactful Hackathon   61

6

Communication and Managing Hacker Teams and Mentors   81

7

Partnerships for Success   109

8

External Communication and Social Media Presence for Hackathon Success   133

Part 3: Introduction to How to Build

9

Taking Citizen-Driven Innovation to the Next Level   157

10

Converting Hackathon Results into Real Tools   173

11

Build for Earth Learnings – How to Make a Startup a Success Fast   197

Preface

What are you curious about?

Right now, I'm hoping you are curious about the content of this book – hackathons and how to create citizen-driven innovation. Furthermore, I hope you will let this book spark your curiosity to explore the possibilities of what you and your organization can do with the *Dream! Hack! Build!* method, and I hope that your curiosity is rooted in what your organization can accomplish and ultimately what impact it can have in the world. The book you are holding in your hand you see, is a guide to becoming a changemaker for the future.

Personally, I have found curiosity to be the number one most important driver for change and development for me no matter the context, in hackathons, and beyond – I would actually go so far as to call curiosity the driver for life itself. I have always been curious. I always wanted to do more, know more, be more, and explore the boundaries of what is possible. The human mind and the communication between us humans is what I have been most curious about during my life, and I still am today. Before we dive into hackathons and citizen-driven innovation, let me take you on a journey to set the stage for why this book is here, and how it is intrinsically joined with the concept of curiosity.

Apart from curiosity, communication intrigued me early on. My first memory of a dream job at the age of four was to be a mailman – I wanted to be the bringer of letters from people to other people, to be the one who delivered the connection between people across the distances in the world. As a little girl, I thought that being a mailman must be the best and most satisfying job in the world, what could be better and feel more purposeful than being the connector between people? Somehow, I think the invoices and bills that came through the mail were not a phenomenon that I, at age four, was aware of yet – to me all letters were good letters.

I didn't become a mailman in my career, but the work I do today as Secretary General and CEO of *Hack for Earth Foundation* is grounded in the same desire that I had at four years old to bring people together – to connect people from across continents, bridging differences in nationalities, age, competence, careers, professions, social background, gender, and more aspects. I do it with the hackathon as a universal tool for creating understanding, building trust, and sparking curiosity – that in turn can lead to real innovation for a better future for us all.

My curiosity for the human mind brought me to study psychology for six years to become a clinical psychologist, and for almost 10 years after that, I had the privilege of working with people who sought help in clinical psychiatry. This extensive experience of psychotherapy, psychological assessment, psychological testing, and psychiatric diagnosis gave me invaluable knowledge of the human mind, and I am forever grateful to the hundreds of patients who trusted me enough to share their life stories with me. I loved my work, but I was not meant to stay in clinical psychiatry it turned out. After a few years working at the local Swedish Public Employment Service in Bromölla in the south of Sweden, I found myself at the Head Office of the Swedish Public Employment Service in Stockholm in 2017.

Here is where there was a sudden plot twist that incidentally brought me, a psychologist, to the hackathon world – a world that is very far from the known waters of psychology. A plot twist is often sudden and unexpected, and this one definitely was that!

Participating in my first hackathon ever, an in-person hackathon event organized by the Digital Innovation Center at the Swedish Public Employment Service at their Head Office in Stockholm in the spring of 2017, I was completely and utterly smitten with the hackathon as a phenomenon. I fell in love with the openness to new ideas, the fast innovation process, the excitement in the air, the connecting and learning with new people with different backgrounds than mine, and the dedicated focus on action – and all of it taking place in an arena that breathed inclusivity, participation, equality, and curiosity in each and every one of its molecules. It was heaven.

I had found my place in the world, and I had to try to get a job working with hackathons! Keep in mind this was the Digital Innovation Center at a public government agency and I was a psychologist working at a completely different department at the time – I did not fit the profile at all. To make quite a long story short – I did apply for a job there and instead of laughing at my lack of competence within digitalization, the manager asked me what I could do, seeing my background as a psychologist as a potential asset and not a liability. He was curious to see what I could do. This taught me to always look to hire people with the right attitude, engagement, and personality traits (including curiosity of course), not the perfect curriculum vitae or formal education background. The effects of hiring the not obvious choice can be hard to foresee, but if you are curious, you will do it. As it turns out, it's all about people, and with the right people anything is possible.

I was appointed Head Project Manager of the Government mission, **Hack for Sweden**, and the rest is as they say history. The synergy effects of my, in this context, odd perspective as a psychologist paired with the Hack for Sweden mission and team members, was evident. Exploring the hackathon method together with my team members during the Hack for Sweden years was a time of fast expansion and learning from trial and error. As we together created a space where exploration of the method was fun and playful, finding the blueprint to Dream! Hack! Build! was still a serious undertaking with an important grander purpose of making an impact on our future.

Hack for Sweden grew into a movement for citizen-driven innovation in less than two years. We crafted the Dream! Hack! Build method as we went along, and it was time to go global. I founded the Hack for Earth Foundation in 2021, and we organized our first global *Hack for Earth* hackathon in the fall of 2021. The first batch of winners entered the newly created Build for Earth acceleration program in early 2022, and we are publishing this first book on the method in 2024.

After my many years of service as an employee in a large public organization, I have learned too well that it was often difficult to take action for several reasons – something that is a reality in many large organizations, maybe yours as well. This is where I find the hackathon method to be like a breath of fresh air and extremely effective: the participants in a hackathon are forced to take action, and in a fun exercise, in merely hours or a few days, tangible results are born. The possibilities seem endless to take the hackathon method into new areas of business, to innovate, bring people together, and more importantly to create a movement and platform where people can take action. This is only the beginning.

So, there you have it: The story of how the Dream! Hack! Build! method was born, and in this book, we will walk you through how you can employ this game-changer in innovation for the benefit of your organization. I'm curious to see where this journey takes us from here, and even more curious to see where it takes you and your organization!

Figure P.1 – The author and the co-authors of this book; from left: Mustafa Sherif, Ann Molin, Love Dager, Carolina Emanuelson, and Dr. Kristofer Vernmark

Who this book is for

This book is for visionary business leaders, C-level executives primarily, who have an ambition to make their organization trailblazers in their field of business, by leading the way as changemakers of the future.

What this book covers

Chapter 1, Redefining the Hackathon Tool, gives you an introduction to what a hackathon is, explores different types of hackathons, and shows you how the hackathon tool can be used to create citizen-driven innovation.

Chapter 2, Making Citizen-Driven Innovation Work for You, explores the concept of citizen-driven innovation and how you can employ it to drive innovation in your organization, turning your challenges into assets and creating the valuable solutions you need to grow your company.

Chapter 3, The Dream! Hack! Build! Method, walks you through an overview of the three pivotal parts of Dream! Hack! and Build! and teaches you how, together, they can create innovative solutions for impact, and how they are intrinsically dependent on each other in a systematic way.

Chapter 4, Creating the Perfect Challenge for Your Hackathon, introduces our systematic way to create the perfect challenges for your hackathon while engaging your audience at the same time. This chapter will enable you to learn the important steps in the Dream! Phase.

Chapter 5, How to Organize an Impactful Hackathon, teaches you the essential parts of organizing a hackathon that serves your purpose, introducing all the important factors, from which platforms to use to how to set up jury criteria and jury work.

Chapter 6, Communication and Managing Hacker Teams and Mentors, focuses on giving you a roadmap to navigating primarily the internal communication channels during the hackathon, and how to create and manage hacker teams throughout the process.

Chapter 7, Partnerships for Success, explores the important factors for signing, creating, and maintaining solid partnerships with relevant stakeholders. This chapter will also guide you on how to sustain a vibrant partner community to deliver value throughout your hackathon journey.

Chapter 8, External Communication and Social Media Presence for Hackathon Success, teaches you how to manage external communication to drive your hackathon, throughout the Dream! Hack! Build! Process, building traction on social media and using your hackathon community to build your brand and more.

Chapter 9, Taking Citizen-Driven Innovation to the Next Level, introduces the idea behind the Build phase, and explains why it is imperative to organize an acceleration program to take care of your winning solutions.

Chapter 10, Converting Hackathon Results into Real Tools, is where the creator of the Build for Earth acceleration program will walk you through the science behind the Build for Earth acceleration program, what results to expect, and you will learn what steps to take in order to create your own acceleration program.

Chapter 11, Build for Earth Learnings – How to Make a Startup a Success Fast, is the final chapter where we share our learnings of hackathon winners we have supported and that are on the market today, and you will learn what important factors to look out for when making a hackathon winner a reality.

There is a *Glossary* and the *Appendices* at the end of this book.

To get the most out of this book

To get the most out of this book, we recommend that you read it in chronological order since the chapters all build upon each other.

Be sure to look up any words, concepts, or phenomena mentioned and highlighted in the Glossary and the Appendices. The Glossary lists a number of words and concepts that you need to be familiar with when reading this book.

In Appendices A and B, there are descriptions of important events and organizations which you also need to be familiar with.

Whether you choose to look through the Glossary and the Appendices before reading the book, or if you choose to look up necessary words or concepts as you read, is a matter of personal preference.

There are also links to relevant material online, which will give you a more illustrative understanding of the book, so feel free to look this up.

Conventions used

There are a number of text conventions used throughout this book.

Bold: Indicates a new term, an important word, or words that you see onscreen. For instance, words in menus or dialog boxes appear in **bold**. Here is an example: "To further contextualize the importance of sustainability in today's corporate landscape, we will explore the 17 **Sustainable Development Goals (SDGs)** established by the United Nations."

> **Tips or important notes**
> Appear like this.

Get in touch

Feedback from our readers is always welcome.

General feedback: If you have questions about any aspect of this book, email us at customercare@packtpub.com and mention the book title in the subject of your message.

Errata: Although we have taken every care to ensure the accuracy of our content, mistakes do happen. If you have found a mistake in this book, we would be grateful if you would report this to us. Please visit www.packtpub.com/support/errata and fill in the form.

Piracy: If you come across any illegal copies of our works in any form on the internet, we would be grateful if you would provide us with the location address or website name. Please contact us at copyright@packt.com with a link to the material.

If you are interested in becoming an author: If there is a topic that you have expertise in and you are interested in either writing or contributing to a book, please visit authors.packtpub.com.

Share Your Thoughts

Once you've read *Dream! Hack! Build!*, we'd love to hear your thoughts! Scan the QR code below to go straight to the Amazon review page for this book and share your feedback.

https://packt.link/r/1-835-08533-4

Your review is important to us and the tech community and will help us make sure we're delivering excellent quality content.

Download a free PDF copy of this book

Thanks for purchasing this book!

Do you like to read on the go but are unable to carry your print books everywhere?

Is your eBook purchase not compatible with the device of your choice?

Don't worry, now with every Packt book you get a DRM-free PDF version of that book at no cost.

Read anywhere, any place, on any device. Search, copy, and paste code from your favorite technical books directly into your application.

The perks don't stop there, you can get exclusive access to discounts, newsletters, and great free content in your inbox daily

Follow these simple steps to get the benefits:

1. Scan the QR code or visit the link below

https://packt.link/free-ebook/9781835085332

2. Submit your proof of purchase
3. That's it! We'll send your free PDF and other benefits to your email directly

Part 1: Why We Hack

Part 1 delves into the reasons hackathons have become a powerful method for fostering innovation in the world of modern business. It guides you through our reinvented approach to utilizing hackathons for meaningful impact, detailing the vision and objectives of citizen-driven innovation. You will learn what outcomes you can expect from using the *Dream! Hack! Build!* Method to address your specific challenges, and how to use a hackathon strategically to build your business and your company brand. You'll explore how the three distinct phases – Dream, Hack, and Build – can be implemented to generate significant synergistic and impactful effects. Additionally, this section highlights the crucial role of core values and a massive transformative purpose, demonstrating how a hackathon can effectively display these concepts and align them with your target audience.

This section has the following chapters:

- *Chapter 1, Redefining the Hackathon Tool*
- *Chapter 2, Making Citizen-driven Innovation Work for You*
- *Chapter 3, The Dream! Hack! Build! Method*

Redefining the Hackathon Tool

In this chapter, we will cover the background to the birth of **citizen-driven innovation**, and in detail, discuss how it can reinvent the hackathon tool. The **hackathon** as a phenomenon within the tech world is not new, so how can this innovation competition have an **impact** in this new context? We will discuss different types of hackathons and how they can serve different purposes and goals you may have for your organization.

The reason this book is here all starts with an odd requirement for a government mission in Sweden back in 2018. An out-of-the-box thinker at the Swedish Public Employment Service decided to hire not the obvious choice. The obvious choice for the role would have been a tech person or a professional project manager – instead, he took a chance on a psychologist at the Swedish Public Employment Service who had expressed a desire to work with digital innovation. This turned out in a completely different way than expected – the psychologist's perspective on innovation, hackathons, and project management added a new flavor that brought about the redefinition of the hackathon tool and the birth of citizen-driven innovation as a concept with the use of hackathons.

From the **Hack for Sweden:** government mission to the *Hack for Earth Foundation*, in just a few years, the concept of citizen-driven innovation with hackathons has taken the world by storm, and the results have been presented at the **United Nations General Assembly** (**UNGA**) in NYC and at TEDxStockholm. Global hackathons in recent times tend to deliver real results. In the past few years, they have been consistently showcasing that real action is possible. In this book, we will show you how we did it and take you with us on the journey from the Government Agency of Employment in Sweden to the global arena of UN **Conference of the Parties** (**COP**) meetings and world exhibitions. We will share our insights and learnings of how we created and built the *Dream! Hack! Build!* **method** and teach you how you can tap into its power to make citizen-driven innovation work for you and your organization.

In this chapter, we will look into the following topics:

- Driving impact through hackathons
- Exploring the types of hackathons
- Understanding the scope of open data in hackathons
- Core values driving the movement

Now that we have set the stage, let's dive into how the hackathon tool can take impact to a new level.

Driving impact through hackathons

A hackathon is a competition in innovation, often organized during a short period of time. A common timeframe is 24-48 hours, and traditionally, this timeframe is set during a weekend so that the participants can devote their time completely to the task at hand. The powerful force of the hackathon setup is that it provides people the possibility to come together to create solutions to difficult problems in a short timeframe, giving them both hope that it's possible to do something about a seemingly very complex problem and the experience that you can accomplish things faster than you would think. Another important aspect is that people are working in teams, and this amplifies the notion that collaboration is the key to success. Connecting minds to create solutions has been a successful way of dealing with complex problems for the human race since the dawn of time.

In large organizations, as well as in society, there is a need for smooth collaboration between departments and people in order to deliver on set goals. This need often collides with the fact that we as humans have a limited amount of relationships that we can handle at a time. As humans, we have an innate limitation in handling relationships, which in reality means that we create subgroups if the organization is too large for us to handle. You cannot handle the same level of relationship with hundreds of people, and therefore we create subgroups of people who cooperate and relate to each other. The downside to this is that the subgroups' need for internal bonding means shutting the door to some extent to relationships outside of the subgroup. How much the door is open depends on the maturity of the group and its overall functioning. High-functioning subgroups, the simple definition being that they deliver on their tasks at hand in a productive way, have a higher level of collaborative relationships with other subgroups.

In short, this means that all groups, formal and nonformal, in society and in organizations need to actively work on collaborating better in order for the overall functioning to excel. This is the basic reason there are conferences and meetings of all kinds: to bridge boundaries between subgroups in organizations and society and provide a platform for them to collaborate and work on the relationships between subgroups. This is where citizen-driven innovation using the hackathon tool is an effective and fast way of making subgroups collaborate effectively by making people from different subgroups work together on commonly perceived **challenges**, thereby building trust and enhancing collaboration and relationships throughout the hackathon. The experience from the hackathon will produce new connections that can serve as a foundation for further collaboration afterward.

This means that the outcome of the hackathon is twofold: you will have real solutions to the challenges you face (that is, the results of the hackathon in the shape of solutions created by the teams), and your organization will be better equipped for collaboration and effective relationships between subgroups. A hackathon makes people collaborate on a common challenge, and this is the key to its power. Collaborating on a common challenge builds trust and relationships on a deeper level than simply talking to others at a conference or during a meeting. If you are to solve a common challenge together, you will inevitably need to get your hands dirty, so to speak. The trust built can be transferred to other areas of collaboration after the hackathon, and one way of ensuring this is to follow up the results of the hackathon with an acceleration program for the solutions.

> **Note**
>
> To summarize, citizen-driven innovation with hackathons is a tool for impact not only on objective challenges perceived but also addresses other non-apparent challenges all large organizations have to work at: making collaboration between groups effective and making the organization run smoothly so that it can better serve its purpose.

Exploring the types of hackathons

Hackathons come in many shapes and forms, and they can be used to accomplish many different things depending on the context, size, content, and desired outcome. In this chapter, we will go through different types of hackathons and learn about their advantages and which usage is best for particular settings and goals.

Traditional hackathon versus non-traditional hackathon

The traditional hackathon format comes from the tech world, where hackathons have been organized since the beginning of 2000 in big tech companies. The word **hackathon** comes from "hack" and "marathon," where the idea is to hack a predefined challenge (problem) in teams and let a jury decide the winner. The common timeframe is 24-48 hours, and often it takes place in person during a weekend. After forming teams, the opening ceremony declares the hackathon open, and the hacking – that is, the work – begins. The resources provided for the hacker teams during the hackathon include **mentors** in relevant fields of expertise, open data sources including **APIs,** workshops, and lectures on relevant topics. Most often, many teams stay up around the clock working on their solution to make it the best possible before the deadline for submissions. When the submission deadline is closed, the jury's work begins, and the hacker teams get to rest a little while before the winners are announced by the jury. This is often done in a prize ceremony on stage, where the **jury members** read the motivation for the winner before announcing who they are – a lot like any gala event with prizes bestowed on winners.

The traditional hackathon has three issues that need to be addressed: the selection of hackers as participants, the formulation of challenges, and what happens after the hackathon with the winning solutions.

Let's look into how a traditional hackathon works:

- First of all, the participant hackers joining traditional hackathons often have similar backgrounds and profiles: they are primarily in the tech business, between the ages of 20-30, caucasian, and most often also male. The problem with this very homogenous group in this context is that science proves that solutions and ideas with high innovation qualities are born out of diversity.

- Second, careful and meticulous formulation of challenges is key to getting the results you are looking for in a hackathon. The types of challenges introduced will determine the quality of the solutions. In a traditional hackathon, challenges are decided by the organizers themselves who perceive the problem from their perspective, and most often the challenges are not given the time, effort, and level of engagement that they deserve. A hackathon is no better than its best challenge, meaning that the quality of challenges will determine the outcome of the solutions to a great extent.

- Third of all, the traditional hackathon ends after the prize ceremony, and in that manner, you have the same issue as with any traditional workshop setting: the work accomplished during the hackathon is not taken to the next step, given the possibility to materialize into tangible tools that make a real difference.

These three issues will be discussed further in this chapter, under the *Core values driving the movement* heading.

The traditional hackathon has a great many advantages too and can create new innovative tech solutions based on new combinations of datasets and APIs in a short timeframe.

An example of a traditional hackathon

A good example of a traditional hackathon is Hack for Sweden 2018, an in-person hackathon with 220 hackers taking place at a venue in Stockholm, Sweden for 48 hours during a weekend in April. The solutions had to be built on data, provided by the 29 Swedish government agencies that were partners in the *Hack for Sweden* community. The participant hackers were tech people, and most of them were students. Challenges were formulated in collaboration with government agencies who provided the data, which made them to a large extent a reflection of the government agencies' own internal challenges. The challenges in *Hack for Sweden 2018* revolved around societal issues such as climate compensation strategies, labor market functioning, especially for immigrants, and biodiversity. The winning solutions were selected by a jury with tech skills, and after the hackathon prize ceremony, the hackathon was over. The winners in the six categories had a wide variety, from the Biologg team (https://www.biologg.se/) using data provided by citizens to preserve biodiversity in nature to a backup system for the internet to be used in a crisis situation. Definitely, this type of hackathon has value in that it can create relevant tech solutions in a short period of time, but it also struggles with a few built-in problems in the setup.

The challenges are key to a successful hackathon in the sense that they will to a large extent determine the outcome of the solutions and their level of innovation. That is why challenges can benefit from being created in collaboration with a larger audience to make them more relevant to more people and more well-rounded. The homogenous group of participant hackers ensures very highly technically advanced solutions, but without the input of other skills in business, creative arts, communication, **storytelling**, or expertise in the specific topic at hand, the solutions have a lesser chance of reaching a high or very high level of innovation. Lastly, the lack of an **acceleration program** or other form of caretaking of solutions after the hackathon has ended makes it highly probable that new solutions will stay on paper. The hackathon might have been a fun weekend but with little or no real impact afterward.

In a non-traditional hackathon, the impactful way of using the hackathon tool from a wider perspective takes into consideration the work to be done before the hackathon starts and the work that continues after. To harness the power of citizen-driven innovation, there are a lot of careful preparations before the actual hackathon starts that involve communicating your vision of the outcome, engaging the participants and potential partners, creating diverse teams with relevant skill sets, and creating challenges that will deliver the right outcome for you. You must also plan from the beginning on how to take care of winning solutions so that they are given the best possible conditions to become a reality after the hackathon has ended.

A good example of a traditional hackathon is the Hack for Sweden 2018 in-person hackathon, which took place at Norrsken House in Stockholm in April 2018. The following image is a picture of one of the winning teams on stage during the prize ceremony.

Figure 1.1 The prize ceremony of Hack for Sweden 2018

The image here shows the winners of the Hack for Sweden Cup, Team Match Yourself, receiving a prize sum of 40.000SEK and praise from the audience. The winners are being cheered on by jury member Susanne Fuglesang, far left, and moderator Elsa Landberg, far right.

An example of a non-traditional hackathon

An example of a non-traditional hackathon is Hack for Earth at the world exhibition **Expo 2020**. Challenges were carefully created over 6 months in the **Dream for Earth** campaign, involving partner organizations and citizens from 121 countries. This way, the challenges had a firm foundation in relevant and accurate real-life problems, and the participants of the hackathon were already invested in the hackathon when it began and felt ownership of the challenges. This ensured that they were committed to doing their best and allocated enough time to deliver on the hackathon. The **Dream for Earth** campaign was also created to attract a different set of participants to the hacker teams, with a wider set of competencies, skills, and experiences than a traditional hackathon attracts. To share your dream for Earth is a task anyone can do, not only tech-savvy people, and this also attracted participants with the right **sustainability** profile that we were looking for. The *Dream for Earth* campaign was a communication strategy to lower the bar for participation in a hackathon for people with other skill sets than technical and throw a wider net to engage people with a relevant but different set of competence than tech.

The *Hack for Earth* at Expo 2020 hackathon was also non-traditional in the sense that it entailed a 6-month online acceleration program for the winning solutions that started right after the hackathon ended – the **Build for Earth** program. Build for Earth was created to support the winning solutions to come to life, either as start-ups or through the support of one or more of the **partner organizations** (government agencies or companies). This ensured that the winning solutions were given the best possible conditions to evolve into working tools addressing challenges in the hackathon.

To summarize, there are benefits to both the traditional and the non-traditional hackathon setup. The traditional setup can certainly deliver on many goals set, but it has limited scope and impact. The non-traditional setup of a hackathon is a more complex endeavor, but in return, your outcome will deliver a wider set of goals with a greater innovation height.

Internal versus external hackathon

Whether you are organizing a traditional or non-traditional hackathon, you also have the choice to organize it within your organization or in collaboration with external customers, partners, and citizens.

The purpose and outcome of an internal hackathon will be different from an external hackathon in the sense that you will own the solutions of an internal hackathon and can then freely decide what to do with them afterward. You can exercise control to a larger extent over challenges, participants, and outcomes with an internal hackathon. The benefit of an internal hackathon includes encouraging cross-department collaboration, which can easily be arranged by letting hacker teams form cross-department-wise. This will strengthen communication between departments internally in your organization and lay the foundation for alignment of the organization's vision among employees. The purpose of an internal hackathon is often to find solutions to challenges that are only relevant to your organization, so you have the opportunity to dig deeper into issues that might not be of interest to a wider audience but are of high relevance to you.

The advantage of an external hackathon is that you can use the hackathon and its outcome as a tool to communicate on a deeper level with your audience, customers, partners, and community. You engage and learn from your external partners and build your brand at the same time. An external hackathon is more complex, with more moving parts and groups of people to communicate with, but the returns will be greater. You will also be perceived as an organization willing to take social responsibility when inviting to an external hackathon, and the hackathon experience alone will make people's perceptions of your organization shift. Challenges can be cocreated by enticing your customers and partners, and in addition to creating challenges that have a firm foundation in real life, you will gain insights into what your customers and partners would like to improve. And you are doing in it a fun way.

Understanding the scope of open data in hackathons

Some would argue that a hackathon is not a hackathon without **open data** resources available and that the entire idea of a hackathon revolves around data. This is how the concept of a hackathon came about, using different data resources and combining them in new ways to create innovative solutions to a challenge. This could be executed within an organization or, as in the example of *Hack for Sweden*, with many organizations offering the hacker teams their datasets and APIs. I often get the question of what kind of data we need for the hackathon at hand, and I always answer that the question is not possible to answer. True innovation knows no boundaries, and therefore it is impossible to say what kind of data should be offered to the hacker teams. Open data sources need to be well organized and sufficient for the task at hand, but data that may seem irrelevant to the naked eye may trigger a great idea for a solution in a hacker team.

So, should you provide your hacker teams with open data or not? The answer depends on what you wish for them to build during the hackathon and, ultimately, what kind of solutions you wish to see. If you are looking for tech solutions only, the answer is obvious, but what if you are looking for a wider spectrum of solutions to complex challenges your organization is struggling with? Then, it is wiser to open up to other types of solutions that are not built on data and that may not be technical at all.

There are tons of open data sources that are published and not being used. If your organization has data of its own, make it accessible to your hacker teams and see what they will come up with during a hackathon, and offer them to combine it with other available data sources accessible outside of your organization. The important part is to offer data sources and APIs in one specific space so that it is easily accessible for the hacker teams to find what they are looking for. The data also needs to be amply described so that it is easy to navigate between the data sources.

> **Tip**
>
> During the hackathon, we recommend that you have mentors available to support the hacker teams when navigating and choosing data sources. If possible, this means that there is one mentor for every organization that has provided data sources to contact and ask necessary questions. This will ensure that the data is used properly and applied in the solutions.

Core values driving the movement

At the Hack for Earth Foundation, we have three core values: *sustainability*, *diversity*, and *impact*. Everything we do is permeated by these values, and together with our mission to create real solutions to the UN's 17 **Sustainable Development Goals** (**SDGs**), they make up the foundation by which we operate. The reason why these three core values are of such importance will be discussed next in further detail.

In a world where global challenges are increasing in complexity and severity by the minute, the core value of sustainability is inevitable. To run your organization in a sustainable way and to communicate openly what your organization is doing to make this planet a better place to live on is not only the right thing to do – it is good business. Any organization that does not have a sustainability agenda of some kind will find it hard to do business in the future, simply because everyone else has a sustainability focus.

Diversity is, in our definition, the key to success when you are working with innovation. It is when people with diverse sets of competencies, backgrounds, ethnicities, genders, and ages come together that truly innovative solutions are born. Homogenous groups tend not to be innovative, due to the simple fact that they are too much alike in their mindset and way of thinking. Science shows that diversity in teams is linked to higher levels of innovation capacity, and a hackathon is, of course, a setting where you are looking to increase levels of innovation as much as possible. When creating your hacker teams for the hackathon, encourage mixing different backgrounds, competencies, genders, and ages. It is also a good idea to include diversity in teams in your jury criteria if the creation of hacker teams is done by the teams themselves. If you know that diversity in the team is a factor you will be judged upon, this will make teams strive for diversity in team constellations. You can also decide to form teams yourself, which will, of course, give you more control over hacker teams.

> **Note**
>
> To understand in greater detail how diversity can spearhead innovation, you can visit this link: `https://www.cs.jhu.edu/~misha/DIReadingSeminar/Papers/Hewlett14.pdf`.

Impact is the third, and to some degree, most important value. To strive for impact means that what you do should have a concrete outcome. For us at the Hack for Earth Foundation, it means that we take action on our goals and that we do what we say we will do. The value of impact cannot be overestimated; it is imperative that the hackathons we deliver result in solutions that are made into real tools that deliver real value for people and the planet. *Without real impact and solutions that have become real tools, a hackathon is just another meeting: people saying great things but no real outcome. This is why the core value of impact is so important.* The Build for Earth acceleration program is the tangible result of these values – a 6-month acceleration program with the primary focus on making winning solutions come to life.

Together, these three core values to keep in mind when you execute your hackathon will ensure that your hackathon is sustainable, diverse, and impactful. A hackathon can highlight all these three values in a more tangible way for the people joining the hackathon, and it can most effectively be communicated as proof of your organization's commitment to these core values. A hackathon is a hands-on way to show the world, your customers, and your employees that you not only talk about your core values – you take action on them.

Summary

In this introductory chapter, we have discussed how the hackathon tool can be reinvented as a tool for impact, creating changes for several levels of an organization's functioning as well as creating real solutions to perceived challenges. We have covered how different types of hackathons can deliver different kinds of value for your organization and how the outcome can be valuable for your organization. We briefly covered how to design your hackathon for impact and how data can drive a hackathon's purpose. These topics will be further developed in *Chapters 2* and *3*. Lastly, we briefly covered how your core values can be integrated into the hackathon process and discussed how this has been done in *Hack for Earth* hackathons.

In the following chapter, we will dive deeper into the prospects and possibilities of the concept of citizen-driven innovation to improve your business. You will learn how to incorporate your organization's vision and purpose in a hackathon setting and tap into the power of citizen-driven innovation. We will start off by defining citizen-driven innovation and why it is a superpower to drive your business – no matter what the purpose is!

2

Making Citizen-Driven Innovation Work for You

In this chapter, you will learn how to make **citizen-driven innovation** work for you and your organization and understand the core values that lie behind the concept of citizen-driven innovation. The purpose of this chapter is to paint the bigger picture of the ideas fueling citizen-driven innovation, with the overall goal being that you will start imagining what the core values of your own organization are that could drive citizen-driven innovation for you. By describing the process of how the concept came about, you will attain an understanding of how citizen-driven innovation can fuel your organization's growth.

The chapter will cover the following topics:

- Understanding citizen-driven innovation
- Sense of urgency
- Massive transformative purpose
- Redefining democracy for the 21st century
- Manifesting core values with the *Dream! Hack! Build!* method

The concept of citizen-driven innovation can be explained through two examples from real life, the **Dream for Earth** campaign at the **Expo 2020** world exhibition in Dubai, and the **Dream for Sweden** campaign in 2019 for **Hack for Sweden** 2019. Both campaigns were open to the public and invited citizens to share their dreams for the future. Moreover, citizen-driven innovation will be described with the driving forces behind it: a **sense of urgency**, **massive transformative purpose**, and the concept of democracy. The three essential elements of citizen-driven innovation – *Dream! Hack! Build!* – will be described, and we will walk you through how you can use it in your own organization.

Understanding citizen-driven innovation

Citizen-driven innovation refers to the process where citizens actively participate in the innovation process, contributing ideas, solutions, and actions to address societal, community, or environmental challenges. This approach leverages the collective intelligence, skills, and experiences of the public to co-create innovations that are more inclusive, sustainable, and aligned with the needs and values of the community. Citizen-driven innovation often involves collaboration between citizens, government, NGOs, and private entities, employing tools such as crowdsourcing, participatory design, and open innovation platforms to engage a wide range of stakeholders in the problem-solving process.

Our journey with citizen-driven innovation

Our journey into citizen-driven innovation took its first steps with the government-backed initiative Hack for Sweden, an endeavor that laid the groundwork for what was to become a more expansive and impactful vision with the Hack for Earth Foundation hackathons. The pivot toward this direction of innovation was propelled by a clear and pressing necessity – the same necessity that has historically been the precursor to invention and progress. Our mission was shaped by the imperative to evolve the **hackathon** concept, to transform it into a vessel for generating superior solutions marked by a higher degree of innovation.

The catalyst for this evolution was the observation that outcomes from traditional hackathons were not soaring to the desired levels of innovative excellence. To address this shortfall, it became clear that a comprehensive reassessment of the hackathon model was essential. The participants, though skilled and driven, were a homogeneous group; they were culled from the same familiar pools of talent. The term "hacker" had become synonymous with individuals who frequently participated in hackathons – usually drawn from the realms of technology, including professions such as programmers, IT specialists, and other technical experts.

To elevate the results of our hackathons and reach new heights of innovation, we recognized the need to diversify our recruitment strategies. Attracting a broader array of participants became paramount. We began seeking individuals with varied backgrounds, not just from the tech sphere, to become the new "hackers" – the thinkers, the creatives, the activists, and the dreamers – who could contribute fresh perspectives and disparate skills to our hackathons.

Furthermore, the **challenges** presented at hackathons required a grander vision. They needed to be more than just problems seeking solutions; they had to embody a purpose, an aspiration to not just innovate for the sake of innovation but to genuinely contribute to the betterment of society. The hackathons needed challenges that were both visionary in their scope and grounded in the potential for real-world impact.

This called for a complete transformation – a total makeover of our hackathon philosophy. We began to construct our events around more ambitious goals, integrating new voices, and placing a significant emphasis on cross-disciplinary collaboration. By redefining who a "hacker" could be, we opened the doors to an array of novel ideas and uncharted possibilities. It was a recalibration of our approach, one that positioned citizen-driven innovation at the forefront, ensuring that the inventive spark could come from anywhere and anyone, reflecting the diverse tapestry of society itself.

Supercharging citizen-driven innovation with Dream for Sweden

The initial foray into citizen-driven innovation was catalyzed during the Dream for Sweden campaign in 2018, an initiative significantly bolstered by the insights and guidance of the Hack for Sweden Advisory Board. The campaign was designed with a distinct and ambitious purpose: to extend the hackathon invitation beyond the traditional hacker circles – beyond those who were well-versed in the concepts and mechanics of such events – and to lower the threshold of participation for the everyday citizen.

The traditional image of a hacker, often associated with a certain set of technical skills and a familiarity with the tech community, needed to be broadened. Our objective was to reach out to a demographic that had not been tapped into before, to communicate with a different segment of the population – those who might not typically see themselves as part of a hackathon but whose insights and contributions could prove invaluable.

In our pursuit of engaging a broader community, we embarked on a series of brainstorming sessions, focusing on how we could create challenges that resonated with the public and how we could bolster community involvement. These deliberations led us to the inception of the Dream for Sweden campaign. This initiative was grounded in the belief that innovation starts with a vision – or a dream, as you might prefer to call it. Such dreams are the seeds of all creation, whether you aspire to construct a new kitchen, devise a new communication strategy or a sustainable energy solution, build a spaceship, or a new type of hackathon.

The act of sharing these visions is foundational to the innovative process. It is the collective dreaming that lays the groundwork for collaborative creation. With this in mind, the Dream for Sweden campaign set out to invite the citizens of Sweden to share their aspirations, and to open up a dialogue about their dreams for the future of their workplaces, their societies, and the urban environments they inhabit.

We recognized that many individuals harbor a deep-seated desire to contribute constructively to their surroundings but often lack a conduit – a platform through which to channel their ideas and expertise. As a result, a wealth of potential innovations and expert knowledge remains untapped. What if there were a dedicated space where citizens could deposit their ideas, a reservoir of collective passion, engagement, experience, and competence?

This question formed the bedrock of our approach to refining citizen-driven innovation. We envisioned a realm where the capacity of individuals to contribute to society was not only recognized but actively encouraged – a domain where every citizen felt empowered to offer solutions, share their dreams, and take part in shaping the future.

The Dream for Sweden campaign was, therefore, more than just a campaign; it was the manifestation of our belief in the power of citizen-driven innovation. It was a testament to our faith that people not only possess the ability but also the eagerness and determination, to foster new and innovative solutions for our society and for the world at large. All that is needed is the right platform to cultivate, harness, and develop their contributions – a platform that the Dream for Sweden campaign turned out to be. There will be more about Dream for Sweden in the example at the end of this chapter.

Why citizen-driven innovation is powerful

The essence of citizen-driven innovation lies in its inclusivity and in empowering the populace to engage at various levels of creativity and implementation. The invitation to innovate is cast wide, embracing all citizens and offering them the autonomy to decide how deeply they wish to be involved. Some individuals may contribute purely at the conceptual stage, providing the seed of an idea. Others may engage more deeply, opting to collaborate in the refinement and evolution of those ideas into concrete strategies or actions.

The distinction between ideators and executors is significant – while some excel in ideating, and drafting blueprints for what could be, others possess the prowess to breathe life into those blueprints, transforming them into functional, real-world solutions. It's an ecosystem of contribution where each role is vital, from the genesis of a thought to the practical manifestation of that thought.

You can easily surmise the multitude of remarkable ideas that go unexplored because their originators lack a proper venue, the necessary connections, or the community to bring them to fruition. By tapping into the collective intellect, and the reservoir of ideas, inspiration, and expertise that citizens hold, and then amalgamating these assets, we can create a world of innovation. Harnessing this collective capability is the lynchpin in making citizen-driven innovation a potent force within any organization.

The challenge and opportunity lie in mobilizing individuals to contribute in ways that are most natural and fulfilling to them, thereby ensuring that each person is motivated to bring their best to the table. But how is this achieved? The answer is multifaceted: provide an inspiring context, a platform that beckons participation, and the autonomy for people to take charge of their ideas. Show them that their contributions are valued and that you have faith in their capacity to generate impactful ideas.

When individuals perceive that their input is genuinely respected and they are entrusted with significant responsibility, they tend to reciprocate with heightened commitment and innovation. They rise to the occasion, inspired to meet and exceed the challenge. This dynamic is a microcosm of a foundational principle of democracy: the trust in the citizenry's ability to add value to the collective society.

Therefore, at its heart, our version of citizen-driven innovation is about reshaping the tenets of democracy to resonate with the needs and mechanics of our contemporary era. It's about evolving the concept of democratic participation beyond traditional venues and channels, creating new spaces where every voice has the potential to be heard and every idea has the chance to be actualized. It's a renaissance of civic engagement, where democracy isn't just about representation but is also about active, creative, and purposeful participation. Trust breeds responsibility, and when people feel that they are trusted and have responsibility, they will respond to that accordingly and rise to the challenge. This is also the foundation of democracy – that we trust in people's ability to contribute and bring value to society.

Hence, reinventing democracy to work in our modern era – that is what citizen-driven innovation is at its core, and that is what we believe is the key to a sustainable future for all.

Generating a sense of urgency

A sense of urgency refers to the perception and mindset that an action or set of actions needs to be taken promptly and with a clear focus to address an issue, achieve a goal, or seize an opportunity. It involves recognizing the importance of timing and the potential consequences of delay. A sense of urgency is important for several reasons in business and in hackathons. It plays a crucial role in driving effective and timely actions to achieve goals, respond to challenges, and capitalize on opportunities. Cultivating a sense of urgency is about balancing the need for quick action with the importance of deliberate and strategic decision-making. It's not about inducing stress or panic but rather about fostering a culture or mindset that recognizes the value of time and the impact of timely action on success and growth.

At the very inception of any endeavor – be it the launch of a business, the planning of an event, or the orchestrating of a hackathon – identifying a compelling sense of urgency is paramount. You must address the fundamental questions.

- Why should this matter to people?
- Why should they engage with your initiative, choose to dedicate their time to your event, or prefer your product over the competition's?

In our experience, this element is often overlooked when organizing hackathons; however, it is absolutely critical when inviting people to participate in a hackathon.

The invitation to a hackathon is, in essence, an invitation to invest time – a resource just as valuable as any financial expenditure. The common oversight is the assumption that the appeal of the hackathon, possibly coupled with substantial monetary rewards, will be enough to draw in participants in droves. However, this is frequently not the reality, since people are not only motivated by money. Crafting a sense of urgency is not about creating pressure; it's about connecting with what is inherently valuable to people, striking a chord with their interests, passions, or professional aspirations to the extent that they're willing to allocate their precious time.

Internal hackathon

Creating this connection in the context of an internal hackathon, targeted toward your organization's employees, can be a straightforward process. The presumption is that employees are already invested in their work and the success of the organization. Yet, even within this scenario, it's essential to communicate effectively, opening channels for employees to express their ideas and contribute their perspectives actively. They should feel that their participation in the hackathon is not only welcomed but essential and that their contributions can lead to tangible changes and improvements.

External hackathon

When the hackathon is open to external participants, cultivating a sense of urgency is even more critical. The challenges and rewards must resonate with potential participants on a deeper level. They need to feel that their contribution could be instrumental in driving change or innovation that aligns with their values or interests. This requires a nuanced understanding of your audience, a precise message that conveys the importance of the event, and incentives that are not just lucrative but also meaningful – tapping into the zeitgeist, aligning with social causes or the UN's 17 Sustainable Development Goals, or presenting opportunities for professional growth that can create a compelling draw. The narrative should be framed in such a way that participation becomes an attractive proposition for personal or professional development, for contributing to a greater cause, or for the sheer excitement of innovation and collective problem-solving.

Whether for an internal or an external audience, establishing a sense of urgency is about crafting a narrative that speaks to the intrinsic motivations of your audience, offers them a role in a larger story, and illustrates the unique opportunity your hackathon represents. It's about showcasing the value of the hackathon not just as an event but also as a pivotal experience that offers growth, community, and the potential to make a significant impact.

To summarize, the sense of urgency is why your hackathon needs a massive transformative purpose, as we'll discuss next.

Living your massive transformative purpose

A **massive transformative purpose** (**MTP**) is a concept that originates from the field of exponential organizations, which are entities whose impact or output is disproportionately large – at least 10 times larger – compared to their peers because of the use of new organizational techniques that leverage accelerating technologies. The term was popularized by Salim Ismail in his book *Exponential Organizations*, and it encapsulates a company or organization's aspirational statement of purpose that is both grand in ambition and able to galvanize large groups of people.

These are the core aspects of an MTP:

- **Ambition**: An MTP is ambitious, aiming to create significant change in its sector, society, or the world at large. It's not just about incremental improvement but about making a quantum leap in impact.

- **Transformative impact**: The purpose outlined by an MTP goes beyond the ordinary; it seeks to transform industries or societal norms, creating new ways of operating, thinking, or impacting communities.

- **Clarity and inspiring nature**: An MTP should be clear and compelling to inspire action. It's formulated in such a way that it communicates a vivid image of what the future could look like and motivates stakeholders to strive toward that vision.

- **Action orientation**: Despite its visionary nature, an MTP is not just a slogan. It is actionable, guiding the strategic decisions and everyday actions of the organization and its members.

- **Scalability**: The MTP is crafted to scale, leveraging the organization's unique capabilities, technologies, and approaches to grow exponentially rather than linearly.

Here are some examples of MTPs:

- Tesla: "*To accelerate the world's transition to sustainable energy.*"

  Tesla's MTP goes beyond the manufacturing of electric vehicles; it is about driving a global shift toward sustainable energy practices. This powerful, forward-looking statement encapsulates a vision for a cleaner, more environmentally responsible future and encompasses not just the automotive industry but energy consumption as a whole.

- TED: "*Spread ideas.*"

  TED's MTP is deceptively simple yet profoundly impactful. By focusing on the spreading of ideas, TED positions itself as a catalyst for global knowledge sharing and education. It champions the power of ideas to change attitudes, lives, and ultimately, the world, by providing a platform for thinkers, innovators, and change-makers to share their insights with a global audience.

- Google: "*To organize the world's information and make it universally accessible and useful.*"

  Google's MTP articulates a commitment to information accessibility and utility. It's not just about building the best search engine; it's about creating an ecosystem where information serves everyone, everywhere, effectively breaking down barriers to knowledge and empowering users worldwide with information at their fingertips.

Each of these MTPs encapsulates a clear, compelling goal that drives the organizations' actions and strategies. They are designed not just as mission statements but as calls to action that resonate with employees, customers, and the broader society, challenging the status quo and aiming for transformative impact.

An MTP is critical because it serves as a north star for an organization, providing a sense of purpose that transcends the profit motive and drives innovation. It attracts talent and resources, not just for the sake of business growth but for the pursuit of the purpose itself. It also becomes a rallying call for customers, partners, and other stakeholders who identify with the MTP and want to be part of realizing that vision.

The presence of an MTP can deeply influence an organization's culture, spurring a more innovative, adaptive, and resilient mindset. It encourages a culture where radical ideas are embraced, where the status quo is questioned, and where the pursuit of lofty goals is seen as a motivator rather than a deterrent. In an age driven by fast-paced technological advancements, having an MTP can be a critical differentiator in attracting the best talent and leading the charge toward revolutionary advancements.

An MTP is not merely a statement but a catalyst for exponential growth and change. It encapsulates a vision bold enough to push the boundaries of what is possible, inspiring collective effort toward transformative change that has the potential to alter the landscape of industries and society.

Crafting your MTP isn't just an exercise in branding – it's a vital strategic endeavor. An MTP acts as the very essence, the heartbeat, of your organization, infusing your objectives with vigor and direction. It's the expression of your enterprise's highest aspirations and imbues every goal with significance and intent.

If your organization's MTP remains unarticulated, it is high time to give it a voice. Defining your MTP is defining the mission that will animate your organization's spirit and direct its energy toward meaningful and deliberate action. Upon crystallizing your MTP, the journey has only just begun. It must be communicated thoroughly – echoed in the halls of your organization and beyond its walls. This declaration serves as a constant reminder to all stakeholders of the larger mission that your daily activities contribute toward. However, merely stating your MTP is not enough. It must be lived and breathed at every level of the organization, manifesting itself through consistent action and decision-making. Your MTP should align with your corporate values and culture and be reflected in every project, campaign, and initiative.

The greater challenge, though, lies in cultivating belief in your MTP among your employees, customers, and partners. It's about transforming your MTP from a statement into a shared conviction, an inspirational force that others rally behind. This is more nuanced and demanding than it initially appears. It requires continuous effort, daily reinforcement, and authentic demonstration of commitment to the MTP's principles.

You need to engage with your stakeholders and your customers and employees in a way that they see and feel the MTP's relevance and potency. Create stories that illustrate the MTP in action, recognize contributions that align with the MTP, and build a narrative that entwines individual roles with the overarching purpose.

In essence, an MTP is not a static line – it is a living, evolving statement that guides your organization's journey. It is a clarion call for innovation, unity, and progress. It is the standard against which you measure success, not just in profit but in purpose, impact, and the legacy you aim to create.

The MTP for Hack for Earth was decided back in 2018 during our time working with Hack for Sweden, but it still holds true to our mission and values:

"From 200 hackers to 2 million in 2 years."

At the same time, we decided that the core values should be **sustainability**, **diversity,** and **impact**. The MTP, together with the core values, formes the cornerstones of our take on citizen-driven innovation, and the idea of reinventing the concept of democracy to fit the 21st century came to life.

In the following image, you can see a world map showcasing that Hack for Earth is working hard to reach our goal of 2 million hackers worldwide. The 125 countries in green are the countries from where there were teams participating in the online hackathon Hack for Earth at COP27 in November 2022.

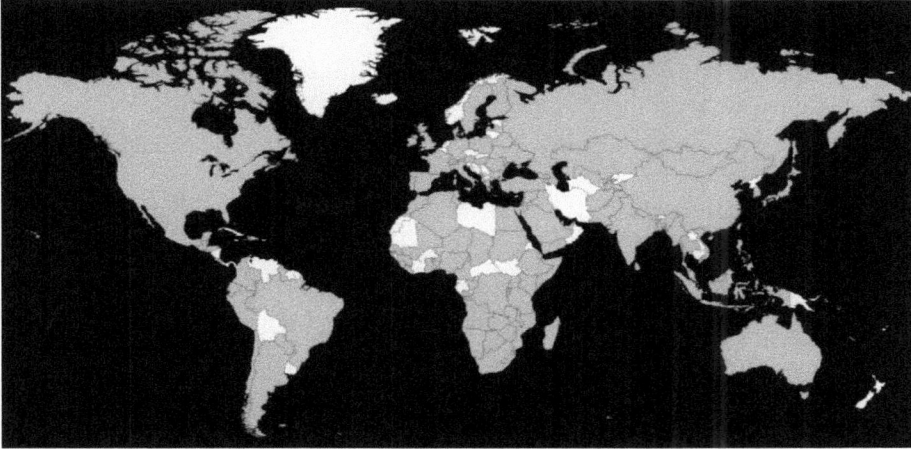

Figure 2.1 – The shaded parts on the map show the 125 countries who participated in the Hack for Earth online hackathon at COP27, Sharm El Sheikh

Making hackathons something for everybody –Redefining democracy for the 21st century

In the ever-accelerating complexity of our global society, the call for collective action rings louder than ever. As we navigate through an era marked by a daunting climate crisis and numerous global challenges, the need for widespread and inclusive collaboration – "all hands on deck" – becomes not just beneficial but essential for survival and prosperity.

Throughout history, human survival has hinged on our instinctive drive to care for our immediate community and inner circle of family and close relatives and friends, a trait that has served humanity well. However, the stakes have changed; the interconnectivity and globalization of our world demand that we extend our concern far beyond our local circles. The decisions we make in the humdrum of our daily lives must now account for the well-being of distant populations and ecosystems, many of which we may never directly encounter.

This is no small feat; as humans, our brains are not inherently wired for this expansive, global stewardship. It requires a deliberate and often challenging shift in human perspective to consider the impact of our actions on a global scale. The common proclivity to prioritize immediate gratification – the allure of air travel, the latest fashion, or the convenience of not sorting our trash – often overshadows the long-term well-being of our planet and future generations. Our evolutionary programming tends to value present desires over future consequences, which can lead to unsustainable choices that ultimately jeopardize the prospects of those who come after us. Yet, within the human psyche lie not only challenges but also remarkable strengths. Among the most potent of our traits is our innate ability to collaborate and unite for the common good. Some anthropologists and historians argue that it is this very capability for cooperation and social connection that has propelled Homo Sapiens to the pinnacle of the Earth's biodiversity.

> **Note**
>
> Here is the link to the research article that support the thesis that cooperation was a vital cornerstone for the emergence of the human race as superior on Earth:
>
> `https://www.scientificamerican.com/article/humans-brain-power-origins/`.

This propensity for collective action is not just a part of our past; it remains a vibrant force that can be harnessed and intensified through citizen-driven innovation.

The hackathon embodies this potential like no other form of collaboration. Unlike traditional conferences or meetings, where interaction is often superficial, the hackathon creates a unique and immersive environment. It fosters a sense of camaraderie and trust as participants roll up their sleeves and dive into the nitty-gritty of tangible challenges. The magic of the hackathon lies in its ability to create a shared sense of purpose, melding individual talents and perspectives into a focused endeavor to solve substantial problems. This not only builds deeper relationships among the participants but also embeds a memorable and rewarding experience of collective achievement. Such shared experiences lay a robust foundation for ongoing relationships and future collaborations. They are especially valuable within an organizational context, where departments or teams might otherwise operate in silos. A hackathon can serve as a melting pot, bringing together diverse departments within an organization to deepen and strengthen their collaborative muscles. The unique quality of the hackathon experience is the secret sauce, the magic so to speak, and it has the power to drive your impact and make your hackathon participants remember the experience as an extraordinary learning and collaborating experience where they connected with others to produce something tangible. The memory of this joint experience will also serve as a foundation for future relationships and possibilities to collaborate on other topics as well – which is very advantageous if you wish for the different departments of your organization to deepen and strengthen their ability for collaboration and cooperation.

By leveraging the hackathon as a tool, we catalyze the coming together of individuals for a common cause, turning the diversity of thought and perspective into a strategic advantage. It's through this alchemy of shared experience, problem-solving, and creation that the **Dream! Hack! Build! method** doesn't just contribute to the immediate goals at hand but also sow the seeds for a culture of enduring cooperation and innovation. *With the hackathon tool, we can make people come together for a common cause, using their different perspectives on the challenge as an advantage – and making citizen-driven innovation come to life, redefining democracy for the 21st century.*

Manifesting your core values with citizen-driven innovation

In the contemporary business landscape, it's almost universal for organizations to tout core values, often dovetailing with the **Sustainable Development Goals** (**SDGs**) that articulate their ethical compass and their commitment to societal and environmental betterment. Ideally, these values are more than familiar to every employee; they are internalized and serve as guiding principles for daily operations. However, the greater challenge for any organization is to keep these values from fading into the background, to prevent them from becoming mere slogans relegated to the office walls or the introductory pages of a website.

For values to be of any real consequence, they must be translated into palpable actions – transformed into living, breathing aspects of the organization's culture. This begs the question: how can an organization authentically manifest that its actions are in sync with its professed ethos? How can it demonstrate to both employees and customers that its declared MTP and sustainability goals are more than just lofty rhetoric?

The answer lies in tangibility – the active embodiment of these values through concrete initiatives. The key to "walking the talk" is to morph these articulated values into active, meaningful content and practice in the everyday life of your organization. It's about extending an invitation to everyone—employees, customers, and the broader audience – to roll up their sleeves and engage in the co-creation of the organization's vision. This collaborative approach not only brings an organization's MTP to life but also harnesses the collective wisdom and input of the community to tackle challenges head-on.

Employing the *Dream! Hack! Build!* method with the hackathon tool as an instrument for this purpose exemplifies proactive engagement with your community. It is a signal that your organization is serious about its commitments – a call to action for collective problem-solving. During a hackathon, the organization's core values and objectives can be put to the test in a dynamic setting, where theory meets practice and strategic goals are pursued through a collaborative effort. It is here, in the trenches of creativity and innovation, where true alignment of values and actions is forged.

By implementing such participatory and action-oriented events, your organization not only reaffirms its dedication to its values but also allows for a community-built and community-led realization of its MTP. This, in turn, can lead to novel solutions and improvements that align with the organization's sustainability agenda, bolstering its integrity and reinforcing trust among stakeholders. Such an approach turns the organization into a living example of its values – a testament to the transformative power of active and engaged citizenship.

Communicating your core values

There are three modules, or parts, to create citizen-driven innovation with the Dream! Hack! Build! method, and they are intricately joined together, in the sense that they all build on the results of the previous part and work together to amplify each other. In this sense, the sum of the three parts is greater than each part is alone. We strongly suggest you use all three to organize your hackathon.

Dream!

In the Dream! part of citizen-driven innovation, you engage your audience of choice to create the challenges you are to use in the hackathon. With a dream campaign where you invite your community to share their dreams for the future, you can build lasting relationships and gain important insights into what is important to your audience and your community. The best part is that you can get expert advice on what the challenges of your organization really are, from the people who see them up close every day, something the leaders of the organization don't often do.

A dream campaign can last for a few days up to a year, depending on the scope and the level of input you wish to create for your campaign. The more people who share their dreams and the more input you get, the more substantial your challenges will be. Another effect is, of course, that you engage with more people too. If the dream campaign is internal within the organization, you can just use the organization's own internal digital platform to collect your dreams, but if you are launching an external dream campaign, you need a website where you can collect the dreams. Preferably, this website can collect both video dreams and text dreams; text dreams can suffice, even though video is always stronger. You will need a function that lets you screen the dreams before they are posted on the website so that no inappropriate dreams are posted. However, this is not a big problem in our experience. The dream campaigns usually attract dreams that are appropriate. Only a very small percentage of dreams are deemed inappropriate and weeded out, in our experience.

The overall purpose of the Dream phase is to create a solid foundation for the challenges in the hackathon and also to engage your audience before the hackathon starts in a positive way. The challenges are crucial to a hackathon, as they determine the outcome of the hackathon, the solutions, and the end result. How you pose a question determines the answer, and the same is true for a hackathon: a good, diverse, well-formulated challenge will set the stage for the hackathon and it will most definitely impact the outcome.

There will be more on how to create the challenges you need to drive the hackathon your organization needs in *Chapter 4* on challenges, where we will delve deeper into the Dream! phase.

Hack!

In the hackathon part, you engage your audience in solving the challenges that you created based on the dream campaign. This way, your hacker teams can be involved and engaged in the challenges offered during the hackathon, and the risk of irrelevant challenges that people feel are not in tune with their reality is removed. **Partner organizations**, **mentors**, and **jury members** contribute and interact, forming new relationships and connections, which can be transferred to new arenas after the hackathon is finished.

If you are organizing an in-person hackathon, you can create a lot of visual content for social media for sharing both during the hackathon itself or afterward, to build your brand and connect with your audience. However, this also brings other demands on the organizers that you don't experience as an organizer of an online hackathon. More about these differences and demands in *Chapter 5*.

Following are a series of pictures from the in-person hackathon Hack for Sweden 2019, showcasing the energy and great vibe you can capture on camera to share in your social media and other channels to promote your in-person hackathon.

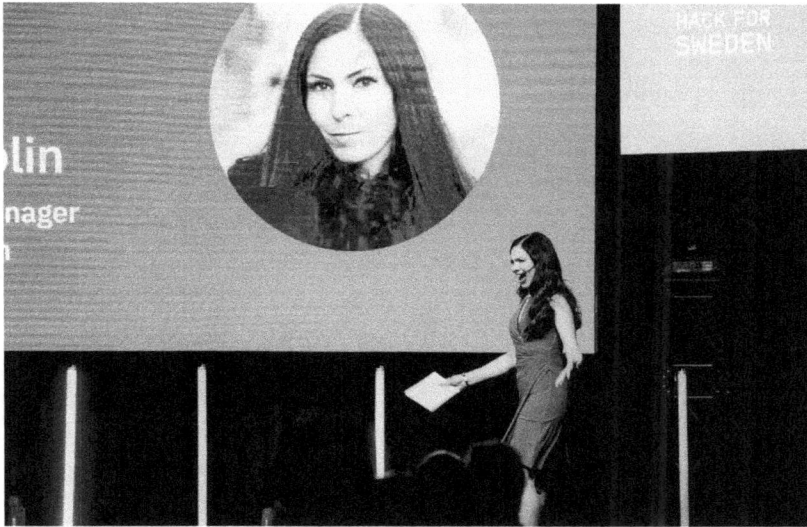

Figure 2.2 – Opening Ceremony at Hack for Sweden 2019, at Stockholmsmässan in April 2019

Figure 2.2 shows Ann Molin, then Head Project Manager of Government mission Hack for Sweden, giving the opening speech at the Opening Ceremony to the 1200 participants joining live: including 420 hackers, 100 mentors, 45 jury members, 88 partner organisations, and 30 lecturers.

In the following image you can see the 420 hackers hard at work during Hack for Sweden 2019, at Stockholmsmässan, in Stockholm, Sweden in April 2019.

Figure 2.3 – Hackers at work at Hack for Sweden 2019 at Stockholmsmässan

Figure 2.3 shows one of the most inspiring messages for a mission of the future. This message was placed to welcome the 420 hackers joining the in-person hackathon Hack for Sweden at Stockholmsmässan, in Stockholm, Sweden in April 2019.

Figure 2.4 – Welcoming the hackers

The following image shows The Hack for Sweden 2019 Head Jury members at the Prize Ceremony, at Stockholmsmässan, Stockholm, Sweden – right after the awards were presented to the winners.

Figure 2.5 – The Hack for Sweden 2019 Head Jury

Figure 2.5 shows the Head Jury members of Hack for Sweden 2019, with Head Project Manager of Hack for Sweden: from left Sara Selldahl, Ishtar Touailat, Mikael Ahlström, Ann Molin, Filippa Jennersjö, Susanne Fuglsang, Magnus Enzell.

There will be more on how to organize your hackathon according to the Dream! Hack! Build! method, what platforms to use, and whether you should have an in-person, online, or hybrid hackathon in *Chapter 5*.

Build!

Build for Earth is the very last part of citizen-driven innovation, where you make the winning solutions in your hackathon come to life. Often, after a hackathon ends, there is no plan for how the winning solutions are going to be realized into working solutions or tools. The prize ceremony is the finale, and when the confetti has landed on the floor and the prize money has possibly been distributed, the winning teams are on their own. In reality, here is where the most impactful part should start, with a customized **acceleration program** for the winning solutions. Depending on how many winners you have, you can create a program that will foster their survival into real solutions. This is important to send the message that real solutions are coming out of your hackathons, and also for the participant hackers – as well as the ones that didn't win. It shows that you are serious about innovation and that you are taking real action on the solutions.

It's important to create an acceleration program that is based on science and experience on what really makes a new solution work in the real world. There will be more on this in *Chapter 10*.

the following diagram:

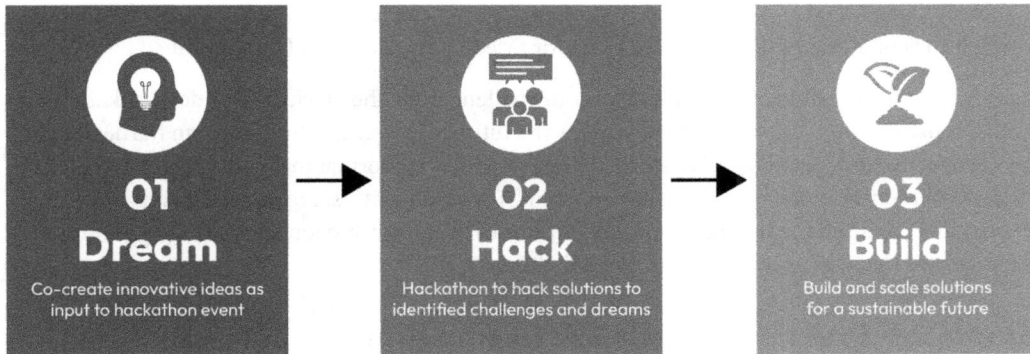

Figure 2.6 – The Hack for Earth innovation process

To exemplify the Dream! phase, the following subsections present two real-life examples describing the process of creating the challenges for a hackathon by inviting an external audience to contribute. A Dream! campaign can also be organized internally in an organization by inviting employees to provide the dreams and the input for the challenge creation; however, these two examples are both from an external audience.

Example 1 – Dream for Sweden campaign

The Dream for Sweden campaign, launched in December 2018, was a pioneering initiative aimed at engaging a wide-ranging audience to bring a rich diversity of skills and expertise to the forefront of the Hack for Sweden 2019 hackathon. This campaign was thoughtfully designed to make the Hack for Sweden hackathon more accessible to the general public, to spark interest, and to stimulate a sense of curiosity about the potential of collective challenge-solving.

At the heart of this campaign was the Dream for Sweden website, which served as the central hub for engagement. Here, citizens were encouraged to envision and articulate their hopes for the Sweden they dreamed of in the year 2045, sharing their visions of the future on a virtual map that represented the country. This interactive map allowed users to dive into a sea of dreams, exploring each vision and gaining insight into the collective aspirations of the nation.

To maximize outreach and captivate a broad demographic, we leveraged the extensive network of the Hack for Sweden community, which encompasses an impressive consortium of 88 partner organizations, including government bodies, major corporations, academia, and non-profits. Utilizing the clout and reach of this community, we disseminated short video clips featuring key figures from these partner organizations. These spokespersons shared their personal visions for Sweden's future, which were then broadcast across the community's social media platforms, supplemented by a comprehensive press release.

The Dream for Sweden campaign was more than just a momentary event; it was a four-month journey that galvanized the public and successfully collected thousands of dreams. These dreams were meticulously categorized and subsequently synthesized into challenge categories for the hackathon, all through the collaborative efforts of the Hack for Sweden organizational community.

This collective journey didn't just result in a set of challenges for the Hack for Sweden hackathon; it fostered a sense of unity and shared direction for the future of Sweden. The campaign harnessed the power of collective imagination and channeled it into a structured format that could then be tackled in a practical, solution-oriented hackathon environment. The result was a set of nuanced, citizen-inspired challenges that captured the true spirit and aspirations of the Swedish people, laying the groundwork for a hackathon that was as impactful as it was inclusive.

Example 2 – Dream for Earth 2021 campaign

In 2021, we embarked on the **Dream for Earth** campaign, which was conceptualized with a singular and distinct objective: to expand our outreach and engage a global audience boasting a rich diversity of talents and skills. This campaign was strategically aligned with the global Hack for Earth hackathon hosted amid the vibrant setting of the world exhibition Expo 2020 in Dubai. Central to this initiative was the portal `dreamforearth.com` – a digital space where individuals were encouraged to articulate their visions for the future, with the option to align their dreams with up to 5 of the 17 UN SDGs.

Spanning a period of six months, the campaign became a mosaic of aspirations, gathering thousands of dreams submitted by people from over 80 countries. These dreams were expressed and shared either through videos or in written narratives. Upon the culmination of this campaign, the multitude of dreams was processed through an advanced AI tool, providing a window into the collective conscience of different regions and cultures, revealing patterns and commonalities in the hopes and aspirations of people worldwide.

The insights gleaned from the Dream for Earth campaign were not confined to data charts or reports; they were disseminated among the Hack for Earth community – a collective that included influential corporates, proactive government agencies, and forward-thinking academic institutions. Together, in a synergistic workshop that spanned three hours, these entities synthesized the data into actionable challenges, distributed among seven core categories pertinent to the hackathon. This collaborative endeavor was not just about addressing the present but about sculpting a future that resonates with the shared dreams of a connected world. Through this approach, the hackathon was transformed from a mere competition to a dynamic platform for genuine global impact, underpinned by the diverse aspirations of people from every corner of the globe.

Summary

This chapter delved into the concept and driving forces behind citizen-driven innovation, providing you with a comprehensive understanding of why this approach is effective and detailing the deployment of the dynamic Dream! Hack! Build! methodology. Through this exploration, you've gained insights into the critical role of establishing a sense of urgency and formulating an MTP. These concepts are not just theoretical – they're practical tools that, when applied through the Dream! Hack! Build! method, can act as catalysts for cultivating innovation and generating significant impact within any organization.

Through the lens of citizen-driven innovation, you've seen the power of inviting and engaging a broad community in the ideation and problem-solving process. Real-world applications of this method have been illustrated with the case studies of the Dream for Earth and Dream for Sweden campaigns, offering tangible examples of how to mobilize and inspire citizens to partake in a collective journey toward change.

The Dream for Earth and Dream for Sweden campaigns serve as exemplars of how diverse perspectives can be united under a shared goal, fostering a collaborative environment where innovation thrives. These initiatives showcased the potential to gather ideas from a spectrum of participants, demonstrating how the inclusion of varied insights and experiences enhances the creative process and leads to more holistic and impactful outcomes.

As we transition from this chapter, we stand on the brink of a deeper exploration into the distinct phases of the Dream! Hack! Build! Methodology in *Chapter 3*. The forthcoming chapter promises to guide you through the nuanced steps of this innovative approach, revealing how each stage contributes to the rapid realization of ideas and the generation of tangible innovation.

You'll learn about the "Dream!" phase, which captures the aspirations and visions of participants; the "Hack!" phase, a crucible of creativity where concepts are challenged and solutions are forged; and the "Build!" phase, where ideas are refined into actionable plans with real-world applications. This methodological journey is not just a blueprint for running successful hackathons but also a formula for accelerating innovation, driving organizational transformation, and delivering outcomes that resonate with both your community and the wider world.

Prepare to be equipped with knowledge and strategies that can revolutionize the way you approach problem-solving and innovation, turning the principles of citizen-driven innovation into a powerful engine for growth and change in your organization and beyond.

3

The Dream! Hack! Build! Method

In this chapter, we will dive further into the three-step **citizen-driven innovation** process – Dream! Hack! Build – which is a much more impactful way to drive innovation than merely hosting a single **hackathon** event.

Dream! Hack! Build! encompasses inviting employees, customers, and **partner organizations** to co-create, fostering engagement, seeing diverse perspectives, and aligning important global missions such as the UN's 17 Sustainable Development Goals. Communication and **storytelling** are key for engagement and showcasing dedication to citizen-driven innovation. Partnerships with other organizations are an important factor in creating impactful solutions and demonstrating **sustainability** leadership, and this is something we will briefly cover in this chapter.

More in-depth coverage of the different parts of the **Dream! Hack! Build! method** will be covered in the subsequent chapters; this chapter is a short overview of the Dream! Hack! Build! method. The purpose of this chapter is to give you, as a reader, some comprehension of the method and why it's important and so impactful. The in-depth details of how to execute the different phases of Dream! Hack! and Build! will follow in the subsequent chapters.

The Dream! Hack! Build! method has storytelling at its core, and the early involvement of marketing and social media teams within your organization is advised. This chapter will showcase the example of the "Hack for Earth" global hackathon at Expo 2020 in Dubai, an online hackathon that highlighted citizen involvement from 120+ countries, which lasted over a year and aligned with the 17 Sustainable Development Goals to create real solutions for impact. In this chapter, you will learn how the Dream! Hack! Build method not only generates impactful solutions but also has the power to strengthen your brand, engage your audience, and build meaningful narratives while showcasing your organization's commitment to a sustainable future.

This chapter will cover the following topics:

- Why the Dream! Hack! Build! method is more impactful than merely hosting a single hackathon event

- The United Nations' 17 Sustainable Development Goals

- Understanding the Dream! Hack! Build! method

- The ABCs of a hackathon's success

Why the Dream! Hack! Build! method is more impactful than merely hosting a single hackathon event

Inviting your employees, customers, and partner organizations to engage with the Dream! Hack! Build! method is essentially inviting them to co-author a transformative narrative regarding your area. This interactive approach transcends conventional one-directional communication, offering a rich, multi-layered dialogue instead, with the collective aim of forging something of greater worth than individual parts can achieve alone. The magic of this method lies in the investment of personal resources: time, creativity, and effort. When individuals and organizations contribute these assets, they inherently place a higher value on the results of their labor.

By involving various stakeholders, your organization is not only showing reverence for their contributions but also displaying a keen interest in their diverse perspectives. This inclusivity signals a willingness to explore novel ideas and perspectives, which can be a foundation for forging new personal and professional relationships. It is a testament to a culture that values humility and curiosity, one that recognizes the wealth of insights its stakeholders hold and extends an invitation to them to play a pivotal role in crafting the solutions.

The Dream! Hack! Build! methodology is versatile in its application; it can be tailored to the specific temporal and resource constraints of your purpose and agenda. Whether it is a year-long journey or condensed into a focused 2–3-month sprint, the key is to ensure the integrity of each phase is maintained. While each segment of this citizen-driven innovation process is potent in isolation, their combined effect is synergistic. To run a hackathon without the preparatory investment of the Dream! phase or the developmental focus of the Build! module is to forsake the full potential of this dynamic triad. Moreover, the absence of a follow-up initiative, akin to the Build for Earth acceleration program, might invite criticism for lack of follow-through.

It's important to emphasize the power of storytelling and community engagement in the Dream! Hack! Build! method, so we wish to highlight this aspect with the following description. A more extended timeline not only allows these elements to flourish but also strengthens the bonds formed during the journey. The Dream! phase lays the groundwork, seeding engagement and gathering the collective aspirations of your audience. It's a call to share visions for a brighter future and an invitation to contribute to the ideation process, whether through democratic voting systems or collaborative decision-making with partners. The excitement and anticipation generated during the Dream! phase lay the groundwork for the Hack! phase, where diverse minds converge to rapidly prototype solutions. The Hack! phase is a catalyst for breaking down barriers, fostering trust, and nurturing new relationships. The crescendo of the Hack! phase – culminating in the submission of solutions, the intense deliberations of the jury, and the announcement of winners – add another layer of community engagement and suspense. The Build! phase then cements this shared journey, demonstrating your commitment to action and honoring the promises made.

Thus, the Dream, Hack, Build! process is not merely a vehicle for problem-solving; it is a strategic approach to brand building, deeper communication with stakeholders, and the crafting of a narrative that embodies the ethos of your organization. It's a holistic experience that not only spawns viable solutions but also reinforces your brand's narrative, engages your audience on a profound level, and solidifies your organization's position as a champion of sustainable and inclusive innovation.

In the modern landscape of brand communication, articulating a commitment to sustainability is not just commendable; it's expected. However, it's not enough to merely espouse an agenda; what truly resonates with consumers, communities, and employees is seeing a brand embody its sustainability ethos through tangible actions. This is the crux of authenticity, where the real measure is in how a company integrates its sustainability promises into the core of its business operations and culture. The execution of this – how a brand transforms its sustainability rhetoric into reality – is where the distinction between aspiration and actualization lies.

Enter the Dream! Hack! Build! method, a strategic process that acts as a conduit between a brand's sustainability ambitions and their realization. This method serves as a powerful demonstration of a brand's commitment to not only envisage but also earnestly pursue a sustainable future for humanity and the planet. It's an approach that goes beyond superficial claims, allowing companies to prove their dedication through collaborative innovation, community engagement, and solution-oriented projects.

As we embark on a deeper examination of the Dream! Hack! Build! methodology, we'll illustrate how it becomes a very practical manifestation of a brand's sustainability pledge. This unique method aligns with the current need for businesses worldwide to be proactive in their sustainability efforts, showcasing not only that they have a sustainability agenda but that they take action on it. Dream! Hack! Build! offers a framework for nurturing ideas that contribute to sustainability, providing a stage for these ideas to evolve from mere concepts to real-world applications.

To further contextualize the importance of sustainability in today's corporate landscape, we will explore the 17 **Sustainable Development Goals (SDGs)** established by the United Nations. These goals serve as a universal call to action to end poverty, protect the planet, and ensure that all people enjoy peace and prosperity. They are integral to the modern hackathon framework, as they provide a clear and ambitious set of objectives for organizations to align with. Understanding these goals is critical for any brand looking to make a significant impact through its sustainability agenda and, frankly, to have an impact overall today.

As we delve into the SDGs, we will demonstrate their relevance and explain how incorporating these goals into the fabric of your brand's mission is not just good practice; it's a strategic imperative. The Dream! Hack! Build! method does not simply pay lip service to these global targets; instead, it offers a structured, engaging way for brands to activate their sustainability strategies, encourage collective participation, and foster innovations that are beneficial not just for business but also for society and the environment at large.

In essence, the Dream! Hack! Build! methodology is not just about showcasing a brand's commitment to sustainability; it's about leading by example. It's about proving that your brand not only understands the importance of sustainable development but is also willing to invest in the collaborative processes necessary to bring about the change we all wish to see in the world. Through this method, brands can demonstrate their resolve to contribute to a sustainable future, where each step taken is a step towards a more responsible and resilient society.

The United Nations' 17 Sustainable Development Goals

Today's global landscape is fraught with complex challenges, and as the clock ticks forward, the window for meaningful action narrows. Bridging the gap between various core groups – employees, customers, and wider audiences – around the pivotal cause of a sustainable future is not just beneficial; it's imperative. The Dream! Hack! Build! method is a hands-on approach that unites these disparate groups in the pursuit of practical solutions that benefit both your organization and the planet's future.

The SDGs, conceived by United Nations member states in 2015 as part of the 2030 Agenda for Sustainable Development, represent a comprehensive framework aimed at achieving a harmonious balance between human prosperity and the planet's well-being today and for the generations to come. These goals are the collective commitment of UN member states to be fulfilled by the year 2030, and their importance in the global narrative of sustainability cannot be overstated; they are the universal adhesive that binds together citizens, nations, and organizations around the world in a concerted effort.

In a world where the realities of climate change are becoming ever more stark and undeniable, the imperative for organizations (globally) to adopt and integrate sustainable practices into their core business strategies is clear. Many organizations now publicly declare which of the SDGs they are focusing on, typically selecting those that resonate most closely with their business operations and values. Such declarations are far more than symbolic; they are commitments that manifest the organization's sustainability initiatives in tangible ways. Moreover, engaging broader audiences in the co-creation of sustainability solutions is increasingly achieved through the Dream! Hack! Build! method, encapsulating the ethos of collaborative innovation.

While the idea of 17 goals may seem daunting, it is crucial to recognize that this marks the first-ever instance of a universally endorsed framework for a sustainable future for all countries that are UN member states—a significant milestone in international cooperation. Each goal encompasses a series of subgoals, laying out a detailed map toward our shared commitment to sustainability.

The escalation of global sustainability crises, especially those related to climate change, underscores the necessity for all growth-oriented organizations to adopt a clear and actionable sustainability agenda. It is not enough to merely have such an agenda; organizations must actively communicate their sustainability endeavors and exemplify their commitment through real-world actions – this is the essence of "walking the talk." By selecting specific SDGs to prioritize and weaving them into a comprehensive public sustainability statement, organizations can clarify their initiatives, making them more accessible and relatable to all stakeholders.

Incorporating the SDGs into an organization's sustainability agenda offers a dual advantage: it contributes to the global mission of a more sustainable future and aligns the organization with universally recognized and respected goals. This alignment not only bolsters the organization's commitment to sustainable development but also enhances its international standing and comprehension among a global audience.

Therefore, it is highly recommended that organizations to integrate the Sustainable Development Goals into their business strategies and utilize them as a guiding compass in their hackathons and broader business endeavors.

Understanding the Dream! Hack! Build! method

"The efficacy of any methodology is intrinsically tied to the proficiency with which it is communicated;" this encapsulates the profound importance of clear and compelling communication, storytelling, and partnerships in any business endeavor. These elements are particularly crucial when it comes to the Dream! Hack! Build! method, where each facet of the approach hinges on the ability to effectively convey ideas, narratives, and shared values.

At the forefront of implementing the Dream! Hack! Build! method must be a strategic communication plan that is not just an afterthought but a central component, crafted with precision and tailored to resonate across various channels and platforms. It demands a harmonization of speed, adaptability, and consistency to navigate the rapidly evolving landscape of audience engagement.

In this comprehensive section, we will embark on a deep dive into the art and science of storytelling and communication, mapping out the key strategies and steps to not only broadcast your message but to ensure it is heard, understood, and embraced by all stakeholders. Storytelling is not merely a tool for engagement; it's an avenue for creating a shared journey, where the narrative becomes a connective tissue between your mission and the audience's values.

Additionally, we will explore the vital role partnerships play in amplifying your reach and reinforcing the credibility of your method. Building strong alliances can catalyze the growth of your initiatives, providing a foundation of support and collaboration that can take your vision from concept to reality. In today's interconnected world, partnerships transcend traditional boundaries, becoming platforms for innovation, resource sharing, and collective impact.

Communication, in its most effective form, goes beyond the transmission of information. It is about interaction, response, and adaptation. It's about crafting a message that is not only heard but also felt and acted upon. Whether through digital mediums, face-to-face interactions, or collaborative platforms, how you communicate can either be the wind that propels your method forward or the resistance that hinders its flight.

You will gain insights into leveraging these tools to their fullest potential, ensuring that your Dream! Hack! Build! method is not just a robust framework for innovation but a resonant call to action that rallies communities, inspires participation, and drives measurable impact.

Storytelling and communication

Storytelling and **communication** are not just elements but the lifeblood of the Dream! Hack! Build! methodology, a truth that will be thoroughly explored and expanded upon in *Chapters 6 and 8*. These tools are far more than mere conveyors of information; they are the vessels through which the very soul of the hackathon process is shared with a multitude of stakeholders—from participants to the wider audience and from employees to the global public. By engaging in effective storytelling and strategic communication, you craft an immersive narrative that can significantly boost engagement and profoundly enhance your brand's perception.

The power of a story is undeniable, and when applied to the Dream! Hack! Build! method, it can transform the abstract into the tangible and the individual into the communal. To leverage this power to its fullest extent, it is prudent to integrate your marketing and social media teams from the onset of the process. Their expertise in capturing and broadcasting the unfolding narrative ensures that every step of the Dream! Hack! Build! journey is shared, celebrated, and built upon, creating a crescendo of momentum and engagement right from the start.

The Dream! Hack! Build! method is intrinsically narrative by nature, as it unfolds in a sequence of action-driven chapters. The narrative arc begins in the Dream! phase, where individuals are encouraged to unveil their aspirations and visions, sowing the seeds of curiosity and excitement. This phase is the prologue to the hackathon saga, setting the stage for the creativity that will flourish.

As the plot advances into the Hack! phase, the co-creation marathon takes center stage, offering a treasure trove of content possibilities. Whether it's the synergy of an in-person event or a virtual hackathon, each moment is ripe for content creation. Encourage participants to document their experiences, share video snippets of breakthrough moments, or post live updates that capture the vibrant pulse of innovation in real-time.

The narrative reaches a pivotal development during the Build! phase. Here lies the opportunity to chronicle the evolution of the winning ideas as they metamorphose from concept to concrete solution. This phase is a story of transformation, ripe with the drama of **challenges** faced and the triumph of obstacles overcome. The Opening and Prize Ceremonies are not just ceremonial; they are chapters that bookmark the hackathon's opening aspirations and its concluding achievements, rich with emotive and inspiring content that can resonate both internally and externally.

Furthermore, interviews with winners, **jury members**, partner organizations, and **mentors** can unearth layers of personal and profound narratives that, when shared, can add depth and humanity to your organization's story. They offer a behind-the-scenes look at the minds and motivations that drive innovation.

By maintaining a steady stream of communication across all channels and throughout each phase of the Dream! Hack! Build! cycle, you reinforce the engagement and paint a picture of an organization not just advocating for citizen-driven innovation but actively embodying it. It is advantageous to create platforms for community participation to invite your audience to contribute their own chapters to the story, perhaps by sharing their dreams during the Dream! phase. This inclusivity not only forges stronger ties of engagement but also weaves a communal narrative where every voice is part of the collective journey toward innovation.

Partnerships

Partnerships are the cornerstone in the architecture of citizen-driven innovation, serving as critical pillars that support and enhance the Dream! Hack! Build! methodology. An exhaustive exploration of the nuances of successful partnerships will be the focus of *Chapter 7*. However, even within the context of this chapter, the importance of partnerships cannot be understated, as they are a foundational element that weaves through the entire Dream! Hack! Build! tapestry.

The cultivation of partnerships in the realm of hackathons transcends the simple inclusion of individuals or customer bases; it's about forging alliances with organizations that share your field of play. In the traditional business landscape, these entities may be seen as competitors, but within the ecosystem of citizen-driven innovation, they become potential allies. This paradigm shift from competition to collaboration is transformative, encouraging a unification of forces to generate a compounded impact for the common clientele.

Embracing this collaborative ethos enables your organization to not only demonstrate leadership in sustainable innovation but also to accept and enact a shared responsibility for devising superior solutions for society. Consider, for instance, a technological enterprise dedicated to delivering innovative products. By inviting peer companies, academic institutions specializing in technology, and pertinent governmental bodies to co-create, you pave the way for groundbreaking solutions that serve the collective welfare. This not only showcases your leadership but also cements lasting partnerships that can evolve into future collaborative endeavors and, in the end, generate growth and more business opportunities.

As the orchestrator of such alliances, your role extends beyond mere invitation. You are tasked with curating the narrative of the hackathon, molding the challenges, and setting the stage for a symphony of collaborative effort. Inviting partners to contribute in the form of mentors, jury members, and knowledge sharers is pivotal. They, in turn, must be invited to become ambassadors of the initiative, expanding its reach through their networks. However, a delicate balance must be struck, ensuring your organization maintains the helm of the hackathon's direction while partners are engaged in clearly defined, contributory roles. This balance is essential to mitigate any potential overlap of leadership that could lead to confusion or dilution of the hackathon's objectives.

Involving partner organizations in the very fabric of the hackathon—be it through co-creating challenges, assembling teams to participate, or offering mentorship and jury members—establishes a fertile ground for mutual benefit. Such involvement is not a mere courtesy; it is a strategic engagement that reinforces the investment of each partner, ensuring they gain tangible value from the collaboration.

As we look forward to the detailed discussion in *Chapter 7*, it's crucial to acknowledge that partnerships in the context of hackathons are more than just support mechanisms; they are dynamic relationships that are nurtured and evolved, enhancing the value and impact of the solutions developed. They are a testament to the fact that when we bridge divides and join hands, the potential for innovation is not only multiplied but also magnified in its ability to effectuate meaningful change, and it can grow our business at the same time.

Example – a global hackathon at Dubai Expo 2020

The Hack for Earth hackathon at the world exhibition Expo 2020 in Dubai was not just an event but a comprehensive journey through the realms of innovation and collaboration, structured around the potent triad of Dream! Hack! Build! This ambitious project spanned a grand total of 13.5 months, capturing the commitment to forge a sustained movement that encouraged citizens from over 120 countries to contribute their ideas for a brighter future.

The journey began with the global **Dream for Earth** campaign, which lasted for 7 months. This initiative took a holistic approach by focusing on the power of dreams – a universally accessible concept that transcends cultural and linguistic barriers. Instead of solely emphasizing the technical aspects of a hackathon, this phase of the project invited individuals from diverse backgrounds, with or without technical expertise, to envisage and share their aspirations. This was a call to dreamers everywhere to partake in a positive and inclusive prelude to the hackathon.

The campaign found its digital home at dreamforearth.com, a virtual gathering place for the shared aspirations of the global community. Here, participants were encouraged to submit their dreams for the future, linking their dreams with the United Nations' 17 Sustainable Development Goals to weave a rich tapestry of global dreams. As the campaign unfolded, an impressive array of over 1,200 dreams from 80 countries was shared and presented through videos and texts. These submissions were processed and analyzed using a state-of-the-art AI tool, providing a revealing glimpse into the myriad hopes and desires of people from various regions.

Participants who contributed their dreams were then extended an invitation to the hackathon at Expo 2020 transitioning from dreamers to active contributors tasked with bringing their dreams to fruition. The dreams collected during the campaign were methodically categorized and converted into actionable challenges with the help of Hack for Earth's partner organizations, solidifying the project's commitment to citizen-driven innovation.

The actual online Hack for Earth hackathon at Expo 2020 which spanned a concentrated two-week period, was a melting pot of ideas and cultures, drawing participants from 121 countries into cohesive teams, each intent on addressing one of the challenges in the seven challenge categories: Water, Sustainable Society, Environment, Education, Health, Human Rights, Partnerships. The hackathon was punctuated with an array of supportive activities, including live-streamed workshops, lectures, and interactive sessions.

Culminating the hackathon was the Prize Ceremony, held at the United Nations Hub within the Expo 2020 venue in Dubai. Winners were celebrated for their innovative contributions across the seven challenge categories, chosen by a diverse jury comprising experts from the sustainable innovation sector.

With the visualization presented in *Figure 3.1*, we are reminded of the scope and impact of the Hack for Earth method of Dream! Hack! Build! This picture is from the Prize Ceremony of Hack for Earth at the Expo 2020 in Dubai in December 2021, an event that took place in our partner organization's venue, the United Nations Hub. From left to right, you can see the team leaders from the winning teams from out of 1,471 competing teams in the seven challenge categories: Winner in Partnerships, team leader: Michael Ojo from Nigeria, Winner in Environment, team leader: Alexander Nobel from Sweden, Winner in Water, team leader: Tessa Dronkers from Netherlands, Winner in Education, team leader: Wanyang Michelle from Kenya, Winner in Health, team leader: Lab Casas from Philippines, and Winner in Human Rights, team leader: Jahir Islam from Bangladesh. (Notably absent is the Winner in Sustainable Society, team leader: Saif Edine Lahlej, who was missing due to corona travel restrictions from Morocco at the time).

Figure 3.1 – Winners of Hack for Earth at Expo2020 in Dubai

Upon securing their victories, the leading teams embarked on the next crucial phase: the Build for Earth **acceleration program**, an intensive six-month journey designed to elevate their winning concepts to fully realized initiatives. The framework of this program was meticulously constructed, drawing upon a rich bedrock of scientific research on innovation as well as a series of insightful interviews with a host of innovation leaders from across the globe. The program's curriculum was meticulously designed to cater to the expansive reach of its international participants, implemented entirely online to bridge the distances between the diverse locales of the winning teams.

The primary objective of the Build for Earth program was to fast-track the transformation of the winning solutions into viable and impactful tools, translating ideas into entities such as startups, non-profits, or other organizational forms capable of implementing the envisioned solutions. This process was not just about speed but also about the efficiency of transition from concept to market-ready solutions, a journey that is often fraught with challenges and obstacles.

The acceleration program was comprehensive, covering various modules that encompassed everything from business model creation, market analysis, and prototyping to securing funding, navigating legal frameworks, and scaling operations. The program's distinct advantage lies in its unique combination of theoretical knowledge, practical application, and mentorship, providing a holistic ecosystem for innovation to thrive.

As we anticipate delving deeper into the intricacies and successes of the Build for Earth acceleration program, *Chapter 10* promises to offer a rich narrative penned by Kristofer Vernmark. This upcoming chapter will unfold the layers of the program, providing valuable insights into its structure, outcomes, and the pioneering journey of the teams as they transitioned from winners at a hackathon to leaders of sustainable innovation initiatives. The chapter will not only serve as a repository of knowledge on acceleration programs but also as a source of inspiration for future innovators who aspire to make a tangible impact on the world through their creativity and dedication.

This example hopefully portrays the scope, dedication, and impactful construct of the Dream! Hack! Build! method.

The ABC of a hackathon's success

Navigating the intricacies of a hackathon's success involves adherence to key steps that, while straightforward, are absolutely crucial to ensuring a favorable outcome. These steps, the ABCs of hackathon planning and execution, are simple in concept yet indispensable for the result you aspire to achieve with your event. Ensure that these pillars are at the forefront of your hackathon strategy to secure the desired outcome.

- **Start by envisioning the outcome you wish to achieve**: The journey of a successful hackathon begins with a vision. Envision the outcome you are striving for. Visualize the day following the hackathon's conclusion: What have you achieved? Who has been impacted? What innovations have emerged? This forward-looking vision will serve as your blueprint for designing a hackathon that aligns seamlessly with your objectives, helping you navigate through the plethora of details and keeping you on track. This imagined outcome becomes your yardstick for measuring every decision's relevance and effectiveness.

When confronted with pivotal choices, always circle back to the fundamental purpose of your hackathon. Ask yourself critical questions: Does this decision move us closer to our goal? Is it conducive to our agenda? A clearly defined, comprehensible objective for the hackathon acts as your guiding star, simplifying the development of a framework that suits your specific needs.

For instance, if your goal is to ignite new solutions to organizational challenges and boost interdepartmental collaboration, then an in-person hackathon would likely yield the best results. Make it a requirement for the relevant departments to be involved, forging teams that cut across different areas of expertise. In such instances, extending invitations beyond the organization might not be necessary, as the focus is on cultivating internal synergy.

Conversely, if the aim is to amplify your sustainability agenda, enhance your brand's reach, and deepen engagement with your customer base or wider audience, then casting a wider net with an online hackathon is advisable. This approach would benefit from the inclusion of external organizations as partners, broadening the scope and impact of your event. Allow your employees to self-organize into teams, thereby fostering a sense of autonomy and internal competition.

- **Set up a small but efficient and autonomous core team**: Forming a dedicated core team is pivotal. This team should ideally consist of a handful of individuals, about 5-6 members, including a leader who shares a commitment to the hackathon's vision and possesses clearly defined roles. Opt for a team structure that values independence and problem-solving agility over size. This enables each member to take charge of their duties effectively and offer support where needed, ensuring that the hackathon operates efficiently.

  This core team must operate with a high degree of autonomy from the overall organizational structure in your organization to facilitate the dynamic requirements of delivering a Dream! Hack! Build! hackathon. They need the freedom to make rapid decisions integral to delivering the innovative spirit that hackathons are known for.

- **Embrace a positive mindset; say "yes" more often than "no"**: Additionally, fostering a culture of positivity and open-mindedness is imperative. A hackathon thrives on innovation, which in turn flourishes in an environment where ideas are welcomed and explored. Encourage your participants to think laterally, to be inventive, and to welcome a diversity of perspectives. By advocating for a 'yes' culture, you create an ecosystem where innovation is not just possible but expected, encouraging participants to push the envelope and think creatively.

By diligently following these guidelines, you create a fertile environment for your Dream! Hack! Build! project that promotes innovation, teamwork, and a positive mindset, all contributing to a successful and impactful hackathon.

Summary

This chapter provides comprehensive guidance on organizing a successful hackathon process adhering to citizen-driven innovation, using the Dream! Hack! Build! method. It emphasizes the importance of setting clear goals and envisioning the desired outcome right from the start. Having a small, efficient core team with defined roles is crucial for effective communication and decision-making throughout the planning and execution process.

The chapter highlights the significance of creating an inclusive and supportive environment for participants. Encouraging diversity and ensuring equal opportunities for all individuals, regardless of their background or expertise, is essential for fostering innovation and creativity. Providing mentorship and resources to participants can further enhance their experience and help them overcome any challenges they may encounter during the hackathon.

Overall, this chapter provides an overview of planning, executing, and fostering a successful hackathon to create citizen-driven innovation using the Dream! Hack! Build! method. By focusing on clear goals, inclusive environments, effective communication, and a positive mindset, organizers can create an engaging and impactful hackathon experience for all participants.

In the next chapter, we will enter into the exciting world of creating challenges for a hackathon and how you can use this opportunity to foster engagement for your hackathon.

Part 2:
Introduction to How to Hack

Part 2 explores the important details of organizing a hackathon event, focusing on engaging participants by crafting urgent and clearly defined challenges. It offers guidance on selecting the appropriate hackathon platforms, establishing effective structures, and implementing strategic communication, both internally and externally. You will gain insights into managing hackers, mentors, juries, and partner organizations, all aligned with your hackathon's objectives to produce meaningful and actionable outcomes based on the Dream! Hack! Build! Method. Co-authors Love Dager, Mustafa Sherif, and Carolina Emanuelson have contributed to this section with one chapter each – on the topic that is their respective expertise.

This section has the following chapters:

- *Chapter 4, Creating the Perfect Challenge for Your Hackathon*
- *Chapter 5, How to Organize an Impactful Hackathon (by Love Dager)*
- *Chapter 6, Communication with Hacker Teams and Mentors (by Mustafa Sherif)*
- *Chapter 7, Partnerships for Success (by Carolina Emanuelson)*
- *Chapter 8, External Communication and Social Media Presence for Hackathon Success*

4

Creating the Perfect Challenge for Your Hackathon

Creating impactful **challenges** is key to a successful **hackathon**, and in this chapter, you will learn how to do this while engaging your audience, employees, and partners at the same time.

We will be using the **Dream for Sweden** and **Dream for Earth** campaigns as examples in this chapter. During the course of this chapter, we will cover the following topics:

- How to create a great challenge that serves your purpose
- The challenge categories – a framework for exploration
- Inviting your audience to find the right challenges
- Learnings of the dream campaigns
- What signifies a great challenge?

Throughout this chapter, you will embark on a step-by-step journey to master the art of crafting challenges with a sharp edge, aimed at yielding solutions that encapsulate real impact. You'll delve into how the essence of **citizen-driven innovation** is rooted in the creation of challenges, and comprehend how to transform your organization's pain points into well-defined challenges. This understanding underscores the significance of challenge creation, revealing how this pivotal process can lay the groundwork for a successful and impactful hackathon. By doing so, you will learn how to devise valuable solutions that meet your organization's needs while actively engaging employees, customers, and your broader audience in the innovation process.

How to create a great challenge that serves your purpose

Much like how the framing of a question influences its answer, the way a hackathon challenge is presented shapes the outcome of the hackathon. A well-defined challenge directs participants toward targeted innovation, ensuring that solutions are not only relevant but also aligned with the hackathon's goals. By specifying the scope and objectives clearly, organizers channel participants' creativity and expertise into generating impactful and actionable solutions. This strategic approach maximizes the event's effectiveness, turning the challenge into a catalyst for focused problem-solving and meaningful innovation.

Crafting effective hackathon challenges – building the foundation of innovation

When orchestrating a hackathon, the creation of challenges stands as a pivotal cornerstone, wielding an immense influence over the event's outcomes. These challenges aren't just prompts; they are the guiding beacons that shape the trajectory of participating teams, determining the depth and breadth of their endeavors. The significance of challenge creation parallels that of a foundation in construction; a well-built foundation ensures stability, while a flawed one risks the structural integrity of the entire edifice.

The formulation of challenges serves as the catalyst that propels the creative thinking and problem-solving prowess of the hackathon participants. Much like the phrasing of a question shapes the contours of an answer, these challenges are instrumental in steering the hackathon's direction and defining its ultimate achievements. Hence, dedicating substantial effort and time to crafting these challenges is not merely a choice but a necessity, especially if one seeks innovative solutions and substantial depth aligned with the organization's objectives.

A challenge, at its core, embodies a query that encapsulates the essence of what the hackathon aims to address. For instance, consider these examples of specific challenges within three different categories (water, health, and environment) posed during the global Hack for Earth event at **Expo 2020:**

- **Water category**: "How can we improve an individual's knowledge of their water footprint to help them make better purchase decisions?"

- **Health category**: "How can public-private partnerships help countries health systems to deliver medicines in a locally affordable context?"

- **Environment category**: "What can be done at the community level to leverage green technology to prevent extreme climate situations and raise climate action?"

These examples underscore the **diversity** and specificity of challenges across various challenge categories, offering a glimpse into the nuanced nature of hackathon challenges. Each challenge serves as a compass, steering participants toward critical issues while also fostering innovation within the defined thematic framework.

Furthermore, the delineation of challenge categories bears immense importance in shaping the hackathon landscape. It enables a focused exploration of multifaceted problems, channeling the diverse skills and interests of participants into distinct realms of problem-solving.

The challenge categories – a framework for exploration

Dividing challenges into categories isn't just organizational; it's strategic. By categorizing challenges under distinct themes—such as water, health, or environment—the hackathon creators strategically channel participants' efforts toward specialized problem domains. This segmentation ensures a deliberate and concentrated approach, allowing teams to delve deep into specific sectors while fostering collaboration and diversity of solutions.

Each category acts as a canvas for innovation, inviting participants to unleash their creativity within well-defined spheres. The choice of categories itself plays a crucial role in inspiring teams, aligning with societal concerns, and catalyzing impactful solutions.

In essence, the creation of hackathon challenges transcends a mere selection of prompts; it's a meticulous art form that shapes the hackathon's ethos, defines its objectives, and steers the path toward innovative solutions. A well-articulated challenge resonates as a clarion call, beckoning participants to embark on a transformative journey of problem-solving, creativity, and collaboration. Thus, investing time, thought, and precision in crafting challenges isn't just a prelude; it's the key to unlocking the doors to innovative solutions that echo far beyond the hackathon itself. To illustrate how a challenge can be molded into a tool that drives your hackathon to success, we will cover a few important key points: how the result of the hackathon is connected to the challenge creation and how you can involve your community to create the challenges, thus building momentum already before the hackathon has begun.

Strategic design of hackathon challenges and categories – fostering innovation and focus

In the realm of hackathons, the construction of challenges and their categorization is a strategic endeavor, intricately woven with the overarching objectives and scale of the event. Designing challenge categories not only dictates the thematic landscape but also influences the depth and diversity of the solutions generated.

The magnitude and goals of a hackathon often steer the decision to employ various challenge categories. These categories encompass multiple challenges, typically ranging from three to five. While the number of challenges within a category can be flexible, understanding the ramifications of this choice is crucial.

Hackathon participants are typically tasked with selecting a single challenge to tackle. Consequently, a surplus of challenges could dilute the focus, resulting in a multitude of solutions that are thinly spread across diverse problem areas. Therefore, if the intention is to solicit comprehensive solutions for specific challenges, maintaining a concise list of challenges becomes paramount. Conversely, opting for a single challenge for all participants fosters a concentrated effort but might limit teams' autonomy in choosing.

Empowering participants through choice

The act of allowing teams to select a challenge instills a sense of ownership and responsibility. Human psychology dictates that the freedom to choose breeds a heightened sense of commitment and accountability for the outcomes. This empowerment leverages intrinsic motivations and fuels a greater drive toward achieving impactful solutions. The availability of multiple challenges offers teams the liberty to align their expertise and passions with a particular problem domain, thus fostering a more dedicated approach.

Communication through challenge categories

Challenge categories serve as an effective medium to introduce clusters of challenges to the participants. They succinctly communicate the hackathon's purpose, instantly outlining its thematic focus. For instance, the Hack the Crisis Sweden hackathon exemplifies this clarity by categorizing challenges into *Save lives*, *Save businesses*, and *Save society*, encapsulating the event's goals concisely and guiding teams toward their area of expertise or interest.

Similarly, the Hack for Earth event at Expo 2020 in Dubai, in collaboration with the United Nations, condensed the 17 **Sustainable Development Goals** (**SDGs**) into 7 challenge categories. This strategic consolidation aimed to prevent participant overwhelm and simplify jury management. For instance, the **Sustainable societies** category encompassed challenges such as leveraging smart societies for sustainable transformation and building resilient communities in the face of climate change.

Illustrating the relationship – challenges within categories

To delve deeper into this relationship, consider the example of the **Sustainable societies** category at the Hack for Earth at Expo 2020 hackathon. Within this category, the hackathon participants were presented with the following suite of challenges:

- How can smart societies accelerate the transformation to sustainable societies?
- How can sustainable infrastructure support societies and make housing more affordable and accessible for all?
- How can we make ethical and fair data available for all to develop sustainable societies?
- How can we make our cities greener?
- How can we build resilience in communities' infrastructure to adapt to climate change?

Each challenge within the **Sustainable societies** category delineates specific problem areas, offering participants varied yet focused avenues to direct their innovative efforts.

In essence, the creation of challenge categories within a hackathon is a strategic maneuver, aligning the participants' skills and interests with the event's thematic objectives. Balancing choice and focus, these categories wield the power to inspire, empower, and guide hackathon participants toward crafting impactful solutions that resonate with the event's overarching goals.

Inviting your audience to find the right challenges

As mentioned before, a hackathon is only as good as its challenges. The challenges will determine the outcome of the hackathon, and that is why the creation of the challenges is of utmost importance.

Creating the challenges is also an opportunity to engage your audience and an excellent way to begin the hackathon journey. By inviting your audience to take part in the creation of the challenges, you at the same time show them that you value their opinion and perspective. You can also get invaluable insights into the challenges perceived at different levels of your organization, insights that you may not have learned about before. These insights may be of utmost importance to improve your organization's overall functioning, so incorporating them into the challenges in the hackathon is a very good way of addressing them purposefully.

Many people don't know what a hackathon is or why they should join one. To communicate your specific hackathon and build engagement for joining the hackathon, you can use the challenge creation as a multifaceted tool. One way to do this is to launch a dream campaign. The purpose of a dream campaign is to level up the perspective of what is possible, in the most positive way—a dream or vision of a future that could be.

Example 1 – Dream for Earth 2021 campaign

The six-month-long global Dream for Earth campaign in 2021 is a more elaborate example of a project to collect dreams to create challenges for the Hack for Earth hackathon at the Expo 2020 world exhibition in Dubai. The Expo 2020 world exhibition was postponed by a year to 2021, due to the coronavirus pandemic, but the exhibition kept its original name, Expo 2020.

The Dream for Earth 2021 campaign, an open platform revolving around the website dreamforearth. com, became a repository of 1,056 dreams from 61 countries, allowing an unprecedented exploration of global consciousness. These dreams, posted between May 17th and August 28th, 2021, were transcribed and subjected to **Natural Language Processing (NLP)**, clustering similar content to unveil thematic and narrative patterns. Metadata, including location and category, was analyzed to reveal geographic and thematic focuses.

Utilizing advanced NLP, dreams were processed to identify common themes. Dreams with akin content were clustered, uncovering recurring narratives. Metadata, such as geographical origin and thematic category, aided in dissecting the dreams' distribution and significance. The dreams were segmented into the 17 SDGs to discern their alignment with the global developmental objectives.

Dreams poured in from 61 countries, representing diverse regions and age groups. The distribution showcased participation from various continents: 8% from Europe, 28% from Africa, 12% from Asia & Pacific, 4% from South/Latin America, 1% from North America, and 47% from the Middle East.

The dreams' contributors spanned various age groups: 53% children (15 or younger),24% adults (20-35), 17% young adults (16-19), 5% adults (35-50), and 1% seniors above 65.

Dreams encompassed multiple SDGs, reflecting interconnected concerns and aspirations. The distribution across SDGs unraveled thematic inclinations and geographical preferences. Notably, the SDGs received varying attention, revealing societal concerns, with each goal reflecting distinctive narratives and garnering differential levels of engagement and support.

The 17 SDGs are listed as follows, showcasing their relationship to the dreams posted in the Dream for Earth campaign. You can also see from which different parts of the world the dreams were from, connected to each of the 17 SDGs:

- **No Poverty** (SDG 1): Highlighting narratives on empowering the poor, providing skill sets, and advocating mental empowerment. This resonated strongly across Uganda, Nigeria, Nepal, Kenya, and Italy. The dreamers emphasized creating equal opportunities and eradicating poverty.

- **Zero Hunger** (SDG 2): Dreams focused on ensuring access to nutritious food for all, particularly vulnerable groups and children. Dreams from Uganda, Nigeria, Nepal, Morocco, and Aruba outlined visions to end hunger and ensure food accessibility.

- **Good Health and Well-being** (SDG 3): Themes revolved around becoming healthcare providers, providing clean water, and advocating for accessible healthcare irrespective of financial status. Contributors from the UAE, South Korea, Australia, Pakistan, and Switzerland envisioned a world free from diseases and accessible healthcare.

- **Quality Education** (SDG 4): Dreams portrayed aspirations for higher education, studying abroad, and equitable access to education through digital platforms. Dreams from Brazil, Pakistan, Malaysia, Tunisia, and China showcased a desire for advanced educational opportunities.

- **Gender Equality** (SDG 5): Dreamers highlighted narratives on eliminating gender-based violence, promoting equality encompassing sexual identity and orientation and destigmatizing menstruation. Notably, Sweden, Chile, Australia, Haiti, and Bangladesh emphasized gender inclusivity and equal rights.

- **Clean Water and Sanitation** (SDG 6): The focus was on clean, safe water access and preserving marine life, particularly in Afghanistan, the Democratic Republic of Congo, Sri Lanka, Singapore, and Moldova. Dreams aimed at cleaner water bodies and waste-free oceans.

- **Affordable and Clean Energy** (SDG 7): Dreams centered on sustainable lifestyles, renewable energy, and reducing reliance on fossil fuels. From the UAE, Singapore, Moldova, Lebanon, and Algeria, dreams envisioned a future driven by renewable energy sources.

- **Decent Work and Economic Growth** (SDG 8): The dreams underscored empowering marginalized groups, ICT skill-building, and equal market access. Dreams from the United States, the United Kingdom, Germany, Bangladesh, and Tunisia emphasized creating job opportunities and skill development.

- **Industry, Innovation, and Infrastructure** (SDG 9): Dreams highlighted environmental concerns, sustainable agriculture, and locally sourced goods. Contributions from Bangladesh, Norway, Myanmar, Mexico, and Iraq revolved around mitigating environmental damage.

- **Reduced Inequality** (SDG 10): Narratives centered on ending discrimination based on race, religion, disability, and sexual orientation. Dreams from Sweden, Brazil, Australia, Switzerland, and Honduras echoed aspirations for an equal and inclusive society.

- **Sustainable Cities and Communities** (SDG 11): Dreams showcased circular economies, scientific interventions, and sustainable urban planning. Contributions from Yemen, Bangladesh, the United Kingdom, Honduras, and Singapore envisioned cleaner, greener cities.

- **Responsible Consumption and Production** (SDG 12): Dreams emphasized responsible consumption, eco-friendly alternatives, and greater respect for nature. Dreams from Italy, Chile, Portugal, Turkey, and the United States focused on sustainable consumption patterns.

- **Climate Action** (SDG 13): Themes encompassed tree planting, environmental consciousness, and technological interventions to combat climate change. Dreams from Zimbabwe, Estonia, the Philippines, Gambia, and India advocated for environmental protection.

- **Life Below Water** (SDG 14): Dreams centered on preserving marine life, reducing oceanic waste, and safeguarding rivers. From Estonia, Peru, South Africa, Egypt, and Lebanon, dreams envisioned cleaner oceans and biodiversity preservation.

- **Life on Land** (SDG 15): Narratives highlighted afforestation, wildlife conservation, and preventing habitat destruction. Dreams from India, Sri Lanka, Zimbabwe, South Africa, and Peru outlined desires for lush, biodiverse landscapes.

- **Peace, Justice, and Strong Institutions** (SDG 16): Dreams spoke of racial, social, and economic justice, global peace, and climate change collaboration. Dreams from various countries echoed aspirations for a world free from discrimination and conflict.

- **Partnerships for the Goals** (SDG 17): Dreams underscored global collaboration, youth participation, and boundary-less cooperation. Contributions from Tunisia, Mexico, Malawi, Croatia, and Russia advocated for cross-border partnerships to address global challenges.

The analysis of dreams within the Dream for Earth initiative unveiled multifaceted global narratives. From aspirations to eradicate poverty and hunger to advocacy for gender equality and climate action, these dreams reflect a shared vision for a more equitable, sustainable, and inclusive world. The thematic analysis of dreams against the backdrop of the SDGs provides insights into global societal concerns, regional focuses, and the collective aspirations of individuals across diverse geographies and age groups.

The preceding-described results of the Dream for Earth campaign were presented to the 32 **partner organizations** in the Hack for Earth community. In a three-hour structured workshop, the 32 partner organizations created the challenges in the 7 challenge categories, based on the results of the Dream for Earth campaign. This way, the challenges were created out of citizen-driven innovation.

Example 2 – Dream for Sweden campaign in 2018-2019

Dream for Sweden was a campaign launched to create the underlying foundation of **Hack for Sweden**, to generate discussions and spark free thinking around how and what people's dreams are for Sweden in the year 2045, raising the bar for what a hackathon can be and steering the projects to a more visionary state as well as inviting a broader audience to participate. It was conceptualized and executed in collaboration with the team at the digital communication company Etablera: Erik Nilsson, Oscar Mörke, Jonathan Gustafsson, and Jisoo Maeng.

Dream for Sweden aimed at creating an inclusive aspect in challenge creation and also, in a data-driven way, giving participants a real sense of purpose around what could be built during the Hack for Sweden 2019 hackathon. The campaign ran for four months, from December 2018 to April 2019.

Dream for Sweden was the first step of the hackathon process, inviting partner organizations, hackers, and a broader audience to dream. This was a new concept in a hackathon setting, since it was inviting a new target group compared to the classic hackathon-goers – the engaged citizen. Via an interactive website, the campaign lowered the threshold for participation in the Dream for Sweden campaign, and users could easily visit, formulate, and share their dreams for the future of Sweden in the year 2045.

The Dream for Sweden campaign was visited by over 110,000 people, and approximately 80% of the dreams shared were related to the environment, highlighting a broad citizen unity around the most urgent and important challenges participants of the hackathon needed to solve. With six areas selected in collaboration with the Ministry of Infrastructure in Sweden (the commissioner of the Hack for Sweden 2019 hackathon), which were considered to be mature in terms of data, the dreams were then analyzed, clustered, and thematized. The result served as a foundation for creating the challenges in collaboration with Hack for Sweden's 88 partner organizations from the public and private sectors.

For further guidance, 18 interviews with people sharing their dreams for the future of Sweden were recorded in a studio. The interviews were with selected ambassadors of the 88 Hack for Sweden partner organizations, and they served as inspiration for citizens visiting the website, showcased there as inspiration. Citizens visiting the website could go and look through how other people communicated their dreams. All the dreams were shown on an interactive map of Sweden, highlighting the wide variety of participants and diversity of dreams. The Dream for Sweden campaign was finalized as an in-person physical exhibition at the Hack for Sweden in-person hackathon in 2019, taking place at Stockholmsmässan in Stockholm, Sweden, in April 2019. Designed by Etablera's collaborator Jisoo Maeng as a wooden, full-size maze made of reusable materials, visitors of the hackathon could view different video dreams shared during the campaign and share their own dreams, in that sense being a part of the Swedish innovation ecosystem.

In conclusion, the campaign invited all of Sweden to create tomorrow's dream society in the spirit of citizen-driven innovation through the Dream for Sweden campaign, a new approach to challenge creation and citizen-driven innovation with hackathons. The purpose was to create greater inclusivity in the Swedish innovation ecosystem and create solutions with a broader aim and target. The goal was to democratize the innovation process by involving citizens' perspectives and ideas to create Sweden's most effective and important digital solutions for society.

The following image shows the interactive map used in the Dream for Sweden campaign in 2019. The language used in the Dream for Sweden campaign was Swedish, since this was a national campaign addressing the citizens of Sweden. This is the reason the language in *Figure 4.1* is Swedish. It says the following: "*What is Sweden dreaming about? Plan for the future, act now. Hack for Sweden invites the whole of Sweden to create the dream society of tomorrow, with our over 50 partner organizations from both the private and public sector. Today the majority of our population is outside of the innovation system, and we want to change that. This initiative aims to democratize the innovation process by listening to the perspectives and ideas of all citizens. We call it citizen-driven innovation. We simply want Sweden to become the society of the future that we all dream of – today!*"

> **Note**
>
> See what the Dream For Sweden website looked like here:
>
> `https://upbeat-meninsky-6f8ebb.netlify.app/`
>
> Learn more about the creation of the Dream for Sweden campaign here:
>
> `https://etablera.co/dream-for-sweden`

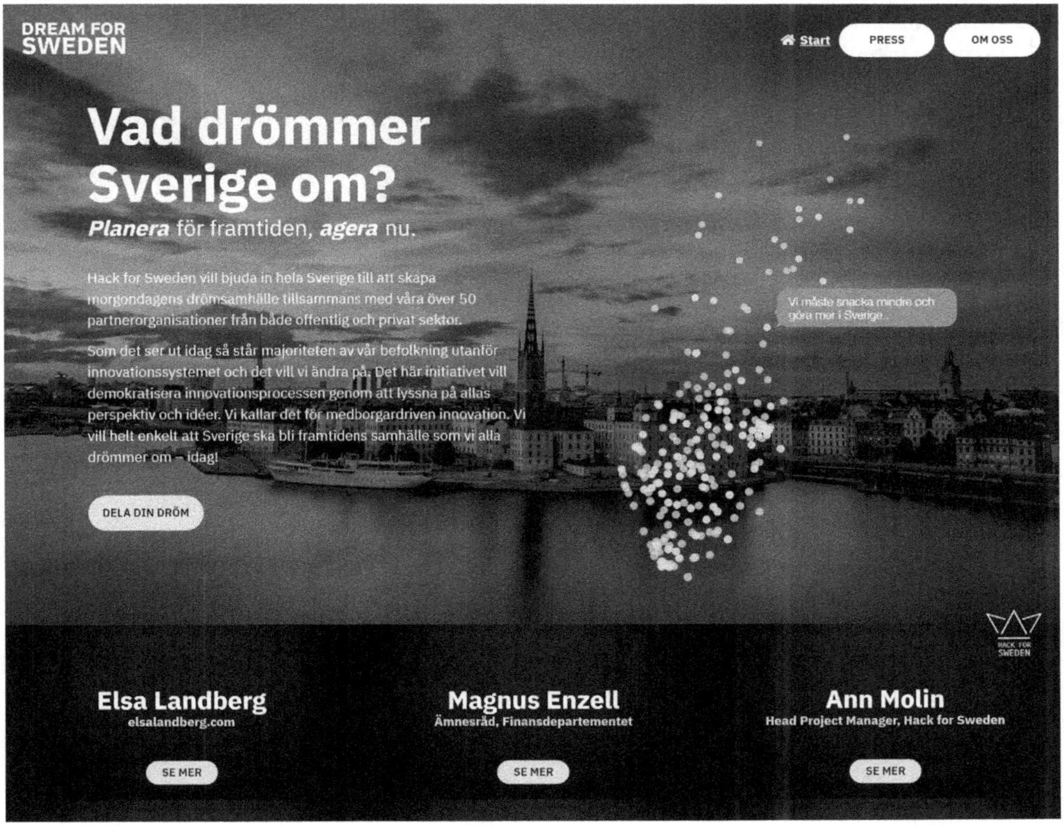

Figure 4.1 – The interactive map used in the Dream for Sweden campaign in 2019

Figure 4.1 shows what the Dream for Sweden campaign looked like on a computer screen, with the interactive map of Sweden in the very top-right corner. The dots represent the dreams shared on the website, and if you moved the mouse on top of the dots, you could read the dream shared. You can see at the bottom of the page the first three ambassador video dreams from the 18 videos with partner organizations' dreams.

Learnings of the Dream for Sweden and Dream for Earth campaigns

The dream campaigns so far executed have shown that citizens want to contribute to the creation of challenges in hackathons and that sharing their dreams can be one way of evoking an interest in joining a hackathon with an audience that doesn't necessarily think of themselves as hackathon-goers. The purpose of the dream campaigns was to open up the hackathon to a more diverse group of people who can contribute to it and its challenges, drawing in a more diverse group of participants too. The results of the dream campaigns show that people of all ages and many different parts of the world are interested in contributing to solutions for a better future and that you can benefit from inviting citizens to be involved in challenge creation. The dream campaigns reached many people and served their purpose as PR for the hackathons as well. It is also a good way of engaging your partner community in creating the challenges, as many partner organizations were very engaged and excited about the sharing of their own personal dreams.

A key learning made during the Dream for Earth campaign was that young people are more likely to share dreams via video, while older people are more likely to share dreams in text format.

You need to be sure to have some sort of screening process for the dreams posted on the website since you don't want inappropriate dreams shared. This, however, did not turn out to be a big problem in either of the dream campaigns; it turns out that this kind of project does not attract a lot of so-called "trolls."

Of course, it can be an option to create a smaller dream campaign within your organization; you don't need a website for people to share their dreams. This could be done in a more simple fashion and the dreams could be shared anonymously. Dreams can, of course, be related to the future of your company or some other joint vision you have.

We recommend adding a competitive touch to the sharing of dreams, meaning that people could vote for the best dream shared. There should be a prize that could be won by the people sharing their dreams so that they feel more motivated to engage in the campaign. One of our learnings from the dream campaigns is that it is more difficult than you would think to incentivize people to share their dreams in a video; meaning the threshold is quite high. One way of making the threshold lower and creating greater incentives is to have a contest built into the campaign, with voting for the best dream and a prize of some kind attached. In our experience, the possibility of winning something is often a good incentive for people.

After you have concluded your dream campaign, you can start creating your challenges! It's advisable to use an AI tool for this; at Hack for Earth, the company Kairos Future, one of our partner organizations for Hack for Earth at Expo 2020, did this.

In the following list, you will find the challenges that were created out of the Dream for Earth campaign, for the Hack for Earth hackathon at Expo 2020. The challenges were created in collaboration with the Hack for Earth partner community, consisting of the United Nations, Amazon Web Services, AstraZeneca, the Nordic Council of Ministers, and many more organizations all over the world. In total, there were 32 partner organizations involved:

> **Note**
>
> You can find out more information about this in the *Appendices (B)*, in the section on Dream for Earth.

- **Education challenge category**:

  - How can we create an educational model that is accessible across the globe for all and that fosters agency to solve global challenges?

  - How can we support teachers to update their curriculum to meet the demands of the future?

  - How can we ensure financing and availability for up-skilling and re-skilling for life-long learning for all?

  - How can tech help educational institutions to combat disinformation?

  - Educational passport: How can we ensure that qualifications get evaluated in a standardized way internationally (alternative educational systems and forms of learning, informal ways, outside-of-classroom skills, soft skills, etc.)?

- **Environment challenge category**:

  - What are the enablers to accelerating the sustainable and just transition toward affordable and clean energy?

  - What are the opportunities to reduce fossil fuels?

  - What can be done at the community/individual level to leverage green technology to prevent extreme climate situations and raise climate action?

  - How do we accelerate the reduction of water consumption and safeguard the quality of water (land/ocean)?

  - How do we incentivize stakeholders to build a supportive environment to co-create solutions for the climate?

- **Health challenge category**:

  - How can we improve healthcare system preparedness for future incidents?

  - How do we empower nurses and community leaders to raise awareness about health (female health, nutrition, and vaccination) in rural areas?

  - How can we have/access true, evidence-based information to address health challenges and inform policymaking?

  - How can public-private partnerships help country health systems to deliver medicines in a locally affordable context?

  - How can we preserve students' mental well-being while studying (this includes positive associations with failure and innovation)?

- **Human rights challenge category**:

  - How can we ensure that children in schools have access to healthy and environmentally friendly produced food?

  - How do we ensure equal access to information through the internet?

  - How do we tackle climate change effects as a global challenge leaving no one behind?

  - How do we provide everyone with the opportunity to be creative and inspired to imagine a better future?

  - How can we ensure equal rights for women and girls and fight discrimination?

- **Partnership challenge category**:

  - How might we engage youths around the world to co-create solutions to some of the world's complex challenges?

  - How can we break cultural, technological, and organizational borders for partnerships to solve complex global challenges?

  - How might we help establish trust between organizations to build effective global partnerships?

  - How can we use **storytelling** to build concrete collaborations for global goals?

  - How might we bridge the digital divide to build unity and remove boundaries?

- **Sustainable society challenge category**:

  - How can smart societies accelerate the transformation to sustainable societies?

  - How can sustainable infrastructure support societies and make housing more affordable and accessible for all?

- How can we make ethical and fair data available for all to develop sustainable societies?

- How can we make our cities greener?

- How can we build resilience in communities' infrastructure to adapt to climate change?

- **Water challenge category**:

    - How can we define the average, fair, and over usage of water consumption relevant to location and communities and region and map it to water distribution?

    - How can we improve an individual's knowledge of their water footprint to help them make better purchase decisions?

    - How can we define which types of plants are suitable for specific climates and locations and the quantity of water needed, when designing green spaces in cities?

    - How can we keep our oceans/natural water resources safe and clean from plastics, for the sake of both us and biodiversity?

    - How can we manage, control, and monitor overfishing and what types of fish are or are not suitable for the fishing season?

The preceding challenges were published at `hackforearth.com` and were offered to the hacker teams to choose from in the hackathon. As this was a global hackathon, covering all the 17 SDGs, the number of challenges was reasonable. In a smaller hackathon with a more defined topic, the delivery of the hackathon would benefit from having a smaller amount of categories and challenges.

This way of creating the challenges of your hackathon is strongly recommended if you want to create challenges that have adequate depth and foundation within your area of business. The Dream for Earth campaign showcases how you can foster engagement and create well-rounded challenges leading up to your hackathon event, drawing upon the ingenuity of your community, employees, and customers.

What signifies a great challenge

The essence of a great challenge is to balance scope, clarity, and creativity. A truly great challenge isn't just a prompt; it's a catalyst that ignites passion, fuels creativity, and drives innovation. Crafting such a challenge requires finesse, where each word holds immense weight and clarity reigns supreme. Within the realm of hackathons and problem-solving ventures, the definition of a "great" challenge is multidimensional, encompassing aspects of comprehension, scope, and creativity.

One hallmark of a great challenge lies in its simplicity and clarity. The challenge statement should be concise and devoid of unnecessary jargon or intricate language that could lead to misinterpretation. When participants read the challenge, they should instantly grasp its essence without confusion. It's an art form to articulate complex ideas in a few words, maintaining a balance between brevity and depth, where the challenge's significance shines through effortlessly.

Another defining characteristic is the challenge's scope. It's a tightrope walk to strike the perfect balance—not too broad that it becomes nebulous, nor too narrow that it stifles creativity. The sweet spot lies in a scope that provides enough leeway for diverse interpretations and innovation to flow freely. This balance ensures that participants can delve into the challenge's core, exploring solutions that address the root problem while allowing room for ingenious ideas.

A great challenge acts as a springboard for imagination. It should entice and inspire hacker teams to embark on the problem-solving journey immediately. Encouraging creativity while maintaining a clear focus on the problem at hand is vital. Too wide a scope might lead to scattered, unfocused solutions, whereas overly restrictive parameters could limit the potential for groundbreaking ideas. The challenge should be tantalizing, offering enough freedom for teams to think outside the box while tethering their ideas to a defined endpoint.

Crafting a great challenge involves a quest for excellence in communication and direction. It's about distilling complexity into simplicity, offering a space where creativity thrives within well-defined boundaries. The challenge should resonate with the hacker teams, sparking a fire within them to explore, innovate, and craft solutions that exceed expectations.

In essence, a remarkable challenge is a fusion of clarity, precision, and creative stimulation. It's an invitation, beckoning participants to unravel complex problems, push boundaries, and illuminate new pathways toward ingenious solutions. Finding this delicate equilibrium between clarity and creativity is the crux of crafting challenges that truly stand out and inspire greatness.

A truly great challenge is one that both addresses the desired topic and appeals to the hacker teams so that they tend to choose this particular challenge. There are many factors that influence why a challenge gets chosen over another, but three factors tend to be recurring.

A great challenge has the following characteristics:

- Is easy to understand
- Has a wide enough scope to make the creativity flow freely
- Has a narrow enough scope to make it plausible to make a solution that addresses it

A great challenge is as short as possible, making it easy to understand. Avoid long sentences with a lot of words, as it only increases the possibility of misinterpreting the challenge. Articulating something rather complex with few words and still making the meaning and substance shine through is an art form, giving the challenge the clarity it needs.

Challenge creation and communication

To create great hackathon engagement you need to master the art of challenge creation and communication. The success of a hackathon extends far beyond its start and end dates. It's about fostering a vibrant, engaged community of hackers invested in both the event itself and its outcomes. Crafting an environment where participants feel connected and passionate about the hackathon requires thoughtful challenge creation and dynamic communication strategies.

The power of co-creation

Imagine the exhilaration of a collaborative journey—inviting your intended audience to co-create challenges with you. This approach transcends conventional hackathon planning; it's an investment in building an engaged community from the outset. Yes, it demands more time and effort, but the dividends in terms of an impassioned hacker community are unparalleled.

By involving the target audience in the challenge creation process, you not only tap into diverse perspectives but also nurture a sense of ownership and anticipation. Their active participation in shaping the challenges fuels a sense of belonging and commitment that extends well beyond the event itself. This communal involvement serves as a catalyst, infusing the hackathon with an electric buzz before it even commences.

Interactive communication to supercharge your challenges

Communication isn't just about relaying information; it's about forging connections. Social media emerges as a potent tool to interactively communicate and engage with your audience throughout the challenge creation process. It's a space where dialogues flourish, ideas spark, and excitement resonates, giving your challenges the well-rounded edge they need to deliver real results.

Leveraging platforms such as Instagram, LinkedIn, or dedicated hackathon forums, you can initiate discussions, seek suggestions, and share snippets of the challenge creation journey. Engaging content such as polls, Q&A sessions, behind-the-scenes glimpses, or teaser challenges can captivate the audience's attention and draw them into the hackathon's narrative.

The interactive nature of social media enables direct engagement, allowing participants to feel heard, valued, and integral to the hackathon's fabric. This two-way communication builds bridges, fosters a sense of community, and piques curiosity, thereby attracting the right mix of hacker teams who resonate with the event's ethos.

In *Chapter 8*, we will delve deeper into the art of communication for the different phases of your hackathon, including the challenge creation phase.

Cultivating anticipation and engagement – citizen-driven innovation

Ultimately, the co-creating of challenges and interactive communication ignites a potent synergy. It cultivates a sense of anticipation, weaving a narrative that goes beyond a mere event; it becomes an experience.

The pre-hackathon engagement, like creating challenges, becomes a vital cornerstone, setting the stage for an energized community eager to dive into the challenges, armed with enthusiasm and a shared sense of purpose. The collaborative effort in crafting challenges, coupled with engaging communication, lays the groundwork for a hackathon that transcends mere participation—it becomes a transformative journey.

In this paradigm, the hackathon doesn't just start when the timer begins; it begins with the initial spark of shared creation and continuous dialogue, fostering a community-driven ethos that resonates throughout the event and beyond. It's the fusion of collaboration, communication, and anticipation that propels hackathons from being events to becoming vibrant, transformative experiences.

Summary

In this chapter, we covered how to create challenges with a sharp edge and pointed at delivering solutions that embody the right level of potential for impact. We covered how you can invite your audience and community to co-create challenges. This was exemplified by two examples of dream campaigns, illustrating how challenges can be created through actively engaging with your employees, customers, and partner organizations. The importance of communication and community-driven activities were highlighted, creating challenges that will be appealing to the hacker teams and also produce the high-quality solutions you need. This chapter also covered specific examples of challenges used in Hack for Earth hackathons. These examples and the descriptions of the two examples of dream campaigns serve as hands-on lessons for readers to create challenges on their own.

In the next chapter, you will learn about the Hack! phase in the Dream! Hack! Build! methodology, taking you through the structure of how to organize an impactful hackathon event, whether it be in person or online, internal or external.

5

How to Organize an Impactful Hackathon

By Love Dager

In this chapter, you will learn all of the technical details of running a **hackathon**; this includes all the relevant communication needed to make sure everyone knows all the important information, what platforms to use to manage the hacker teams, the **mentors**, the **jury members**, and the submitted solutions, and last but not least, how to manage the scoring procedure. This chapter will also cover how to set up the jury and jury criteria for a successful hackathon.

In this chapter, we will look into the following topics:

- Creating diverse teams
- Hackathon platforms
- Submission and evaluation
- Online hackathon versus **In Real Life** (**IRL**) hackathon
- Jury process and setup
- Opening, closing, and prize ceremonies

Creating diverse teams

A lot of science from different fields of study shows that diversity is a key part of innovation – you need people to spark each other's creativity, and that comes from thinking differently. For example, workers at companies embracing two-dimensional diversity are 45% more likely to see an increase in market share from the previous year and 70% more likely to report that their company entered a new market (reference: *Harvard Business Review*, December 2013, by Sylvia Ann Hewlett, Melinda Marshall, and Laura Sherbin).

> **Note**
>
> To understand this in greater detail, you can visit the following links:
>
> `https://hbr.org/2013/12/how-diversity-can-drive-innovation`
>
> `https://vbn.aau.dk/ws/portalfiles/portal/203812913/Diverstity_RP_2011.pdf`

And, when we talk about **diversity,** we mean it in every possible way – diversity in gender, age, nationality, ethnicity, background, field of study, profession, and more.

At Hack for Earth, we encourage diversity in a multitude of ways:

- We communicate it in all our presentations and livestreams to keep it top of mind

- We include it in the jury criteria, making it something the teams are required to think about

- We keep the majority of our hackathons online so that as many people as possible can join, making them inclusive to everyone around the world

- We let hackers create diverse teams in a few different ways so that we don't limit team structures to ones only we have thought of

So, what are the types of teams you can create?

First of all, we don't recommend setting a limit on how many team members you can have in your hacker team; this will most likely create unnecessary boundaries that will create more questions than will be necessary for the result. We do, however, recommend to the joining participants in the hackathon to form teams with a size of 3-8 people per team, but this is merely a recommendation based on our experience with optimal team dynamics. We allow participants to join as **solo hackers**, meaning they join as a team of one person, if they want to. However, it is good to point out the advantages of having more members in your team, to get multiple perspectives in the endeavor of creating an innovative solution. We also allow bigger teams than 8. We once had a whole school class of very enthusiastic young girls join as a team of 30. In the latter example, we of course recommended they split up into multiple teams of approximately 8 hackers in each, but they insisted they wanted to keep their team of 30. The reason for letting teams decide themselves on their size is that it simplifies matters for you as an organizer and it gives the teams themselves a sense of self-determination.

As a final check, when teams sign up for a hackathon, we ask them if they are open to new team members. In the course of our registration process, we ask them to select from the following options:

- *A*: I have a team and do not want more team members

- *B*: I have a team but want to find more team members

- *C*: I don't have a team and want to find team members

- *D*: I want to hack solo

This is because options *B* and *C* will go on to join our Meet & Match sessions, explained in the next section.

Meet & Match – team creation and networking session

Meet & Match is our solution to the question from participants: *"How do I meet new people to join my team if the hackathon is online?"* The Meet & Match sessions are, however, a method that can work just as well in person, at a physical hackathon.

What is Meet & Match, then? Meet & Match is a free form of networking activity where we invite all hackers who are looking to meet new people and form teams. We recommend hosting approximately three Meet & Match sessions before an international online hackathon to cater to different time zones and other individual needs, each session lasting an hour. The activity is based on "stations," one for each **challenge category**, and the task for the participants is to go to each challenge they would be interested in creating a solution for and talk to other people interested in the same challenge. It aims to mimic a physical networking activity where you'd simply walk around in a room with different signs or tables, one for each challenge.

You will learn exactly how we do this in the next section about hackathon platforms.

Hackathon platforms

Hackathon platforms are where you communicate with stakeholders and where the hackathon takes place, so to speak. In this section, we will delve into the communication channels needed and the types of platforms we recommend using in these communication channels.

As you've probably noticed by now, there's a lot of information that needs to be communicated to a lot of different stakeholders; mainly, these stakeholders are hackers, juries, mentors, and partners. As partners and mentors are easily managed over email, this chapter is going to focus on hackers and juries.

In addition to communication, we're also going to cover submission and evaluation of the solutions that hackers create during the hackathon, as well as how the Meet & Match team creation activity works in practice.

Communication channels

We at Hack for Earth mainly use five communication channels. The following setup has slowly evolved over the years and now functions like a well-oiled machine for our global online hackathons. Adapt it to your needs, depending on your hackathon size, geography, and audience, and select platforms that resonate with your audience and your needs:

- **Website**: For keeping all hackathon information gathered in one place, and to refer to in all other communication. Example: *"Announcing the 8 Challenge Categories for Hack for Earth at COP28; read all about them on our website."*

- **Social media**: For reach and generating buzz around the hackathon; also, our main way of recruiting hackers.

- **Emails**: For all the most important information, such as sign-up links, deadlines, announcements, and so on.

- **Videos and livestreams**: All our ceremonies are live-streamed on YouTube, and we also post instructional videos and trailers for our hackathons here. After trying out a few different platforms for videos, we decided on YouTube as it works well regardless of the country and internet speed that our hackers might have access to.

- **Chat room – using, for example, Discord**: During the actual hackathon, it is crucial to have quick instant messaging for all questions that pop up from participants, mentors, jury members, and **partner organizations**. For this purpose, having an open platform (we use Discord, but there are of course other options) makes it easy for all participants to communicate with each other, speak to mentors and partners, as well as contact the project management team/organizing team. Discord is a free option that works well.

The aforementioned platforms are examples of what we use at Hack for Earth. Always look into your audience, and use platforms that everyone in your audience is familiar with or can easily learn. Nothing kills engagement for participants more than someone not understanding how a platform works or, even worse, why they should bother to join the platform in the first place. Either way, the recommendation is to make sure you have at least one very fast and instant communication channel; in our case, this is livestreams and a chat room. Email is another option, but not everyone checks their emails very often, and you can lose a lot of engagement from using email as the sole communication channel.

More on communication channels for both internal and external purposes in *Chapters 6* and *8*.

Communication timeline

In this section, we will go through the strategy and different pushes for sending out information about the hackathon and explain in which channels we do them.

Before the hackathon

In this section, we focus on the communication timeline of the hackathon, where we meticulously chart the journey from initial announcement to post-event wrap-up, ensuring that every pivotal moment is captured and communicated effectively. Understanding when and where to share information on your hackathon will maximize participation and engagement and set the stage for a successful hackathon event. This timeline serves as a roadmap, guiding you through various stages of the hackathon, from generating initial interest through social media teasers to invites via email, and timely updates through dedicated platforms such as the website and more. We emphasize the importance of choosing the right channels at the right times to engage our audience, keeping them informed, excited, and ready to participate in the hackathon. This approach ensures a seamless flow of information, optimizing engagement and ensuring a successful, structured, easily managed, and well-coordinated hackathon event.

2-6 months before the hackathon

These are the key to-dos you need to focus on when you start communicating about your hackathon. Launch the website with general information about the hackathon, such as dates and challenges:

- Initial promotion in social media and over email newsletters
- Information about *"What is a hackathon?"*, *"How can I join?"*, *"What is needed of me as a hacker?"*, *"challenge categories,"* and *"jury criteria"*

2-4 months before the hackathon

After the initial communication, these are the key things to do and to communicate next:

- Open up for registrations or applications (depending on your chosen strategy for accepting hackers)
- Large-scale promotion in all external channels

1 month before the hackathon

These are the most important things to communicate 4 weeks before the hackathon starts:

- Publishing important details, such as sub-challenges in each challenge category and the jury criteria
- Publishing the time and location for the opening ceremony
- Publishing the time and location for the closing ceremony
- Publishing the time and location for the award ceremony

The weeks before the hackathon

Make sure to reiterate all details in all channels to maximize reach. Most hackers sign up at the last minute – this we know from experience – so many have most likely not seen the content you've published earlier.

Also, publish info on how hackers can prepare for the hackathon, such as reading up on the topic for the hackathon, reading up on the challenges, and the jury criteria. If you have a partner zone (see *Chapter 7*), make sure to mention that they can take advantage of partners' offerings such as workshops, livestreams, open data, and so on.

1 week before the hackathon

Send out a list of deadlines to apply and information on how to join the different platforms required for the hackathon. Reiterate the time and date for the opening ceremony and the importance of joining it.

The day before the hackathon

Send out a short and simple email with a link to the livestream where they can watch the hackathon opening ceremony. This way, even people who've skipped the other info because it was extensive or too long to read won't miss the opening ceremony!

During the hackathon

During the hackathon, communication is split into two parts: **proactive** and **reactive**.

Proactive

The proactive part centers on the different ceremonies, where all of the information and instructions should be communicated. You can read more about the ceremonies later in this chapter, but as a teaser, you should go through all of the info already communicated, then all of the info about the hackathon details. So, it is a lot of information to communicate. Hence, it is very important to mirror the information from the different ceremonies onto other channels you are using.

We recommend having a website or section of the website called **Hackathon Info** that builds up with all the information hackers have received so that they can always go back to this page if they are confused or missed something. The **Hackathon Info** page acts a bit like *Wikipedia* for your hackathon, one could say. It should feature a good overview of the content and be kept well-structured and easily searchable.

In addition to the website, which should always be kept up to date with *all* the relevant information, we always send out an email to all participants after each ceremony, with a summary of *the information from that ceremony or livestream*.

> **Note**
> Here is the difference – the website acts as a library but the emails act as a newspaper.

Reactive

The reactive part mainly takes place in the chat room (in our case, Discord), in different comments on livestreams, and – potentially – in emails sent to the organizers. If you are doing an in-person offline hackathon, then this represents hackers coming up to you at the info desk.

As one can never know exactly what questions will be asked, we can only give general advice here, but we've built a process around this to make it as smooth as possible, and here are the key important takeaways:

- **Keep as much as possible public**: Answering a question that everyone in the hackathon can see benefits all hackers and also lowers your workload in answering the same question multiple times. The easiest way is to keep as much as possible of the "help desk" in the chat room so that it is public by itself, but it could also mean that if you get an email with a question, you later post the question and answer in the chat room just as a heads up for the rest of the participants. In this case, make sure to keep the original asker anonymous.

- **Create occasions where it is easy to ask questions**: We schedule livestream Q&As with the team multiple times a day during the hackathon so that hackers can tune in and get immediate answers. We as organizers also make sure to be available in the chat room by simply asking every now and then if anyone has questions.

- **Take notes and adapt quickly**: For every question that seems like more than one hacker might be wondering about, we write it down and publish it on the website on quite an extensive FAQ page so that during the hackathon, you build up a good amount of knowledge that way. But more importantly, if you notice that a lot of people are asking the same questions at the same time, take action quickly! We do this by organizing a very short livestream (or sometimes just a video call) on this exact topic. Announce in the chat room that you've noticed a lot of hackers having this same question and that all participants interested in the answer can join a video call or livestream starting in 15 minutes. Post the link in the chat, and voilà – you've solved potentially many hackers' frustrations very effectively.

After the hackathon

After the hackathon is finished, the main piece of information to communicate is, of course, the results. Make sure everyone knows exactly who won and why, the *why* being the motivation of the jury. What does the solution do? Why was it the best? What was the motivation of the jury? And what happens next for the winners after the hackathon, and also for the rest of the participants (if you have any programs they can join, or an alumni club or similar)?

We also recommend "closing down" the website, changing the information to reflect that the hackathon is now over, and publishing on the website what was accomplished. If you are soon hosting another hackathon, you can also open up pre-registrations for that.

When it comes to post-hackathon communication, the most important thing is simply to make sure that the winners get their well-deserved moment in the spotlight, with digital diplomas sent to all winners and diplomas of participation sent to all who have participated in the hackathon.

Submission and evaluation

At Hack for Earth, we tend to use the same platform for submitting and evaluating the solutions of hacker teams, even though this is not strictly necessary. When we started out making hackathons, we asked the teams to send in their solutions over email, and then we made an Excel spreadsheet for the jury to mark their scores in! Those were exciting times, and although it probably still works well for smaller hackathons (fewer than 20 teams), most of the time you'd need to have some better structure to the process to make it more clear to everyone involved how solutions will be made, submitted, and scored and what is required to win. There are several hackathon platforms on the market, and all of them have their respective pros and cons. At Hack for Earth, we have tested a lot of them, and we choose the platform according to our needs for the hackathon at hand – different hackathons need different hackathon submission platforms. We will delve deeper into the importance of submission structure later in this chapter.

Networking and Meet & Match

As explained in the previous section, we use a method called Meet & Match for hackers to network and find team members to join up with and create hacker teams. This is, of course, most relevant to hackers who sign up for the hackathon alone but want to create a team, but Meet & Match sessions are always open to anyone who is registered for the hackathon.

To run Meet & Match sessions, one needs a platform where all hackers can log in at the same time and meet each other freely, like in a physical mingle event. This rules out video call platforms such as Zoom, Google Meet, or Microsoft Teams as either everyone is in the same conversation and only one person at a time can speak, or if you are using a breakout feature, it is instead limited to predetermined groups, also ruining the spontaneity of a mingle event.

After a lot of research, we found a platform called **HyHyve** (hyhyve.com) that works exactly the right way for our needs. HyHyve allows each hacker to log into a virtual networking room where their avatars can "walk around" and speak to each other. You can also create sections of the room that have specific themes, which we use to have an area for each of the hackathon challenges.

How to run a 1-hour Meet & Match event

Before the event, an invitation with a date and time is sent out to all hackers by the hackathon organizer team, explaining that they can join Meet & Match to find new team members, discuss the topics of the hackathon, and generally network with each other. This invitation includes a link to the HyHyve platform. We in the team also prepare the virtual room with a corner for each hackathon challenge, and also an additional one called "Help Desk" in case participant hackers want to speak to us in the hackathon team.

When the event starts, we make sure hackers have joined in (potentially waiting a few minutes if we see that people are still coming in), and then we kick off with a welcome speech (10 min) by us in the team to all participants using the **Broadcast** feature where we explain how the platform and the Meet & Match method work and explain that the goal is to find new team members and form teams for the hackathon.

The hackers are free to mingle for the remainder of the session, and we in the organizer team stay at the Help Desk to answer any questions that come up. We also take turns to mingle around with the hackers to make sure conversations are flowing well, as well as helping out any hacker who hasn't found any team or who is struggling to join a conversation for whatever reason.

When there are 15 min left of the Meet & Match session, we make another **Broadcast** to all participants to remind them to take each other's contact information so that they can stay in touch before and during the hackathon. We then encourage one person per newly formed team to act as the Team Leader who has the task of registering the team on the hackathon platform.

We then wrap up by asking if anyone has any final questions before our hackathon team leaves and explain that the hackers themselves are free to stay and continue discussing as we don't close the Meet & Match platform when we leave.

Online hackathon versus IRL hackathon

One of the key decisions one has to make early in the hackathon planning is this: Are we creating an online hackathon (also called virtual or digital) or an offline hackathon (also called physical or IRL)?

Most of the hackathon process is the same regardless of whether it's online or offline, but here are some differences worth mentioning:

- Information and communication are much more important for an online hackathon, as hackers can't simply walk up to the staff and ask for clarification as they can at an offline hackathon.
- Livestreams have to be more concise than stage appearances as the attention span is shorter while watching a livestream. In our experience, a livestream at an online hackathon can never be longer than 1 hour, while an opening ceremony live on stage at an offline hackathon can easily be upward of 3 hours as long as it is entertaining.

- Everything takes longer online, meaning that the overall hackathon schedule should be longer, the time for jury work should be longer, and so on. This comes from the increased levels of outside distraction for the participants in an online hackathon, which you simply don't have if everyone is in the same physical room with food catering provided and no other matters outside of the hackathon to attend to.

Quality or quantity? In a way, it comes down to this question many times, as venue and catering and hotels and travel all cost money, but in return, almost all metrics are better at an offline physical hackathon.

But how should one choose? See *Table 5.1* and *Table 5.2* for a classic pros/cons comparison, to help guide you on how to choose the best setup for your hackathon, depending on your resources, your budget, and your purpose for organizing the hackathon:

Pros	Cons
Global reach, anyone can join	Much harder to engage participants virtually than physically
Convenience of no travel	
More cost-effective if you are planning on a large number of participants	Often lower-quality engagement and, hence, solutions
Relatively easy to get a high-quality production	Livestreaming has a relatively set minimum cost for small hackathons

Table 5.1: Pros and cons for an online hackathon

For an offline hackathon, also known as a physical or in-person hackathon, the pros and cons are different than for an online hackathon. There are obviously a few advantages that come with having all the people in the same room together, but as you can see from *Table 5.2*, there are also disadvantages to be considered. Again, be sure to keep your purpose for organizing your hackathon in mind, and choose a setup that suits your needs and your budget best:

Pros	Cons
Much easier to engage participants with everyone in the same room	More expensive if a venue has to be rented, technicians hired, and so on
A fun activity to gather around, leading to more team building/community building	Much more expensive if participants' travels are to be paid for by the organizer
Higher-quality solutions due to more engaged participants and fewer distractions	More difficult to plan, set up, and deliver as an event
Relatively easy and cheap for small groups as there's low overhead to set up	

Table 5.2: Pros and cons for an offline hackathon

These are our guidelines for choosing the right hackathon type for you:

- **Small internal hackathon in your own venue/office/school, and so on**: Offline
- **Small external hackathons**: Online
- **Large hackathons**: Online, except in the following scenarios:

  - Where the quality of the solutions is worth the additional cost: Offline
  - Where the teambuilding element is key: Offline

In this first section, we have delved into pivotal elements essential for orchestrating an impactful hackathon. The topics covered so far are tangible tools you need to learn, and our recommendations here are based on years of experience working with setting up different types of hackathons.

We started out with a discussion on the criticality of assembling diverse teams, emphasizing how varied backgrounds and skill sets can significantly enhance the innovative output of the hackathon. Following this, we evaluated different hackathon platforms, detailing how these tools can lend structure and efficiency to the hackathon's organization and delivery. A comparative analysis of online versus in-person hackathons was then provided, outlining their unique advantages and challenges, guiding you as an organizer in selecting a format that best aligns with your objectives and logistical constraints. This section has also brought you insights on crafting a strategic communication timeline, aimed at ensuring all participants, from hackers to partner organizations, are well-informed and engaged throughout the hackathon's progression. To summarize, this serves as a crucial guide for anyone looking to harness the full potential of how to use a hackathon as a catalyst for innovation and collaboration.

We will now continue our exploration of the hackathon setup by looking closer at the jury process and setup, something that needs a thought-through strategy to run smoothly and efficiently.

Jury process and setup

After all the hacker teams have submitted their solutions to the hackathon platform, their work is done and the jury or juries take over. Their role is to go through the submitted solutions and select the best few from a pool of potentially thousands. It is not an easy task, so we use a few tools to make it easier.

First, we'll discuss the importance of jury criteria, then the submission structure, and lastly, how the process can be segmented to streamline jury work.

Importance of jury criteria

The main tool the jury uses to evaluate the solutions is, of course, the jury criteria. We use a carefully chosen selection of six jury criteria when we evaluate Hack for Earth hackathons, and we believe most of them are quite applicable to all hackathons where you are looking for innovations that are not necessarily code-based (but could be). If your hackathon is strictly code-based solutions, then you might want to include input from a technical architect to define some additional jury criteria to measure this area. Remember to not have too many jury criteria – this will make it more difficult for the jury to assess the solutions and also for teams to create good solutions that meet the criteria. Jury criteria also need to be clear, direct, and easy to understand for both hackers and jury members.

Jury criteria from Hack for Earth at COP28

Next are the jury criteria we employed specifically for Hack for Earth at COP28, our online hackathon held from COP28 in Dubai in December 2023.

Each jury criteria is structured in the same way, with a name and a short description, and then a number of questions that both the hackers and the jury can ask themselves about the solution to help them evaluate if the solution meets these criteria and whether it has a good chance of winning or not. This setup is used to frame the jury criteria in a manner that will ensure that as many as possible understand them fully and is designed to avoid unnecessary questions from the organizing team about how to interpret the jury criteria:

- Innovativeness – Innovativeness of the idea behind the solution, as well as the intended technology to be used in the implementation of the solution (if applicable):

  - In what way is this solution innovative?

  - Are there existing or similar solutions?

  - How does the solution differ from any existing solutions?

- Realizability – Realizability of the solution from its current idea stage to implemented solution, used by its intended users in its problem context:

  - How realistic is the time plan?
  - Does the solution have access to all the needed data (if applicable)?
  - How well are potential risks calculated?
  - How soon can the solution be available to the intended users?
  - Is the technology mature enough (if applicable)?
  - Can a **minimum viable product** (**MVP**) be created within 3 months?
  - Can a **proof of concept** (**POC**) be created within 6 months?

- Comprehensibility – Comprehensibility of the solution proposal's value proposition and main use case:

  - Is it easy to understand the solution?
  - Is it easy to understand how the solution works and how it will be implemented to solve the challenge?
  - How well detailed is the description of the solution?
  - Does it include an understanding of key stakeholders and ecosystems that are relevant to the realization of the solution?
  - Will the end users of the solution understand it too, or do they need special skills to take part in it or use it?

- Diversity – Diversity in teams is an important factor in achieving a high level of innovation:

  - How diverse is your team?
  - Is there a good balance regarding gender, skills, competence, background, and age?
  - Solving the Sustainable Development Goals (SDGs) – Does this solution correlate to the United Nations' 17 SDGs, and how well does it solve the challenge it is intended to address?

- Scalability – Scalability of the solution if it is implemented and realized:

  - How many are experiencing the problem that this solution is intended to solve (if applicable)?
  - How well does this solution scale?

- How well does the solution correlate to the SDGs?

  - In what respect does the solution solve one or more of the SDGs?
  - How many in the solution's target audience would experience an improvement, and how extensive would that improvement be?

For Hack for Earth hackathons, we put extra emphasis on the first criterion (*Diversity*) and we instruct jury and hacker teams to always include this in the solution. This is to slightly nudge our solutions to include diversity, a criterion that is extra important to our solutions and to our hackathons.

Adapting the jury criteria to your needs

The aforementioned first three jury criteria are the essential foundation of any good set of hackathon jury criteria. Is the solution innovative (*Innovativeness*), can it be done (*Realizability*), and can one understand what the solution is about (*Comprehensibility*) are really the basics. It happens more often than one might think that the solution has an oversight already here, though.

Some common issues of submitted solutions in hackathons are the following:

- **Comprehensibility**: Especially if technical teams can't explain the solution in an easy enough way, so that is why this jury criteria needs to be included

- **Realizability**: The solution is so advanced that some parts are simply not possible until well in the future or are out of budget to implement. This is a jury criterion you need to include if you are looking for solutions from your hackathon to be implemented.

- **Innovativeness**: Simply because the solution might already exist on the market and there's no need to reinvent it, this jury criterion is essential to any hackathon aimed at creating new solutions to a challenge.

The latter jury criteria are more nuanced and can be applied depending on the focus and goal of your hackathon:

- Scalability could regard how well the business model scales if you create a hackathon looking for business models, but could also regard how many employees in your organization are struggling with the problem the solution applies to. In a simplified way, scalability is all about the quantity of the solution. *It is easy to think that this criteria is not relevant if the solutions are meant to be used internally, but this is most likely the wrong way of looking at it.* Instead, think about how you can quantify the solutions against each other. Is it a matter of cost or of how many developers are needed to implement this? I'm certain your hackathon has some level of quantifiable measure that could be translated into a criterion.

- Diversity is easily defined but just as easily overlooked, but as we described previously in this chapter, it is a key part of forming successful teams. See the previous section for details.

Solving the SDGs is, of course, only applicable to hackathons focusing on global goals, but use this sixth criterion to add your main topic to the jury criteria. This criterion could be called "Relevancy" to make a generic name for it. Imagine an amazingly great idea, with a full score on all criteria but not actually relevant to the results you are looking to achieve with your hackathon. That is where this criterion comes into play.

Jury criteria are one of the important tools to get the outcome that you are looking for in your hackathon, so it's good advice to put in effort in designing jury criteria that are well-defined and shaped to align well with your purpose. The preceding examples are well tested in our hackathons, for the purpose our hackathons have, but this is not necessarily what your hackathon is aiming to achieve. Be sure to align your jury criteria with what you aim to accomplish with your hackathon, and remember to communicate these jury criteria well to your jury and your hacker teams. This way, you steer your hackathon outcome on the right path.

Importance of submission structure

The structure of the hackathon platform and the submissions in themselves mainly act to make things efficient.

Imagine a small hackathon of just five teams and no structure on the submission. They are just told to create their solution in any way they want and see fit. This would make it a little bit harder to compare the submissions and choose a winner, but if you also had five members of the jury, they could still probably read through 100% of the submission materials and decide between themselves a winner.

Now, imagine the hackathon grows, and the next year you have 50 teams handing in solutions; this system already implodes. Even if you scaled the jury to 50 members, it would be impossible to align and compare everything, and this is where structure comes into play.

Basically, we recommend starting with the number of teams you expect to have in your hackathon, together with how many jury members and how much time the jury can allocate in total. Combine all this with some simple math, and you have a good starting point.

> **Math**
>
> (Jury members X Minutes they have available)/Submitted solutions to evaluate
>
> 10 jury members X 2 hours (120 minutes) = 1,200 minutes
>
> 1200/50 teams = 24 minutes per submission

So, with 10 jury members allocating 2 hours to evaluate 50 teams' solutions, they can spend 24 min per solution, giving plenty of time to go through a detailed document of the solution.

This fails to include that it wouldn't be a fair evaluation if only one jury member reviewed each solution. To limit the amount of bias from individual jury members, we recommend having at least five different jury members evaluate each submitted solution, and during Hack for Earth in 2023, our average was nine.

If we go with our recommendation of five jury members evaluating each submission, the math changes dramatically.

> **Math**
>
> (Jury members X Minutes they have available)/(Submitted solutions to evaluate*jury members reviewing each submission)
>
> 10 jury members X 2 hours (120 minutes) = 1,200 minutes
>
> 50 submitted solutions X 5 evaluations per solution = 250 evaluations to be made in total
>
> 1,200/250 teams = 4.8 minutes per submission (let's call it an even 5 minutes)

Now, you see why it is important to think of the submission structure, as realizing that your jury members need to spend day and night for 2 weeks going through all their submissions is a nightmare you don't want to happen. Instead, we have this very clear number of 5 min that can be spent per evaluation, and we can work with this to make a good structure.

Opening, closing, and prize ceremonies

The ceremonies of a hackathon are the glue that sticks the hackathon together, and they set the tone and the structure for your hackathon, getting all your participants on the same page – in essence, they give your hackathon a face. In this section, we will look at the important aspects of the ceremonies, explain why they are so necessary for your hackathon event, and guide you on how to best organize your own ceremonies – whether online or in person.

Importance of the ceremonies

The ceremonies, of course, mark important parts of the hackathon but also serve some other purposes, so let's look into that:

- **Marking the start and end of the hackathon**: First and foremost, the ceremonies exist to mark the start and end of the hackathon, with a separate one for giving out awards to the winning teams. We separate the closing ceremony and prize ceremony to give a sense of achievement to the hacking teams after submitting their solutions, and then give the jury plenty of time to go through the solutions before handing out the awards. If you have a smaller-scale hackathon, these two could be combined.

- **Making sure everyone has all essential information**: Another main purpose of the ceremonies is to make sure all hackers are up to date with the instructions. They should already be, considering the information has been sent out over email (and/or other communication channels of your choice), but the ceremonies serve as a point of collection for the busiest of hackers who have not read the information, as well as a reminder for those eager to read it all and who therefore might have forgotten already if some time has passed since it was sent out.

- **Giving the hackathon a face**: Certainly more important for an online hackathon than an offline one, but key in either case. The ceremonies act to show the team behind the scenes, say hello, and cheer on the brave teams that are part of the competition. We at Hack for Earth many times choose to livestream our ceremonies from a strategic location also to amplify our message. As an example, Hack for Earth at **Expo 2020** in 2021 was aired from the Expo 2020 world exhibition in Dubai, to show the message of global collaboration, and the *Hack for Earth* hackathon in 2023 was aired from the United Nations' COP28 climate change conference in Dubai to show the importance of climate action.

The focus of each ceremony

Every ceremony in a hackathon has a special focus, and here, we will guide you on what signifies each ceremony and what are the key aspects to communicate in them. Since they have different purposes, they also have different content and ambiance, so next, you can find a description of the ceremonies you need to have in your hackathon, along with a description of what content is important to include in them.

Opening ceremony

The opening ceremony is the most information-heavy and focuses on the following:

- Welcoming everyone to the hackathon
- Walking through the schedule of the hackathon and important deadlines
- Explaining what is a hackathon for first-timers
- Explaining the hackathon's goal and procedure
- Going through hackathon platforms, submission structure, and jury criteria
- Introducing the sponsors, partners, staff, and jury members
- Kicking off the hackathon with high energy

Closing ceremony

The closing ceremony is a milestone for hackers having submitted their solutions after the intense hackathon. Therefore, it is much lighter in topics, such as the following:

- Congratulating all hackers for their hard work
- A few key messages from sponsors, partner organizations, staff, and jury members
- Explaining what happens next and the jury process
- Clearly instructing when and how they will be contacted in case they win and get to join the prize ceremony

Prize ceremony

The award ceremony is a celebration of innovation, with its content being very flexible but of course including an announcement of the winners:

- Thanking all sponsors, partners, staff, and jury members, as well as all hackers, for spending the time to join the hackathon

- Announcing the winning solutions, usually including having them pitch their solutions at the ceremony so that all participants can learn about the winning solutions and the teams behind them

- Having the jury on stage to explain why they chose the winners and comment on the submitted solutions in general

- Presenting the different options and support available to teams that want to bring their solutions forward and continue working on them after the hackathon is over

- A warm send-off

Summary

Now that you have finished reading this chapter, you should have a good understanding of the different aspects of organizing a hackathon. You've delved deep into the technical intricacies of organizing a hackathon, covering a range of crucial aspects.

This chapter underlines the components essential for orchestrating successful hackathons, with a particular emphasis on the vital role of assembling diverse teams. To cultivate this inclusivity, we recommend implementing strategies that promote wide-ranging participation. These strategies include creating opportunities for individuals from different backgrounds to join teams, as well as organizing events such as Meet & Match.

Further detailed within this chapter is the indispensable nature of effective communication in the planning and execution of hackathons. It stresses the importance of leveraging a variety of channels – from websites and social media platforms to emails, videos, and interactive chat rooms – to ensure that information reaches all stakeholders in an efficient manner. A carefully structured communication timeline is highlighted as a critical tool for ensuring that essential information is conveyed at the right moments.

This chapter stresses the importance of having a well-organized submission process coupled with clear, transparent criteria for the jury's evaluation. These criteria should encompass a range of aspects to achieve your hackathon's goal.

In addressing the modalities of hackathons, the chapter contrasts the advantages and challenges associated with both online and offline formats.

The role of the jury in the evaluation process is underscored, with the chapter emphasizing the importance of establishing clear evaluation criteria, creating a structured submission framework, and dedicating ample time for thorough assessment.

The narrative also delves into the ceremonial aspects of hackathons, including opening, closing, and prize ceremonies.

In conclusion, the chapter articulates that the organization of a successful hackathon demands thorough planning, the employment of the right tools and platforms, effective communication strategies, the formation of inclusive teams, structured evaluation processes, and the hosting of engaging ceremonies. These elements, when combined, empower organizers to create hackathons that are not only impactful but also memorable and inspiring for all participants. Further insights on this topic are promised in the subsequent chapter, inviting readers to explore the deeper implications of community engagement in the success of hackathons.

In the next chapter, we will dive into community engagement and how to manage hacker teams and mentors during a hackathon, a topic of utmost importance due to its power to attract attention to your hackathon.

6
Communication and Managing Hacker Teams and Mentors

By Mustafa Sherif

A **hackathon** is about passionate people coming together to create innovative and impactful solutions. It's a challenge to have diverse people from different backgrounds and geographical locations walking toward one vision and working to achieve one common goal in a short amount of time as a hackathon. Therefore, communication is key in hackathons. Clear and simple communication is one of the key factors in making a successful hackathon and achieving the aim and goals of a hackathon. In this chapter, you will read about and learn how to communicate and tell a hackathon story before, during, and after a hackathon with different target groups through different physical and digital channels. You will also learn how to bring people together to build a hacker team and how to bring skilled and experienced people to mentor and guide hacker teams. Lastly, you will explore best practices from local, national, and international hackathons about how to build an active and creative hackathon community and manage it in an efficient and structured manner.

So, in this chapter, we will look into the following topics:

- The importance of communication
- Communication channels
- Communication with hackers and mentors
- Creating the right hackathon vibe in your channels of communication

Now that we have set the framework of this chapter, let's explore what is needed to communicate to different target groups and how to bring people together to build a hackathon community.

The importance of communication

Communication is one of the key factors in making a successful hackathon and achieving the aim and goals of a hackathon. Communication as a tool can be very powerful and help a lot in achieving hackathon goals, or it can backfire and cause misunderstanding and unclarity, which affects the achievement of hackathon goals and repatriation of hackathon organizers. Being clear and simple in communication serves many important fundamental purposes and helps to achieve many goals:

- Raise awareness about various local and global challenges on different levels – for example, individuals, organizations, communities, cities, and the entire planet – communicating about the climate crisis and raising awareness about it. Hackathon organizers can spread a message and communicate the vision, mission, and values that they stand for.

- Attract people to participate in the hackathon as hackers to create solutions to different **challenges**.

- Attract people to participate in the hackathon as **mentors** to help hackers create solutions.

- Attract partners to contribute with resources (funds, open data, workshops, and so on) to organize a hackathon.

- Attract the press and media to communicate about the hackathon to spread the word about the hackathon and cover it.

- Attract the general public to follow the hackathon from a distance even if they are not actively participating in it. This can be important to attract more participants for the next hackathons, and also attract partners and investors to collaborate with the winners of a hackathon.

- Make it easier for the hackathon organizers' team to run a hackathon.

Clear and simple communication is a key tool to help achieve the goals of organizing a hackathon.

A flexible communication plan

A flexible communication plan is a plan that is easy to follow, has very few steps to implement, is flexible to change and adapt, and is very clear about what, when, to whom, and where to communicate. *A communication plan can be divided into three main phases: the pre-hackathon, during, and after a hackathon*. It's important to create a continuous story and journey of a hackathon and not only communicate about it during hackathon time, which can last for a few hours or a few days. In this way, continuous communication will serve the purpose and achieve the goals that we mentioned previously.

One might wonder, what does flexibility mean here?

The answer is that a communication plan should not be locked, fixed, unchangeable, and difficult to adapt to different situations. During any event, especially events such as a hackathon, many things pop up during the time of an event. A hackathon organizer team should be flexible and ready for any changes in the plan; for example, activities might be canceled, new activities might be added, activities might be rescheduled, and so on. The point is to stay relevant and up-to-date with what is happening in a hackathon and the atmosphere around and outside a hackathon. A smart hackathon organizer team can be flexible and use different circumstances to survey hackers with information and inspiration so that they can create relevant solutions to hackathon challenges.

For example, during the *Hack for Earth* hackathon at *COP27*, the activity that the *Hack for Earth* team was supposed to communicate according to the plan was a reminder about the deadline for the hackathon. But then, we had an expert reaching out who wanted to have a session about how to present a solution and talk about pitching and **storytelling**. According to the communication plan, the *Hack for Earth* project management team should have said: "*No, sorry – we do not have time in our schedule now and we need only to communicate about the deadline, and so on.*" But then, hackers would have lost a big opportunity to get inspired to make their pitch as a way to tell their story better.

It's because flexibility is a key aspect in a communication plan that the *Hack for Earth* team adjusted the communication plan, invited the expert to a session, recorded that session, and informed the hackers about the deadline and the recorded session. The hackers got information about the deadline and inspiration for their pitch as well.

Internal communication

When we mention clear and simple communication, the focus might be on external communication. But this is not only the case. Let's not forget about internal communication in the hackathon organizer team that organizes and runs a hackathon. Usually, hackathons are short in terms of time. Some hackathons take only a few hours, some other hackathons take 1 to 3 days. During each hackathon, there are a lot of sub-events and activities that happen inside and outside a hackathon, and people pop up with interesting ideas and inspiration for hackers. New things that are happening all the time might affect an organized team and shift them from the main plan and delivery of a hackathon. That is why it's very important to have clear and simple communication within the core project management team so that each member of the project management team knows and understands what are the activities that a hackathon organizing team is supposed to deliver during a hackathon. An internal communication plan is more about the following:

- Making clear what is the main responsibility of each member and making sure everyone in the team understands it.
- Deciding about the platform/platforms that will be used for internal communication between different team members; for example, Gmail, WhatsApp, Discord, Teams, and so on. It's very important to make sure everyone in a team knows how to use the platform and has access to it.
- Deciding what storage service the core team is going to use to store their files; for example, OneDrive, Google Drive, or another cloud storage service.
- Making sure that each member of the team understands the mission, goals, different phases of a hackathon, and what the team will deliver.

A well-communicated, well-synchronized, and well-organized hackathon organizing team creates an easy and effective workflow for themselves, which can lead them to create a great experience for people who are following a hackathon from social media or for people who are participating in a hackathon and creating real solutions. Always follow this saying: *"Leave no one behind."* It helps a lot as a rule to get everyone on the same page and make sure hackathon organizers' team members have the knowledge to use and communicate with each other internally and externally with different target groups.

To whom are we communicating?

Usually, there are many different groups of people and organizations involved in a hackathon. Depending on the aim and goals of a hackathon, it's important to identify target groups that will be addressed in communication. The usual groups that can be part of a hackathon can be divided into two categories: active (hacker community: people and organizations who take an active part in a hackathon) and nonactive (the general public or people and organizations who follow a hackathon but are not involved actively in any part of it).

The active category (hacker community) comprises the following:

- **Hackers (participants in a hackathon)**: Individuals who apply to be part of a hackathon. They actively want to create a team and compete to create solutions to solve hackathons' challenges.

- **Mentors**: Individuals who apply to be part of a hackathon and want to actively contribute with their expertise to help hackers create their solutions.

- **Partners**: Organizations and networks who contribute to a hackathon with different resources (read more on this in *Chapter 7*).

The nonactive category (general public) comprises the following:

- **The general public**: People who are following the hackathon on different channels (digitally or physically) but are not participating in it. They are just an audience. They might not be actively involved in participating and creating solutions in a hackathon, but they like to follow a hackathon journey, see challenges, see solutions, and all the different events that happen in between during a hackathon. (It's like when we like to follow an event on TV, social media, or other platforms. We are not involved in the event, but we as an audience enjoy following it for different reasons.)

- **Press**: Media channels and platforms, networks, and influencers who might be interested in covering a hackathon or some parts of it in different ways.

- **Organizations** who are following the hackathon from different channels (digitally or physically). They are not involved actively in contributing to the hackathon as partners, but they like to follow the journey, see the challenges, see the solutions, and all the different events that happen in between during a hackathon.

We can turn a lot of the general public audience, organizations, and media from inactive to active by having clear and simple communication. This is important because many individuals from the general public might be motivated to participate in the next hackathon. This leads to an increased number of participating hacker teams who can contribute impactful solutions to the global goals. Also, when it comes to organizations, it's important to bring related organizations to the journey of hackathons. Depending on how each organization contributes, their contribution can help hackers find solutions and also make their solutions come to reality later after a hackathon.

Sometimes there are people, organizations, and media who are interested in joining a hackathon but they are not sure about it. This can be because of different reasons. But there might also be communication about a hackathon that could be clearer; for example, there is a lack of information about a hackathon and how to join a hackathon, which makes a person decide whether to participate or not.

Communication channels

So, what communication channels work best, and which ones to choose for the hackathon outcome you are looking for? As we all know, there are hundreds of different communication channels, physical and digital. People in different countries use different platforms to communicate for different purposes. Generations use different channels to communicate. You might notice that a younger person in your family or in a family that you know uses different platforms than what you as an adult use to communicate. Sometimes, it differs in using the same app but in different ways, and so on. WhatsApp in some countries is used as a mobile texting application for family and close friends only, while in some other countries it's used as a communication app for not only family and friends but also for work colleagues in an organization.

On top of these differences in using communication channels between generations, nations, and organizations, every couple of months we see a new communication platform has been developed, upgraded, or completely invented; for example, Clubhouse, TikTok, Instagram Threads, Telegram, X, WeChat, Facebook (Meta), and many more.

According to *Global Social Media Statistics* (`https://datareportal.com/social-media-users`), there were 4.95 billion social media users around the world in October 2023, equating to 61.4 percent of the total global population. The good news is that people can afford to have a smartphone and can connect to the internet. This can lead to a lot of people getting and sending information to other people in the world and can be part of different online activities such as a hackathon.

As a hackathon organizing team, we want to include people from different nations, genders, backgrounds, , and so on. We aim for **diversity**. This means that we need to tell the story of the hackathon and send and receive information in different communication channels that suit different people.

Depending on the hackathon budget, there may be different solutions for hackathon communication channels. As we mentioned at the beginning of this chapter, the communication method depends on the aim of a hackathon that is being organized. At *Hack for Earth*, we have been organizing national and global hackathons based on **citizen-driven innovation**. We want to attract the general public to join our hackathon and also to follow it if they do not join. That is why when we tell a story of each hackathon we organize, we include as an audience both the active target group (people and organizations who are taking actively part in a hackathon) and the nonactive target group (people and organizations who are following the hackathon on social media but not taking actively part of it). Let's look at this in more detail:

Target group (audience)	Nonactive (general public)	Active (hacker community)
Who? Description of a target group	People and organizations who like to follow a hackathon but do not take an active part in it.	People and organizations who are taking an active part in a hackathon by, for example, creating solutions or contributing with knowledge or other resources to help create solutions.
Why? Aim and purpose of communication with this specific target group	To tell them the story of a hackathon to raise awareness of the challenges of that specific hackathon. To build an online audience that shares the word of hackathon around the globe. To show them how a hackathon works and how they can be part of upcoming hackathons as hackers, mentors, or partners.	All the points that we mentioned for the nonactive target group are on the left in this table. To inform them about different details of how to apply to be part of a hackathon.
Where? Communication channel	On social media to communicate and tell stories about a hackathon. Social media platforms offer the chance for online engagement with an audience. Digital or physical events.	Social media to communicate and tell stories about a hackathon. Social media platforms offer the chance for online engagement with the audience. Other specific communication channels help to give detailed information, receive information, and create a space for communication between hackathon community members.

Table 6.1 – Communication roadmap and target groups

The preceding table shows the two target groups of audiences' communication channels and purposes. During this chapter, we will build on this table and fill it with more detailed information.

Social media as a communication channel

For communicating with the two audience groups by covering and telling a story of a hackathon, social media is the easiest method. It's accessible to people in most countries and for different ages (with age limitations for youth/children depending on the platform). As we read at the beginning of this chapter, there is already 61.4 percent of the total global population using different social media platforms as a communication channel, so which social media platform should we choose? There are two ways of choosing which social media platforms should be used to communicate with the audience:

- The first one is to stay where we are. We stick to platforms that we are already using and wait for people to join us there and take part in the stories and information that we share. The upside of this way of choosing social media platforms is we do not need to spend time and money on establishing new channels. The downside is that the already existing channels that we have are not actively used by our target audience for a hackathon. This means that we are not going to have a large audience of nonactive or even active target groups. This can lead to the fact that we need to spend money to market our social media channels and content to reach out to people and welcome them to follow us (but once again, it depends on the aim of a hackathon).

- The second way of choosing social media platforms as a communication channel, which is the one recommended, is to find and reach out to people to go where they are already gathering. It means looking at the top-used social media platforms and starting to communicate there. This book was written between the years 2023-2024. A the time of writing, Facebook still has a high amount of users, according to *DataReportal Global Social Media Statistics*. In the top 10 list, we have the following:

  - Facebook

  - YouTube

  - WhatsApp

  - Instagram

  - WeChat

  - TikTok

  - Facebook Messenger

  - Telegram

  - Snapchat

  - Douyin

The Hack for Earth project management team is actively telling stories about our hackathons on Facebook, Instagram, YouTube, and LinkedIn. LinkedIn doesn't publish monthly active user data. That's why we can't see it included in the top 10 list by DataReportal. LinkedIn has 1 billion users in 200 countries worldwide, according to LinkedIn in 2023, making it one of the world's largest social media platforms, with a focus on target groups such as students, businesses, governments, professional organizations, and networks.

In *Chapter 8,* you will read more about how to use social media to drive a hackathon, how to interact and engage to grow your audience and hacker community, how to build a strong community of partners, hackers, mentors, and juries, and the importance of timing for posting on social media.

Communication channels with the active hacker community

On social media channels, we communicate and tell a story about a hackathon in general. It's like a TV channel covering an event for the general public.

We still need another type of communication channel to communicate with this group, which we call the active hackers community. As we mentioned previously, the active group is the hacker community, which includes the following:

- **Hackers (participants in a hackathon)**: Individuals who apply to be part of a hackathon. They actively want to create a team and compete to create solutions that contribute to solving hackathons' challenges.

- **Mentors**: Individuals who applied to be part of a hackathon and want to actively contribute with their expertise to help hackers create their solutions.

- **Partners**: Organizations and networks that contribute to a hackathon with different resources.

The communication channels we use are mostly to survey the purpose of sending and receiving information to a specific person; for example, deadlines, dates, files, and applications. The following communication channels are needed to run a successful and well-structured hackathon:

- A website to publish all details and important information about a hackathon, such as the following:

  - Background and aim of a hackathon

  - Challenges that hackers will solve

  - Instructions on how to join a hackathon as a hacker team

  - Instructions on how to join a hackathon as a mentor

  - Instructions on how to join a hackathon as a partner

  - Information and profiles of different mentors

  - Jury criteria for a winning solution

- Hackathon prize

- Hackathon timeline and important dates

- Hackathon important links for resources and other useful information/websites

- Useful material for press and media

- Link to events and livestream

- Contact information for hackathon organizers

- Application forms that are linked to the website. These forms are important for receiving communication from the following:

  - Hacker teams

  - Mentors

  - Partners

- Evaluation and feedback about a hackathon:

  - Based on these forms, you can collect emails and information; for example, the number of team members, countries, ages, backgrounds, and other data that is useful for measuring hackathon objectives and goals

- A mass email communication platform to send out important information via email to all collected emails from application forms. You can communicate the following:

  - Acceptance and welcoming letter to hackers

  - Acceptance and welcoming letter to mentors

  - Instructions about the next steps of a hackathon timeline and deadlines

  - A reminder of deadlines before each important deadline

  - A reminder of important live events

  - Links to recorded events that are important for the community to watch

  - Links to important resources such as workshops, open-source data, e-books, lectures, and so on

  - Links to hackathon social media platforms and home page so that they also follow the coverage of the hackathon

  - Contact information for the hackathon project management team or a specific team member whom they can reach out to when they need help

In mass email communication, be very clear and simple about the information so that you minimize the number of questions that you receive afterward. If information is unclear and unstructured, this increases the chance of having many hackers or mentors emailing and asking for clarification. This will consume a lot of a hackathon organizer teams' time to answer. It's better to avoid this kind of extra work and instead spend time simply writing clear information and explaining it very well.

During *Hack for Earth*'s recent hackathons (for example, *Hack for Earth* at **Expo 2020** in Dubai and *COP27* in Egypt), there were more than 1,000+ teams in each hackathon and more than 200+ mentors as well. These are big numbers of people to contact and to communicate with. So, imagine if we had unclear instructions and information. Imagine the time we'd need to spend answering questions from different teams and mentors. That is why clear and simple communication is a key factor for delivering a successful hackathon.

Another important example is the amount of information we send during these hackathons. The *Hack for Earth* team divides information and instructions into different steps. We don't overload hackers or mentors with information at once in one big and long email.

Based on our experience from local, national, and global hackathons, it's better to divide information and instructions up rather than send everything at one time. Short emails will make hacker teams less stressed in a hackathon. Recommended channels include the following:

- An email service (Gmail, Outlook, or other email services) to communicate and respond to different emails that will come from hackers, mentors, and partners.

- A YouTube channel to livestream different events; for example:

  - A promo video about a hackathon and challenges

  - Opening ceremony

  - Q&A sessions with hackers, where hackers use chat functions to ask questions or write comments (this can also be done by a video call meeting, not necessarily on YouTube)

  - Q&A session with mentors, where mentors use chat functions to ask questions or write comments (this can also be done by a video call meeting, not necessarily on YouTube)

  - Lectures related to a hackathon's topic

  - Instructional videos about how to submit an idea, or videos to explain other important activities

  - Closing ceremony

  - Prize ceremony

The aforementioned communication channels are mostly one way of communication (information from the *Hack for Earth* project management team to different active parts). Sometimes, it's also two ways of communication when the different parts respond to the *Hack for Earth* project management team. This type of communication is not building a community of people who can interact with each other and exchange their knowledge and experiences. That is why a community needs a platform that brings together all people in one place to collaborate.

Once again, there are many digital applications such as Slack, Discord, Trello, Confluence, and many more. It's very important to choose a platform that has the needed functions without the need to pay to access the platform; this is important because users don't have to pay to join. A paid platform will lower the number of participants in a hackathon; especially when a hackathon is on a national level or a global level, or the target group is civil society, then a platform should be free to use. In this way, hackathons are more accessible for many people to join and create a community that creates solutions. More aspects to think about while choosing a platform are how simple it is to use and if it's available on smartphones as well.

For example, the *Hack for Earth* community uses the Discord digital application. It's an application with channels to discuss topics and collaborate. It even works to send files between users. On Discord, there is an important function where community members can have a label next to their username. Examples of labels are *Mentors*, *Hackers*, or *Hack for Earth Team*. These labels help in communication. It is easier for everyone to understand who is posting and who is answering.

On Discord, we create different channels that fill different purposes; for example:

- A channel for announcements of information and instructions.

- A channel for mentors where they can share and exchange their experiences and also help each other. For example, if a mentor gets a question from a team about a specific topic that is not within this mentor's expertise, this mentor can contact mentors on the Discord channel and ask if other mentors have expertise within this specific topic and can help hackers.

- A channel for each challenge so that community members can post related websites, comments, questions, and other material that can inspire them to create solutions for that specific challenge.

- A channel to ask questions for the hackathon organizing team. These questions can be related to information about hackathons; for example, deadlines, who to submit, where to find X lecture, and so on. This channel is important because it can work as a **frequently asked question (FAQ)**. When community members ask, all questions and answers will be there for all community members.

- A channel for random stuff that community members can post. This kind of channel is more to make the hackathon atmosphere more fun and contribute to community-building purposes. *Hack for Earth* believes in fun and joy as an important element to create solutions for big challenges. During every hackathon that we have organized, there are a lot of memes, fun videos, and inspiring material posted on this channel. This boosts, motivates, and inspires the hacker community.

- A channel for introducing community members, where members can post a picture of themselves and write a brief summary about themselves. It works as an icebreaker between our community members from different countries.

- A channel to find a team member. In this channel, community members can post to find more team members. Also, **solo hackers** who need a team can post there to find a team that can take them to be part of it. It's like a match-making channel.

- A channel for hackathon organizing teams for internal communication.

For each target group externally and internally, there are different channels to communicate by sending and receiving information at the hackathon. To include as many citizens in a hackathon as possible, different communication channels should be accessible and should not cost anything for the users.

Communication channels in a physical hackathon

For a physical hackathon that takes place in a specific physical building or place, the same digital channels that are mentioned previously can be used here as well. The only difference is that hackathon organizers should take opportunities for face-to-face meetings. In a physical place, various communication channels can be used:

- A stage or place can be established to announce important information and run the main activities for a hackathon; for example, the opening ceremony, lectures, Q&A sessions, closing ceremony, announcing winners of a hackathon, and so on

- Mentors can walk around and coach different hacker teams

- The hackathon organizing team can walk around and make sure the hacker teams have everything they need to hack

It's a combination of a physical place and digital platforms. To have everything clear and accessible all the time, it's important to publish all information and instructions about a hackathon digitally to all teams so that they can go back and read this.

Just as in a digital hackathon, there are X number of hackathon organizing team members who coordinate different digital platforms, in a physical hackathon, there should be a team of coordinators to synchronize between a digital world and a physical world. In a digital hackathon, there is always a person who fronts a hackathon, acts as a host, and presents different activities during the hackathon. In a physical hackathon, a *host* is necessary to act as the main communicator for a hackathon. This person acts as a host on the stage, introduces different activities, and announces important information.

When to communicate?

An introduction on when and what to communicate was covered in *Chapter 5*, and here, we take a deeper plunge into this most important part of a well-structured hackathon.

When there are many communication channels, it might be difficult for the hacker community to navigate where to find what. Here comes the responsibility of simple and clear communication for the hackathon project management team. This team should tell community members about the different communication channels and what purpose each channel of them have.

Based on *Hack for Earth* local, national, and international hackathons, we observed that some hacker teams might be stressed due to different reasons, and it affects the way they think and how they look for and find information. That is why it's very important to gather all information in one place to start with. The *Hack for Earth* project management team uses the *Hack for Earth* website. This one place for gathering all the needed information makes life easier for community members and also for the hackathon organizer team to find information or to refer to when they get a question.

Different types of information need to be sent out and communicated at different times and in different channels. What time is the best to send out information? At *Hack for Earth*, we have a rule of thumb that we call "*Days, hours, minutes, and repeat.*" So, let's start exploring what each of these rules means.

Days and hours

Communicating information in advance is helpful so that community members can plan their schedules and synchronize their teams well in advance. Especially when it's an international hackathon, there are hackers from different countries, which means people who are living in different time zones. Thus communication in advance will help them to plan and follow a hackathon. For example, before the start of a hackathon, a few days in advance, send out information about what are the different communication channels that will be used in the hackathon so that hacker community members have the time to download and register on different platforms and learn how to use them before the hackathon starts. This will ensure that valuable time for hacking is not eaten up by participants trying to figure out how the platforms work.

Hours and minutes

Then, a reminder is always a good idea. The hacker community needs reminders about deadlines and activities. These can be reminders of important application and submission deadlines, important events, and other activities during a hackathon. Usually, hacker team members are very busy working on their solution and developing it. They might read instructions and information about deadlines or other events, but later on, they might forget or miss them because of working hard. This reminder can be done in a few hours or a few minutes before a deadline or an activity. For example, during a hackathon, before a deadline, send out a reminder a few hours before about it. Another example is before a live Q&A session, send a reminder a few minutes before, and so on.

Repeat

In the *Hack for Earth* rule of thumb, when it comes to communication timing, we have the word "*repeat.*" This means that we send out information about what happened. Depending on the activity, we send out a summary of that specific activity. This is useful for community members who missed that activity. Here are a few examples to make "*repeat*" more clear:

- A summary of the opening ceremony; this can be a recorded video and information in text format
- A summary of a Q&A session
- A summary of the prize ceremony and a list of winners with information about their solutions

One might question whether this method of *"Days, hours, minutes, and repeat"* is an overload of information for the hacker community. The answer based on our experience is no. Because hacker teams will get very busy during a hackathon, they will be diving deep into creating innovative and impactful solutions. They need information to be gathered in a place where they can access it when they have time. Also, they need a reminder about this information in case they forget about it because of their hacking work. If a team feels that it's too much of a notification, they always can mute a communication channel on communication platforms. But from many years of experience with thousands of hacker teams from different hackathons, the *Hack for Earth* team never received feedback about information overload. The feedback was the opposite. Many of the hacker teams were very grateful to receive information in advance, receiving a notification with a reminder and also a summary.

As a hackathon organizer team, it's very helpful to think that we do our best to support our community members in their journey. You give information to support them in creating impactful solutions for hackathon challenges. Always communicate information in advance, remind them about it, and repeat information. With clear and simple communication that is happening in a timely manner, the hacker community will understand the hackathon process. An understanding of how a hackathon works and what are the important deadlines and activities will make the hacker community part of this hackathon and enable them to engage and contribute with solutions.

Let's go back to our communication table and fill it with more information:

Target group (audience)	Nonactive (general public audience)	Active (hacker community)
Who? Description of a target group	People and organizations who like to follow a hackathon but do not take an active part in it.	People and organizations who are taking an active part in a hackathon by, for example, creating solutions or contributing with knowledge or other resources to help create solutions.
Why? The aim/purpose of communication with this specific target group	To tell them the story of a hackathon to raise awareness of the challenges of that specific hackathon. To build an online audience that shares the word of hackathon around the globe. To show them how a hackathon works and how they can be part of upcoming hackathons as hackers, mentors, or partners.	All the points that we mentioned for the nonactive target group are on the left in this table, and also: To inform them about different details of parts of a hackathon; for example: The application process Criteria for a hacker team Deadlines for submitting an idea The application process for being a mentor Jury criteria for submitted solutions A schedule of different events Partnership process Award and the process of the Build for Earth acceleration program

Target group (audience)	Nonactive (general public audience)	Active (hacker community)
Where? Communication channels	A website Social media platforms that offer the chance for online engagement with the audience; for example: Facebook Instagram YouTube Linkedin	A website The same communication social media platforms that are used for the general public audience. Specific communication channels that are used only for this active hackers' community group: Mass email Application forums A platform for digital meetings A platform for community collaboration
What? Content to communicate	All information about a hackathon can be on a website. Social media channels can be used to communicate important information about a hackathon to the general public and also be used to cover a hackathon. Stories can be shared about the hackathon's different phases (from application to the opening ceremony to updates about the hackathon, the closing ceremony, the winner announcement, and so on).	All information about a hackathon can be on a website. Social media to communicate and tell stories about a hackathon. Other platforms can be used to send detailed information and instructions about a hackathon. These platforms help us to send and receive information and create a space for communication between a hackathon community.

Target group (audience)	Nonactive (general public audience)	Active (hacker community)
When? A time frame	Days (weeks) before the start of a hackathon to communicate important information about the hackathon and open for registration. A few hours before important deadlines and events that are open to the public. Everyday stories and content (images, short videos, lives, events, and so on) during a hackathon. A few days after the end of a hackathon with a summary of the hackathon and the next steps.	Days before the start of a hackathon, for sending instructions about registration steps. A reminder before deadlines or important activities. Always a few hours in advance so that a community can prepare themselves for the next steps. 1 hour or half-an-hour reminder before deadlines or an important activity ASAP, a summary of previous events or activities. This can be information, a recorded video, and so on. This is useful for community members who might missed an event or activity. A few days after the end of a hackathon with a summary of the hackathon and the next steps.

Table 6.2 – Communication roadmap and target groups

After making a communication plan and launching communication channels, it's now time to welcome people who want to be active in a hackathon and be part of the hacker community.

Communication with hackers and mentors

In this section, we will focus on hackers and mentors as hacker community members.

Hacker communication

Hackers are individuals from different backgrounds who believe in hackathons as a method and process to create useful solutions in a short amount of time. Many other reasons make a person sign up for a hackathon; for example, to collaborate and network with new people, make a better world by creating impactful solutions, get a hackathon and teamwork experience, get a certification for their CV, win a prize, make their idea come true (in case there is an **acceleration program** such as *Build For Earth*), and many more.

At the national and international hackathons that *Hack for Earth* organizes, we don't specify and select one type of people to join hackathons. We always advocate for diversity in competencies in teams. We want to include people and bring people together from different nations, genders, backgrounds, knowledge, and so on. To make this happen, *Diversity* is one of the criteria of the *Hack for Earth* jury at all *Hack for Earth* hackathons. It's a must criteria to fulfill for a hacker team to get more points to win a hackathon. There are usually two different types of hackers when it comes to having a hacker team:

- **Hackers with a team**: Hackers who sign up for a hackathon and already have a team of hackers. They already have a communication channel internally and divide roles in their hacker team. They are ready to go. They are ready to hack. A hacker can be part of only one team and not two hacker teams. This is to make a hacker focus on their teamwork to deliver high-quality solutions with a high level of innovation. Many hackers have great energy and want to create as much and as big a change as possible. Some hackers want to be part of two or three teams. But based on experience, being part of many hacker teams will affect the output and participation of a hacker. Also, a hacker cannot be a mentor and vice versa due to the same productivity reasons mentioned previously.

- **Solo hackers**: Some individuals are interested in being part of a hackathon, but they are alone without a hacker team. Fantastic individuals such as these are very important to have in a hackathon. They can bring very valuable, interesting, and impactful ideas and inspiration to a hackathon community. A way to create a diverse team is the *Meet & Match* method that *Hack for Earth* uses to bring solo hackers together to build a team.

Meet & Match sessions

This most effective way of connecting participant hackers who do not have a team or need additional team members for their team was first introduced to you in *Chapter 5*. We will only briefly cover it here; for more details on how to organize a Meet & Match session, see *Chapter 5*.

The method explains itself by the name *Meet & Match*. It's a method we use to create an opportunity for solo hackers to build a team together or join an existing team in need of additional competence.

The timing of the Meet & Match meeting is before the start of a hackathon to give new teams a chance to talk to each other, explore their competencies, and organize themselves before the start of a hackathon.

There will always be people who might miss different Meet & Match meetings or attend Meet & Match meetings but could manage to join a team due to different reasons. But no worries for them when they sign up for a hackathon and join the Discord community platform, where there is a specific channel for finding a team or a team member. They can introduce themselves in that channel and ask to join a team. The Discord channel works as a second option if a solo hacker doesn't get the chance to join a team.

Hacker engagement through communication

Communication with hackers starts in the very early stages of a hackathon, even before the start of a hackathon. It's the stage of announcing a hackathon and welcoming hackers to join it through marketing, social media posts, and so on. Then, after Meet & Match meetings and sending out application forms, it's time to bring them into the Discord platform as a digital place for the community to gather and collaborate. Making hackers feel excited and included in this hackathon has a lot to do with communication. It has a lot to do with making them feel welcomed, respected, and appreciated and showing them what a hackathon is about and how it works. We stress again the importance of simple and clear communication. Moreover, a hackathon project management team must guide the hacker community with information and instructions and walk them through the journey of a hackathon. This means explaining to hackers about this hackathon and its challenges, what the different phases of this hackathon are, when the main deadlines are, how hackers can navigate and use different platforms, what purpose every channel and platform has, and so forth.

The following is a summary of the main communication with hackers:

- Marketing and invitation with an application form to apply for a hackathon

- A welcoming letter

- Information and instruction about a hackathon and how to join different hackathon channels

- The rules of communication in the hackathon and what the consequences are for violating them, including not promoting your own company and that no harassment of any kind will be tolerated. Important with explicit rules of the concrete consequences if the rules are broken by a hacker and how to get in touch with the project management team if you have a complaint.

- Invitation to watch the hackathon opening ceremony

- Information and invitations to different lectures, workshops, and Q&A sessions

- Instructions about submission format and deadlines

- Reminders about deadlines and other important activities

- Invitation to hackathon closing ceremony

- Invitation to the winner announcement

- Certification of participation for all hackers

- Winners diploma for all winning teams

- A thank-you letter for all hackers

- Information and instructions about the next step for winning teams

When it's a physical hackathon, the same rules apply. It's important to welcome hackers and explain to them about a hackathon and the different details of it. It doesn't matter if it's a digital or a physical hackathon. Information should always be accessible digitally as well to all teams, even if it's a physical hackathon.

This section was about how to bring together different people from different backgrounds to create a team that competes in a hackathon. In the next section, we will explore how to bring in mentors who will have the duty of coaching hacker teams in a hackathon and guiding them to create impactful solutions.

Mentor communication

Mentors are expert individuals who have valuable expertise in some area relevant to the hackathon topic to share with competing teams. They also believe in hackathons as a method and process to generate ideas and create solutions. Usually, mentors are people who have already started their careers and have knowledge and experience to share with other people in the hackathon community.

Hack for Earth is always advocating for diversity in competencies, not only for hackers but also for mentors. In the different *Hack for Earth* hackathons, we are looking for tech or industry experts in tech, data application, **artificial intelligence (AI)**, blockchain, business, climate change, **Sustainable Development Goals (SDGs)**, communication, and other competencies that are relevant to hackathon themes and challenges. In other words, we invite a wide range of mentors from different backgrounds who can offer help and advice to the hacker community.

When a person applies to be a mentor at a *Hack for Earth* hackathon, this person will be asked to provide the following:

- Name and surname
- Expertise and skills specific to the hackathon
- Link to their LinkedIn profile
- An email address to communicate with
- A profile picture

This information will be published on the website and will be accessible to the hacker community to find a suitable mentor with skills that they are looking for and need help with.

Mentors with different skill sets can be the most valuable asset in a hackathon. The strategy of *Hack for Earth* mentorship is not to assign one mentor to one specific team because a mentor might have less experience in a specific topic and can't help the hacker team with that specific topic. So, it's better to free all mentors from having one team to mentor. Instead, they can be available to be asked for help by any hacker team. In this way, we can make sure that a hacker team has a wide range of mentors to ask for help on different topics, from ideas and brainstorming to open data to storytelling and pitching a solution to a jury. When it's a physical hackathon, it works the same as a digital hackathon. There is no mentor assigned to one team. Mentors are available and present in the hackathon room and can be reached by the hacker team anytime during a hackathon.

Moreover, a mentor cannot be a hacker or join a hacker team that creates solutions and competes to win a hackathon because this might lead to bias from a mentor against other teams; for example, a mentor is only helping their own team and not helping other teams who might have the same ideas in order to not let them win.

Overall, there is often less communication between organizers and mentors compared to the communication levels between the organizing team and the hacker teams because mentors will have a responsibility to coach and give advice, which is less work than creating solutions like hacker teams do. Hackathon communications are addressed to both hackers and mentors; for example, information about the hackathon, challenges, jury criteria, different deadlines, submission format, and so on. Some other communication is addressed to only mentors. After people apply as mentors and get accepted, there will be specific communication that is addressed to them as mentors:

- A welcoming letter to them with information about the hackathon, challenges, and jury criteria. Mentors need to know what the hackathon's challenges are about so that they can give relevant advice. Also, they need to know what are the jury criteria. So, while they are mentoring hackers, they help them to achieve jury criteria; for example, scalability, innovativeness, realizability, and so on. That is why it's important, as we mentioned before, that a website has all the useful information about a hackathon so that mentors can read it.

- Information about their role as mentors and what it entails in a hackathon. All mentors participate virtually and must be available online most of the time during the hackathon. The mentors' task will be to share their knowledge with competing teams and answer questions they have. Their task is not to come up with a solution; it's to support and inspire. The hacker team will create a solution. For example, the *Hack for Earth* project management team brings in an expert to speak to inspire hackathon mentors about how they can be useful and inspiring mentors in a hackathon.

- Information about how mentors can mentor hacker teams and which platform they will use to do that. In most hackathons, all help is provided on the Discord program digitally. On Discord, there are different channels for different challenges; hacker teams write their questions there, and mentors with relevant information can answer. Everyone in the hacker community can read this also, so it might benefit others who might have wondered about the same question. There are other ways for hackers and mentors to get in touch with each other; for example, by email or LinkedIn. Sometimes, mentors find it easier to have a video call with a hacker team or get in touch on WhatsApp. It's totally up to the mentor and hacker team to decide where they want to communicate.

- Information about deadlines and submission format so that mentors understand when and what hackers need to submit to help them and inspire them with ideas and references.

- Information and invitation to different events that are happening during a hackathon; for example, opening ceremony, Q&A sessions, inspiring lectures and workshops, closing ceremony, and prize ceremony.

- Information about hackathon winners and their solutions.

- A certificate of mentorship. All mentors receive a certificate from *Hack for Earth* for their mentorship and contribution to different teams after the hackathon is completed. This is a way to show appreciation to all mentors for giving their valuable time and energy and sharing their knowledge with the hacker community.

Many mentors are looking for opportunities other than only helping hacker teams during a hackathon. Some mentors are looking to network with other mentors and develop their knowledge and skills. That is why there is a mentors' community within the big hacker community. This community has a digital place to meet on a Discord channel that is only accessible to mentors in a hackathon. In this channel, all mentors can interact with each other, introduce themselves, and exchange contact information, ideas, and knowledge.

Based on different hackathons that *Hack for Earth* organized, this mentor channel is also being used by mentors to get help from each other; for example, a hacker team asks mentor X about a topic that is not related to mentor X's expertise (let's call it Y topic). Using the Discord mentors channel, mentor X shares with other mentors that there is a hacker team who is asking about Y topic. Then, any mentor shows support and replies to mentor X on Discord, taking the conversation further with the hacker team.

Just as with hacker teams, mentors have also questions about a hackathon. That's why it's necessary to have specific mentor Q&A sessions in video call format that are only open for mentors to attend and be part of. This session often works as a Q&A session and also a digital meeting for the mentor community to talk with each other and discuss topics related to hackathons and other subjects. So, these meetings function as a digital meeting place for mentors to exchange and share their knowledge and ideas. Mentors can always send questions in text format on the Discord channel or in a chat in case they are not available during a Q&A session.

Mentors already learn mentorship skills by helping different hacker teams during a hackathon. By having a channel for mentors, facilitating it, and creating opportunities for them to get in touch with each other and interact, a hackathon can suddenly be much more valuable for mentors' personal development and networking.

Creating the right hackathon vibe in your channels of communication

After creating a communication plan and identifying the who, why, where, what, when, and starting to execute this plan, a foundation for community interaction is built. All different communication channels are there and can be used based on their purpose. There are key aspects that we should be aware of when it comes to creating a hackathon vibe and community interaction. Let's look at these next.

- Create a *code of conduct* for the hacker community. A code of conduct is defined by rules, values, principles, and behaviors that guide people from different backgrounds toward building a hacker community and a common vision. An example of a code of conduct could be never using bad language during a hackathon, with other team members, and in communication in general. By having a code of conduct, both hackathon organizers and participants will have a common ground and understanding about what community they will build and what rules to adhere to. It's just an agreement to make sure that all community members are on the same page and working toward one clear vision.

All groups of a hackathon community *should be on the same page* when it comes to information and hackathon phases/steps. By that, we mean when hacker teams receive information about a submission format and a deadline, then mentors should also receive information about when the deadline for a hackathon is and what hacker teams will submit so that mentors and hackers are on the same page. This allows both groups to work together as one community toward one deadline and target.

For example, if hacker teams receive information about the submission format that will be a 2-minute video and mentors don't receive this information, this will affect communication between them. Hackers will ask questions about how to pitch an idea in a 2-minute video, and mentors who didn't receive information about the submission format will maybe talk about a PowerPoint presentation. Not having a community on the same page will create a misunderstanding between community members. The amount and level of details of information don't necessarily have to be the same as communicated to hacker teams and mentors, but both groups must know about what the status of a hackathon is now and what the next steps are.

- *Lead by example and ice break* in different communication channels. Here, we are focusing on Discord as a platform for all community members to interact with each other on different channels. Usually, there will be many people from different backgrounds who have different social behaviors. Not all community members are socially active and ready to interact from the first second of a hackathon. This is because of many reasons; for example, it's an online hackathon, and people do not see who is sitting behind a screen on the other side of the Discord channel. It might also be because it's a physical hackathon, so people are too shy to interact face-to-face But there is also a possible reason, which is community members don't know how to use a specific channel and they don't want to post something that might not fit with a channel purpose and they then see it as a mistake. Here comes the responsibility of a hackathon organizer team to lead by example and ice break. Hackathon organizers should initiate a conversation and activate different channels by posting, explaining, and motivating other community members to post and interact. In this way, community members will feel sure about what to post and start to engage and interact with each other online or physically. A community needs to see a leader who is leading communication so that they can follow and start taking action. Sometimes, this leader is another member of the community who just starts and everyone follows; sometimes, hackathon organizers should start a first post.

For example, during **Hack for Earth at COP27**, the community on Discord was quite silent at the beginning of the hackathon, and there was not so much interaction at all in different channels online. That was a red flag for us as a project management team because a hackathon is about collaboration, exchanging ideas, and inspiring each other. We followed *"lead by example and ice break."* The *Hack for Earth* project management team took a selfie and posted it on the Discord channel with a short text about who we were in the selfie picture and a few inspiring and motivational words to the hacker community. Just a few minutes later, many hacker community members sent pictures of themselves or their team members sitting together, introduced themselves, and wrote about their feelings and excitement for this hackathon and for finding impactful solutions. This Discord channel was continuously active during the *Hack for Earth at COP27* hackathon, and community members were posting different stuff that was about themselves or just to cheer up the community and motivate them. It created such a fantastic and energetic vibe in the community.

In the following photo, you can see the *Hack for Earth* project management team from the operating room during the *Hack for Earth* hackathon at *COP27*, in November 2022. 1,800 teams from 125 countries were working on solutions to the 7 challenge categories, and it was a very busy time for the three members of the project management team (from left to right: Ann Molin, Head Project Manager, Mustafa Sherif, Community Manager, and Love Dager, Hackathon Manager):

Figure 6.1– The Hack for Earth project management team from the operating room during the Hack for Earth hackathon at COP27, in November 2022

Another example: during the Hack for Earth at Expo 2020 hackathon, in Discord there was a specific channel to find new team members. This channel was dedicated to solo hackers who had not joined a team during Meet & Match sessions. In this channel, solo hackers could introduce themselves, write about their skills, and state what challenge category they would like to find a solution for. When they provided this information on this specific Discord channel, other teams in the community could read it and ask the solo hacker to join their team. It was all about matchmaking for teams and solo hackers. During the Hack for Earth at Expo 2020 hackathon, there was very little activity on this channel. At the same time, the Hack for Earth project management team received questions from solo hackers about wanting to find a team. What we did was also "lead by example and ice break." We posted in the channel a post explaining to the solo hackers how they could do it and also motivating them to post. After this post, many solo hackers posted about themselves, and other teams started to like and comment and ask them to join their teams. The problem was solved for solo hackers. The learning is this: even though the channel description was very clear about what this channel is used for and how community members can post, people might be shy or not read a channel description, or for other reasons they want someone else to start. If everyone waits, then nothing will happen, and hackathon time passes quickly. The hackathon project management team needs to be fast-moving and react to motivate community members to interact at the very early beginning of a hackathon.

- *Warn and disqualify community members* for their inappropriate behavior, including bad language and/or bad attitude. There is a chance that a community member does not behave according to the code of conduct of a hackathon. This could be by using bad language in communication, posting inappropriate videos and pictures, or texting in a chat with other community members and disturbing them. If this happens, this hacker will receive a warning and a second chance from the hackathon project management team, to give this hacker a chance to behave well, be part of the community, and create a good hackathon experience for everyone. If this person doesn't listen to the first warning, disqualification is the second step. This person will be disqualified from the hackathon by removing the hacker from Discord as a platform for the community and also as a member of the hacker team. A hackathon project management team needs to act immediately and not let a person disturb other community members and create unpleasant experiences for them over a long period of time. This might affect the output of their solutions and the outcome of a hackathon.

For example, during one hackathon, there was a hacker who was writing and posting things that were unrelated to a hackathon and also disrespectful to some other community members. This hacker got a warning for the *Hack for Earth* project management team in a private chat on Discord. After that warning, this person stopped posting, and the *Hack for Earth* team removed all previous posts by this hacker that were inappropriate on different channels. It's important to act immediately before other community members read these kinds of unacceptable posts or comments.

Another example is about a hacker who was part of two teams. It's not allowed by *Hack for Earth* to be part of two hacker teams. This is against the rules. So, this person also got a warning and selected one team to compete with. Thus, warnings are not only about what people write and post but also if they are following hackathon rules or not.

- *Don't be a friend* – make sure that project management team members treat all hacker community members equally. In any hacker community, there will be social interactions and networking during a hackathon. This is an amazing thing that can come out of an event, creating a real network between people. But if a friendship starts between the hackathon project management team and community members, it might have a backfire effect on both parties. We are not against friendship or other kinds of active networking between these two parties. However, it is important to set firm boundaries and delay friendships and networking with hackers starting until after a hackathon period. Having close community members as friends for a hackathon organizer team can cause a bias toward specific community members. These close hackers might get extra help, or a deadline might be extended for them just because they are close and have good relationships and contact with a hackathon-organizing team member. This can create an unfair hackathon for other community members. This aspect can destroy a hackathon experience and community when community members are being treated unfairly. Having these kinds of relationships and communication with specific community members can also affect a hacker team's performance, output, and solution quality. A hacker team that receives special treatment might think it is fine if they don't fulfill all the jury criteria or it's fine if they don't submit a solution in time according to a deadline, and so on. All these aspects will affect their solution negatively. Equal treatment is a key aspect of creating good and a fair hackathon. After a hackathon period, when a hackathon is done and winners are announced, then it is fine for project management team members to network and create connections because these connections and close communication will not affect a team's performance, solutions, and results of a hackathon.

For example, during each hackathon, the *Hack for Earth* team receives many connection requests on different social media and communication platforms. That's a very usual thing that happens. The *Hack for Earth* project management team makes sure not to communicate and offer help related to a hackathon outside formal hackathon communication channels. We do not answer any questions related to a hackathon on platforms other than the official ones. We ask hackers and mentors to kindly respect that and stick to the rules. By this, we avoid the backfire effect of connections from a hackathon and do our best to treat all community members equally.

Engage community members in social media and storytelling of a hackathon. A hackathon is about citizen-driven solutions, collaboration, and co-creation of solutions. This co-creation can be extended to how we tell a story and cover a hackathon. Community members are a big asset to a hackathon. They are the hackathon. Without them, there would be no hackathon. Community members can engage in storytelling by being active on their social media channels. This can be done by providing them with material (images, text, videos) so that they can use it to tell a story about the hackathon and their participation. One further step can also be taken by collaborating with some hacker community members and getting quotes from them to be published on your main social media channels. In this way, community members feel extra empowerment, and they are part of the hackathon story when they are also part of social media and storytelling.

For example, at the *Hack for Earth COP27* hackathon, the *Hack for Earth* project management team asked community members to send short videos of them describing their experiences of the hackathon. Many hackers and mentors sent their videos, and these videos were shared on social media platforms and also in our ceremonies, such as closing and award ceremonies. This not only created contact for *Hack for Earth* social media channels but also a big engagement on Discord between community members when they watched each other's videos.

- *Have an ambassador and a spokesperson onboard.* To spread the word about a hackathon more, it's always good to have ambassadors who talk about and promote a hackathon. This helps a lot to get more people to know about a hackathon, which increases the possibility of several people applying to be part of a hackathon and creating impactful solutions. An ambassador should be a person who is studying, working, or somehow active within a topic of a hackathon. This will give more authenticity to a hackathon when an ambassador is credible and the hackathon target group can relate to this person.

To create the right ambiance in hackathons and to make hacker teams deliver high-quality solutions with a high level of innovation, communication is a key element. People will already see a high standard of a hackathon by the first impression they get from social media. Then, they see it in how a hackathon is communicated, the structure of communication channels, clear and simple information and instruction, possibilities for the community to interact and collaborate, help and answers from hackathon organizers, how well and fairly a community is treated, and so on. All these aspects help hackers to create high-quality and high-level innovative solutions and help mentors coach hackers to do that.

Summary

In this chapter, we went on a journey of how to communicate and how to build an active and creative hackathon community. We talked about the importance of a clear, simple, and flexible communication plan to communicate the hackathon mission and goals to different target groups of people. We covered how to create a communication plan, identify the whom, why, where, what, and when, and start to execute this plan. We highlighted the different communication channels, both digital and physical, that can be used to communicate internally with a hackathon organizer team and externally with different target groups; for example, hackers, mentors, and a general public audience. We have covered how to bring together hackers and mentors in one place to build a community of passionate people on a digital platform. Lastly, we shared experiences from different local, national, and international hackathons about how to create hackathon vibes so that hackathon community members will interact and inspire each other to achieve hackathon goals by creating impactful solutions.

In the following chapter, we will dive deep into how to find partner organizations that help in making a successful hackathon. You will learn about the purpose of having partner organizations, where and how to find relevant partner organizations, and how to create a partner package and make a hackathon attractive to them. Moreover, you will get an insight into how to manage hackathon partners and make them contribute to a hackathon.

7
Partnerships for Success

By Carolina Emanuelson

To maximize the impact of a **hackathon**, it is in most cases crucial to establish partnerships with various organizations. This has proven to be successful not only in national hackathons but also on a global scale. Involving diverse **partner organizations** and encouraging them to be part of addressing as well as supporting solutions to solve a variety of **challenges** or problems will in most cases be a factor contributing to the success of your hackathon.

This chapter will cover the following topics:

- The power and purpose of a strong partnership community
- The importance of a diverse partner community
- Finding suitable partner organizations
- Crafting competitive partner packages
- Managing your partner community
- Partner communities in a national and international context
- Value for partner organizations – communication, branding, and recruiting talent
- Relevant resources offered by partner organizations

The power and purpose of a strong partnership community

Establishing and engaging with a partner community can offer substantial benefits throughout every stage of the hackathon, whether it is in the development phase of the hackathon, creating tangible challenges; participant outreach; resource provision throughout the entire event; or in the final stage, supporting teams in actualizing their solutions. There is no doubt that a robust network of partners becomes an invaluable asset to the success of a hackathon.

Establishing solid partnerships with reputable organizations offers unparalleled benefits. Collaborating with industry leaders may not only enhance the event's credibility but also attract a diverse range of participants. Open resources from public organizations can elevate the hackathon's capabilities, being important components resulting in more comprehensive and impactful solutions to the challenges at hand. Partner support with critical resources, such as funding and technology, can not only amplify the hackathon's impact but also foster innovative solutions.

The value derived from partner organizations also extends beyond the event itself, and that is something that should be included in the strategic plan when reaching out to potential partner organizations and building your partner community. Post-hackathon, your partner collaborations can evolve into long-term relationships, opening avenues for sustained innovation and joint initiatives. By nurturing these connections, as a hackathon organizer, you will have the basic instruments to create a dynamic ecosystem that transcends the boundaries of a single event, fostering continuous learning, collaboration, and advancement.

The importance of a diverse partner community

The benefits of establishing partnerships with a variety of organizations are many. Not only do such collaborations bring a variety of skill sets to the table but, more importantly, they introduce a spectrum of perspectives where the participants get access to a rich tapestry of knowledge and insights, crucial for solution development. The **diversity** of organizations in your partner community will become a cornerstone for the participants of the hackathon to rely on.

The examples of how a diverse partner community brings value to your event and its participants are many. Getting the most out of your collaborations and how you nurture your relationships will depend on your creativity.

Collaborating with tech companies can add technical expertise, while partnerships with non-profit organizations may offer a humanitarian perspective. In this brief example, the synergy of these different viewpoints can fuel innovative problem-solving, and also ensure that the solutions generated during the hackathon are not only technical solutions or have technical robustness but also address broader societal and user experience aspects of the challenges that are to be solved. Organizations offering tools such as open data along with the perspective of tech start-ups for successful methods for innovation and an entrepreneurial way of working can be a great combination for using existing data in solutions development with an efficient and experience-based go-to-market strategy.

Establishing and harnessing a strong, solid, and diverse community of partner organizations can also act as a catalyst for broadening the hackathon's reach and participant base. Partnerships create an ecosystem where the collective networks of collaborating entities converge, casting a wider net across diverse industries, sectors, and geographical regions.

For instance, teaming up with a technology corporation might draw in participants from the tech sector, while a partnership with an educational institution has the potential to bring in students and researchers. The cumulative effect is a melting pot of expertise and backgrounds, ensuring a more comprehensive exploration of ideas and solutions. This diversity not only enriches the hackathon experience but also enhances the potential for groundbreaking, interdisciplinary solutions.

Moreover, partnerships can facilitate targeted outreach strategies. If a partner organization has a strong presence in a particular sector or community, their network becomes a conduit for reaching individuals with specific expertise or local insights. This targeted approach ensures that the hackathon attracts participants with a nuanced understanding of the challenges at hand, contributing to the development of contextually relevant and impactful solutions.

Expanding the participant base in this manner, through your partner community, not only fosters innovation but also creates a more inclusive and representative environment. It encourages individuals from varied backgrounds, skill sets, and experiences to collaborate, generating a synergy that is crucial in addressing complex challenges and finding solutions that really can make a change. The variety of partners in your community is to be seen as part of creating a hackathon platform for creative minds to meet, bringing in different experiences and backgrounds.

Aligning with established organizations also lends credibility to the hackathon, signaling to participants, sponsors, and stakeholders that the event is recognized and supported by reputable entities within and outside industries. It also facilitates knowledge exchange between organizations and participants, fostering a collaborative learning environment from both sides.

Sustainable partnerships can also extend beyond the hackathon event itself, creating a foundation for collaboration. This continued collaboration allows for the exploration of long-term initiatives and projects. In our experience, partner organizations also get inspired to use their learnings from this kind of innovation method as a useful tool for innovation within the company.

From a financial perspective, strong partnerships can increase sponsorship opportunities. Despite the size of the hackathon event, you will always be dependent on your financial budget. It's important to establish a strong relationship with your partner organizations since they may be more inclined to provide sponsorships or in-kind support, alleviating financial burdens within their own company and enabling the hackathon or other events related to the hackathon to operate at a larger scale.

In addition to the financial part and the possibility of outreach to potential participants with the help of partner organizations, through your partner community, you are also able to find people who can serve as **mentors** or experts during the hackathon. Organizations often have experienced professionals with a deep knowledge in areas that from a participant hacker perspective can be highly appreciated and even crucial in developing solutions addressing the given challenges of the hackathon. These professionals can serve as mentors, both during the hackathon and in the solution development phase. This mentorship not only benefits participants but also enhances the overall quality of the solutions developed.

By strategically establishing partnerships with different organizations, you can increase the visibility and prestige of the hackathon and tap into a multitude of resources, expertise, and networks, increase sponsorship opportunities, and, in the end, ensure a more successful and impactful event.

An illustrative example of such a strategic alliance, where the augmentation of visibility was important to the hackathon's purpose, can be exemplified by the global online hackathon Hack for Earth at **Expo 2020**, which took place at the world exhibition Expo 2020 in Dubai. In this example, the collaboration with the United Nations Hub at the Expo 2020 world exhibition in Dubai marked a strategic maneuver. The hackathon aimed to tackle the important issues outlined in the United Nation's 17 **Sustainable Development Goals (SDGs)**. For the hackathon, having the United Nations as an official collaborating organization in the partner community was important, to give weight and credibility, to raise awareness and interest among potential participants and partner organizations, and in the development of the challenges and potential collaboration in developing the solutions as well as bringing the solutions to life – for instance, the **Build for Earth acceleration program.**

The United Nation's presence at the Expo 2020 was to "inform, inspire and engage visitors to take impactful action towards a thriving future for people and the planet" *(Maher Nasser, Commissioner-General for UN at Expo)*, and that aligned very well with the purpose of the Hack for Earth at Expo 2020 hackathon. The hackathon was also used as a platform to bring people together to find solutions to different global challenges.

Finding suitable partner organizations

As you now know, identifying and securing suitable partner organizations will in most cases be a critical aspect of success.

To optimize the process of finding suitable partner organizations, it is essential to adopt diverse approaches that allow you to find a broad spectrum of potential partner organizations. The key to success is quite simple. Don't limit yourself when considering organizations for inclusion in your partner community. By embracing a variety of entities, each contributing resource enhances the overall value provided to the participants, not only before or during the hackathon but also in the post-event phase.

- **Targeting a wide variety – casting a wide net across industries, sectors, and geographical regions**

  When embarking on the journey of finding relevant partner organizations, one important strategy involves casting a wide net across industries, sectors, and geographical regions. Consider both established entities and emerging players, as the variety of different perspectives often sparks creativity in finding great and realistic solutions and also in making them become a reality. By fostering an inclusive partner community, you have the right conditions to create an environment rich in diversity, harnessing a range of expertise and insights that can not only elevate the hackathon experience but also support the participants in several ways and from a variety of perspectives.

- **Strategic crafting of win-win partnerships**

  Moreover, when engaging with potential partner organizations, it's crucial to articulate the mutual benefits of the collaboration. It is not unusual for organizers to forget that a partnership should benefit both parties. Just as you need to be creative when searching for partner organizations, you need to think of how your partners will benefit from your collaboration. To do that, read up about the vision of the company, the strategic goals from a short- and longer-term perspective, and their views on social responsibility. What does their employer value proposition look like to attract talent, and how can the purpose of your hackathon tap into that?

- **Customized collaboration – crafting persuasive pitches tailored to diverse industries**

    As you approach organizations from different industries, consider tailoring your pitch to showcase how their unique expertise aligns with the hackathon's goals. For instance, if targeting a technology company, emphasize the role they can play in providing cutting-edge solutions or technical mentorship. Similarly, for organizations in the public sector, underscore the potential for civic innovation and community impact through their involvement.

- **Unlocking the full potential – highlighting the value**

    Clearly communicate how a partnership involvement goes beyond mere sponsorship and contributes to the holistic success of the hackathon. Highlight the value they bring to the participants, emphasizing the diverse resources they can provide, such as mentorship, access to industry networks, or even opportunities for project implementation.

- **Nurturing lasting partnerships for continued impact**

    Don't forget the post-hackathon phase, the Build for Earth, that can serve as a valuable asset in attracting partnerships. In your eagerness to recruit a variety of partners and establish a strong and tangible partner community at the same time that you are making the plans for your hackathon, it's easy to forget that there is also a post-hackathon phase that is as important as the hackathon event itself. More on the post-hackathon phase, the Build! phase, in *Chapter 9*.

- **Fostering future collaboration – demonstrating long-term value for post-hackathon success**

    To create a partner relationship that will also provide you with the support you will need after the hackathon event for the Build! phase, make sure to showcase how the partner organizations can support and benefit from the tangible outcomes of the hackathon, whether it's successful project implementations, innovative solutions, or the personal and professional growth of participants. By highlighting the lasting impact of the collaboration, you not only express gratitude but also solidify the foundation for future partnerships and sustained engagement.

- **Elevate your partnership – empowering organizations with strategic communication tools and recognition plans**

    Also, when finding suitable partner organizations, provide them with your communication plan and how they will be recognized and celebrated as they decide to be part of your partner community. Provide them with a well-prepared communication kit and instructions and suggestions for how to use it to push your partnership in their own preferred communication channels.

Identifying and securing partner organizations is not a one-size-fits-all endeavor. Embrace diversity in your approach, cast a wide net, and articulate the mutual benefits of collaboration. As you engage with potential partners, tailor your pitch to align with their unique expertise, and ensure that the post-event phase emphasizes the tangible impact of their support. This comprehensive strategy not only optimizes the partner selection process but also establishes a robust foundation for ongoing collaboration and success in future hackathons.

Crafting competitive partner packages

Crafting a competitive partner package is equally crucial in attracting organizations willing to collaborate as making sure you have a diverse group of organizations in your partner community.

To create an attractive and realistic partner package, you need to have partner packages at different levels, so different kinds of organizations can find an option that suits them and their needs. As you would like to have diversity with organizations from various industries, sizes, and interests, they will have different capabilities and resources. Depending on the capabilities and resources the organizations will bring to the table, you should investigate in which phases they will bring the most value to the hackathon – in Dream!, Hack!, or Build!. More importantly, to create the diversity you need in your partner community, there needs to be at least one partner package that is for non-profit organizations and does not include a monetary investment by the partner to you as an organizer. Non-profit organizations may have a lot of valuable resources to offer the hackers (mentors, open data, **jury members**, a great network of potential hackers, etc.) and that will provide value for your hackathon, so be sure to have an offer that suits them too.

To entice non-profit organizations, your partner packages can be tailored to focus on how their mission aligns with the goals of your hackathon, particularly in terms of engagement and how they agree to actively participate in the event. This may include promoting participation among its members or providing mentorship and expertise.

To establish partnerships with corporate companies and offer a competitive partner package to them, your agreement will include what we previously discussed but also a monetary investment. Here, you can have different levels: each level will include a different set of communication/market set up, different levels of impact in the creation of the challenges, and a differentiation of access in supporting the winning solutions.

Tailoring the offerings to align with each organization's strengths and objectives not only enhances the appeal of your partnership proposal but also fosters a sense of mutual benefit. Not limited to the different levels of partnerships you offer, your partnership package should articulate the tangible benefits of the partnership, emphasizing the unique value each organization brings to the table. For example, a technology company may provide infrastructure support, while an educational institution contributes research and studies on the specific topic. Whether financial contributions, technological resources, mentorship, prizes, or promotional opportunities, a comprehensive partner package communicates a compelling proposition, making it more likely that organizations will actively engage.

Diversifying your partner portfolio goes beyond mere quantity; it encompasses the strategic inclusion of organizations that complement one another. This synergy amplifies the overall impact, creating a collaborative ecosystem where each partner's contribution enhances the hackathon's comprehensive support system.

In conclusion, the pursuit of partner organizations is not just about quantity, even though the numbers sometimes can be important. It is about cultivating a diverse network that elevates the hackathon experience. From identifying potential collaborators to crafting enticing partner packages, the process is a strategic journey that shapes the success and sustainability of the hackathon ecosystem.

How can it be executed?

Expanding on the process of building a robust partner community for your hackathon involves several steps:

- Strategically reaching out to potential partner organizations
- Clarifying the purpose of the collaboration
- Leveraging your network effectively

In orchestrating the development of a thriving partner community for your hackathon, the utilization of your existing network (personal and professional) is a valuable asset that should not be underestimated. Armed with a clearly articulated purpose and a well-defined set of resources you seek from potential partners, you possess the foundational elements needed to initiate outreach to organizations. Don't underestimate the possibilities that may arise from personal connections by the people in the project management team of the hackathon.

To commence this outreach journey, it is imperative to conduct a thorough examination of the resources required to achieve the hackathon's objectives. Whether the goal is to address local challenges, tackle national issues, or contribute to global solutions, the purpose of the hackathon becomes a guiding beacon, helping you pinpoint the starting point for collaboration and identify organizations aligned with the hackathon's mission.

Recognizing that partner organizations play a dual role is paramount. Firstly, they contribute with essential resources that not only facilitate the execution of the hackathon but also transform conceptual solutions into tangible realities. With engagement in acceleration programs, mentoring winning teams, and supporting them with knowledge or other tools needed, they are part of transforming ideas into reality.

Secondly, they serve as catalysts for participant engagement, acting as conduits to attract and recruit individuals to the hackathon. The significance of partnering with organizations boasting strong brands, impeccable reputations, and a clear sense of purpose cannot be overstated. As mentioned, their involvement not only enhances the event's credibility but also adds a layer of prestige that attracts both participants and sponsors.

Equally important is the alignment of values between your hackathon and the organizations you intend to approach. While their support can undoubtedly boost your event's credibility, it is crucial to ensure that their ethos resonates with yours. A harmonious alignment of values not only enhances the collaborative spirit but also safeguards against potential mismatches that could compromise the integrity of the hackathon. As an example, Hack for Earth Foundation would not consider collaborations with companies or organizations that manufacture products that don't serve people or the planet, because their core values rest on the United Nations 17 SDGs and Agenda 2030. These core values thus exclude companies that sell, for instance, weapons, alcohol, or tobacco as potential partner organizations. It just would not rhyme well with the overall purpose. Keep this in mind when creating the list of organizations you wish to approach: what are your core values and what organizations would be a good fit in line with this?

As you navigate the intricate process of establishing partnerships, consider developing a comprehensive strategy that addresses both short-term needs and long-term sustainability. A well-thought-out plan should encompass clear communication, adaptable partner packages, and a commitment to nurturing relationships beyond the hackathon event.

In essence, the orchestration of a successful hackathon partnership community is a multifaceted endeavor that involves leveraging your network intelligently, aligning with organizations that share the same values as you as the organizer, and recognizing the dual role that partners play in providing both resources and participant engagement. This strategic approach sets the stage for a collaborative ecosystem that extends beyond the confines of a singular event, fostering lasting connections and sustained innovation.

Managing your partner community

Effectively managing your partner community is a critical aspect of ensuring the success and impact of your hackathon and also your partner relationships. Building and nurturing strong relationships with partner organizations from an early stage is essential not only for smooth collaboration but also for maximizing the collective benefits derived from the involvement of your partner organizations. In the dynamic landscape of hackathon management, where variables such as the event's size, the number of participants, and overarching goals vary, a strategic and adaptable approach to handling diverse partner organizations becomes imperative.

The magnitude of the hackathon, whether it is on a very local scale, national level, or a large-scale international event, can guide you on an array of the number of partner organizations you should aim for as well as the types of partner organizations to be part of the community you are building. But at the same time, a small hackathon event can also be in need of a lot of partner organizations and variety in terms of sectors, sizes, and missions. Regardless of the scale of the hackathon and the number of partners involved, the foundation of successful partner collaboration lies in establishing relationships based on both trust and collaboration.

For successful partner management, from the very beginning, prioritize open communication and transparency, ensuring that partners feel integral to the process.

To build trust, build engagement. A strategic angle is to make sure that your partner organizations in some way will have an impact on the solutions resulting from the hackathon. In this way, you will not only have the potential to establish long-lasting engagement but also earn more engagement from your partners. This is because when partners feel that they will be involved in different ways and over a long period, they tend to be more engaged, which will help you when planning how and when you will need their involvement.

One key aspect of managing your partner community is also to recognize the multifaceted role that different organizations play. Each partner brings a unique set of resources, expertise, and networks, contributing to the overall success of the hackathon. By being well aware of the strengths of each organization you have in your community, you can also plan and prepare for when you will need them and in what way. By acknowledging and valuing these diverse contributions, you lay the groundwork for a collaborative environment where partners feel not only appreciated but also integral to the event's success.

Maintaining a transparent line of communication with your partners is pivotal. Regular updates, progress reports, and inclusive decision-making processes foster a sense of ownership among partners. Consider implementing a collaborative platform or regular meetings to facilitate discussions, share insights, and address any concerns promptly. This approach ensures that partners are informed and engaged throughout the hackathon journey and will also help you to have a close communication line. When unexpected things occur and you need your partner or your whole partner community to act fast, this will be more than helpful. You as a hackathon organizer would know not only what partner organizations to reach out to but also how they can contribute.

Furthermore, involving partners in strategic decision-making goes beyond just transparency; it cultivates a sense of shared responsibility and investment. Seek their input on matters such as challenge ideation, participant outreach strategies, and post-hackathon initiatives. By incorporating their perspectives, you not only enhance the quality of decision-making but also lay the foundation of a collaborative spirit that underpins a successful partner community.

The success of your hackathon is intrinsically tied to the success of the management of your partner community. Recognizing partners as integral stakeholders rather than mere contributors amplifies their commitment and enthusiasm. Encourage a culture of mutual support, where the hackathon becomes a shared endeavor, and the impact extends beyond the event itself.

Mentorships

Here are examples of some of the steps to engage your partner organizations in offering people from their organization as mentors before, during, or after the hackathon:

- **Early engagement and alignment**: Begin by engaging partner organizations early in the planning phase of the hackathon. Clearly communicate the vision, objectives, and expected outcomes of the event. Ensure that partners align with the hackathon's goals and are enthusiastic about contributing not only as sponsors but also as mentors. Invite partner organizations to actively contribute to the hackathon. One way of doing this is by inviting the partners to provide inputs to the challenges. In fact, many of our partners have found it to be a rewarding experience to collaborate with the Hack for Earth project management team to develop and refine the challenge content. This activity has consistently been well-received and appreciated.

- **Identify mentorship expertise**: Understand the specific expertise and knowledge areas within each partner organization. This could range from technical experts in relevant fields to professionals with a strong background in problem-solving and innovation. Ensure diversity in mentorship to cover many areas and topics that could be valuable to the participants.

- **Recognition and appreciation**: Acknowledge and appreciate the contributions of mentors publicly. This not only recognizes their commitment but also shows appreciation to your partner organizations.

Jury duty

Incorporating partner organizations as jury members in a hackathon is a strategic move that not only strengthens the relationship between the hackathon organizers and partners but also enhances the credibility of the partner organizations within their networks:

- **Selection of jury members**: To select jury members, identify individuals with expertise relevant to the hackathon's focus areas. This ensures that the jury possesses the knowledge and experience needed to evaluate the projects effectively.

- **Diverse perspectives**: Curate a diverse panel of jury members from different partner organizations, covering various industries and skill sets. This diversity ensures a well-rounded evaluation process and brings a range of perspectives to the table. A multidimensional approach to judging reflects the hackathon's commitment to inclusivity.

- **Recognition of jury members**: Make sure to highlight the names and profiles of jury members in promotional materials, during opening and closing ceremonies. This recognition serves as a mark of credibility for both the hackathon and the partner organizations.

In conclusion, effective management of your partner community involves cultivating trust, fostering collaboration, and embracing transparency. Regardless of the scale of the hackathon, treating partners as valued collaborators and involving them in key decisions creates a robust foundation for success. This approach not only ensures the smooth execution of the event but also establishes a lasting and mutually beneficial relationship with your partner organizations.

Partner communities in a national and international context

As mentioned earlier, it's essential that your partner network aligns closely with the goals you've set for your hackathon. Just like in any other scenario, the ability to adjust to changing circumstances is crucial, and this principle applies equally to hackathons. We will use four examples from hackathons to illustrate this aspect. First, we have **Hack for Sweden** 2019.

Example 1 – Hack for Sweden 2019

"We are bigger, better, and we're gonna shine so much more this year."

Ann Molin – Head Project Manager, Hack for Sweden 2019

The Swedish Government's Hack for Sweden mission emerged as a yearly hackathon and a collaborative platform designed to raise awareness and demonstrate the value and use of open data. To begin with, the platform was a space for government agencies to converge their expertise and resources to collectively tackle specific challenges, with an open invitation to citizens in Sweden to engage in the mission.

As the initiative gained traction, drawing interest from a diverse array of participants and organizations from not only the public sector but also other sectors, the vision of the hackathon became more ambitious. With a more bold and ambitious vision, starting from a small event and transforming into a nationwide movement with tangible impact, the approach needed a new strategy. With that transformation, it also became imperative to develop the partner community and not limit the community to only include government agencies. With the new approach, important resources such as funding, technical resources, and knowledge; outreach to a higher diversity of participants; and entrepreneurial expertise were necessary to benefit the overall goal – creating real solutions to the most important challenges Sweden was facing.

The organic growth of the initiative itself mirrors the strategic outreach to potential partner organizations that was made. The network had to grow exponentially to transform Hack for Sweden into a nationwide movement.

Since Hack for Sweden was a hackathon where open data was a requirement for the solutions submitted by the hacker teams, the organizations in the partner community needed to all provide open data assets. There were already 29 organizations from the public sector that were part of the partner community in 2018. Heading into 2019, it was important to retain these organizations, but more government agencies, companies, and municipalities had to be recruited, and it was especially imperative to invite organizations from the private sector too. The vision was to have all parts of society join in the making of the future solutions for a better society in Sweden, not only government agencies but also private companies, academia, and citizens.

To gain interest and also share insights about the upcoming hackathon with existing and potential partner organizations, an open in-person partner meetup event, free of charge, was organized for the existing and potential partner organizations to attend. The agenda of the partner meetup was to share the goal and vision of the upcoming hackathon, but also, in a very dynamic way, to showcase how organizations from the public and private sectors, which normally don't collaborate much in Sweden, could do so and how sharing expertise and collaboration could be done by serving a well-defined cause, facilitated by the hackathon organizers.

At this partner meetup, the challenge categories of the upcoming Hack for Sweden 2019 hackathon were introduced in an interactive workshop. The representatives from the 88 partner organizations discussed and started to generate ideas for specific challenges for each of the challenge categories the hackers were to compete in at the Hack for Sweden 2019 hackathon.

This structure and way of working with an open invitation and a collaborative setting was a very successful way of starting the recruitment process of finding new potential partnerships and also retaining existing partners, which was imperative for the success of the upcoming hackathon.

The attending organizations at the event recognized the clear advantages of working together, transcending traditional borders, and how that benefitted the common goal of finding solutions to pressing challenges, in this case on a national scale. Fostering collaboration among diverse sectors was a unique opportunity.

One of the key takeaways from this approach on how to evolve the partner network significantly was the importance of showcasing to the attendees, at a very early stage, the synergy effect of organizations collaborating cross-sector and the unique opportunity to pool resources, expertise, and insights to make the hackathon successful. New partner organizations were interested in being part of the community and the foundation for the coming partner recruitment journey had been established.

Moving from one inspirational and productive event to the next phase was a pivotal journey involving the signing of partner agreements and crafting competitive partner packages. The crucial part was to ensure that these agreements were tailored to suit the specific needs and characteristics of each organization, but at the same time follow the standard agreement as much as possible. The packages were categorized into standard types: government agencies, private organizations, and non-profit organizations. The intention of the partnership agreement was clear – every participating partner organization had to bring a resource to the hackathon that would genuinely benefit the participants.

The agreements were designed not only to define the specific contributions but also to cater to the unique strengths of each organizational sector – government agencies bringing organizational weight to the table, private organizations injecting innovation and entrepreneurial spirit, and non-profit organizations infusing the hackathon with a sense of mission and social responsibility. With this approach, it was obvious how the collective of the partner community was a distinctive resource that would enhance not only the hackathon experience but also the value each partner would bring to the hackathon, contributing with something vital. With this approach, the partner agreements went beyond paperwork, starting to shape the foundation of an engaged partner community with common goals and where the collective effort was the way forward.

The outreach efforts and the strategic approach to broaden the Hack for Sweden partner community proved to be immensely successful. What initially comprised 30 organizations soon became an alliance of 90 partner organizations. This expansion wasn't just about quantity; it was a deliberate strategy to amplify the diversity within the collaborative network, bringing together stakeholders from the public sector, the private sector, and non-profit organizations.

The transition from only having public organizations as part of the partner community to inviting a variety of organizations showed the vision of Hack for Sweden was compelling and that it resonated across the diverse organizational landscape. Not only did the expansion pave the way for a more dynamic and inclusive hackathon environment, but it also showcased the power of a partner community focusing on collaboration, transcending boundaries, and harnessing collective strengths, turning the Hack for Sweden initiative into a platform of shared ideas, resources, and commitment.

Example 2 – Hack the Crisis Sweden

In 2019, coronavirus hit the world. As a response, many hackathon organizations in Europe and around the world arranged hackathons to find solutions to the most pressing challenges the world was facing. Our second example is from Hack the Crisis Sweden, a global online hackathon in 2020.

Hack the Crisis Sweden, organized by the government mission Hack for Sweden, emerged as a powerful response to the challenges Sweden as a country and its citizens were facing. This initiative, an online hackathon, was not like a traditional hackathon and was very different from the in-person Hack for Sweden 2019 in the previous year. It was a collective effort to fight the effects of the coronavirus pandemic on society, business, and health, harnessing the agility and creativity of diverse minds to develop solutions that could make a tangible impact on the societal challenges posed by the pandemic. It was also a digital event with no physical interaction, where everything from creating a team to mentor sessions was provided through the hackathon platform. The timeframe for setting everything up, including recruiting all 130 partner organizations, was less than two weeks. This was the order from the Swedish Government at the time. The website and the official promotional video with a voiceover from the Swedish Prime Minister at the time, Stefan Löfvén, were created in a matter of days.

In the following figure, you can see what the official website looked like.

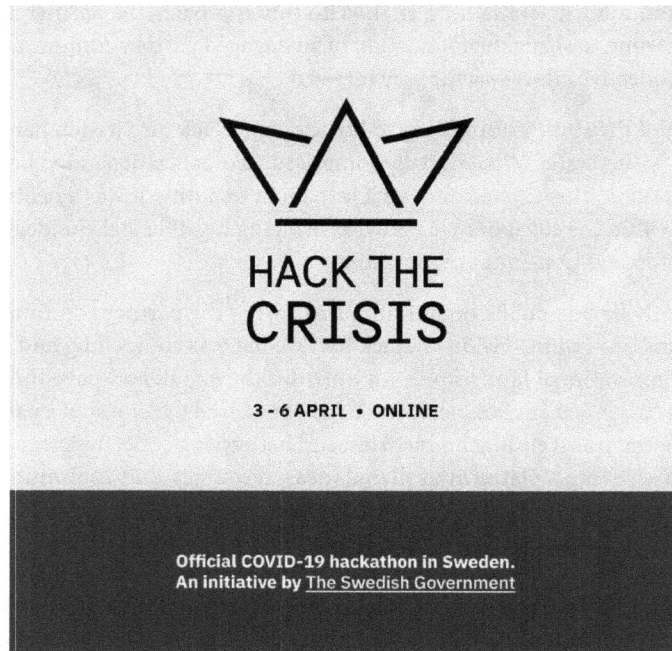

Figure 7.1 – The official website of the Hack the Crisis Sweden online hackathon, April 3-6, 2020

The success of the hackathon was huge. More than 7,400 participants and 130 partner organizations signed up and participated in the hackathon, and this all happened in a matter of days. What was the secret sauce to this winning method?

The foundation of Hack the Crisis Sweden's success partly lies in the experience and dedication of its existing partner community. These stakeholders and the partner organizations of Hack for Sweden 2019 had already navigated the collaborative landscape, understanding the importance of their involvement and commitment. This familiarity with the process was crucial in shaping their role in the initiative.

Unlike previous hackathons, where involvement and commitment were discussed internally over time, the urgency of the pandemic demanded a more immediate decision-making process. The partner organizations found themselves faced with the challenge of deciding almost instantly whether they wished to be part of this rapid-response initiative. This shift in dynamics reflected the accelerated pace at which the world was responding to the impacts of COVID-19.

The partners' decision to join was not a mere formality; it was a commitment to contribute actively and meaningfully to the cause. With limited guidance, due to the short and limited timeframe, they had to identify how they could leverage their unique strengths, resources, and expertise to support the goal of the hackathon. This proactive engagement marked a departure from the traditional approach, emphasizing the need for swift and decisive action in the face of a global crisis.

Simultaneously recognizing the enormity of the challenges at hand and the diverse expertise required to address them, the initiative needed to expand the partner community network. While the existing partners brought valuable experience, new perspectives and resources, and the potential for outreach to new and more participants, were essential to comprehensively tackle the multifaceted issues posed by the pandemic.

Recruiting new partner organizations became a strategic imperative to evolve the hackathon's capabilities. This expansion wasn't only about numbers; it was about diversifying the pool of resources available to the participants. Each new partner organization brought with them unique skills, resources, knowledge, support, or connections that complimented or enriched the existing collaborative partner community and ecosystem.

The recruitment process was very different compared to how it was done in Hack for Sweden 2019. The qualifying process was more or less excluded because of the very tight timeframe until the opening of the hackathon. Instead, the qualification was more based on the organization's attitude to problem-solving and the willingness to collaborate, where every partner had an important part to play, no matter whether you were contributing with open data, jury members, recruiting participants, or more specific resources.

The expansion and recalibration of the partner community in Hack the Crisis Sweden reflected not only the urgency of the situation but also the adaptability and resilience of the collaborative model. It demonstrated that, when faced with a global crisis, the ability to swiftly mobilize and integrate a diverse range of 130 partner organizations could be a powerful catalyst for innovative solutions and meaningful impact.

> **Note**
>
> Here is a link to the official Hack the Crisis Sweden video, with a voiceover by the then Swedish Prime Minister Stefan Löfvén:
>
> ```
> https://www.instagram.com/p/B-iP16kp2OC/?utm_source=ig_web_copy_
> link&igsh=MzRlODBiNWFlZA==
> ```

Example 3 – EUvsVirus

The EUvsVirus hackathon emerged as a collective response to the challenges posed by the COVID-19 pandemic. The focus of this hackathon was on the challenges Europe was facing. Conceived as a pan-European initiative, it aimed to harness the power of innovation, technology, and collaboration to develop solutions that could address the diverse array of issues stemming from the public health crisis. It was organized at the end of April 2020.

The hackathon kicked off with a call to action, inviting participants from all **European Union (EU)** member states and beyond to join forces in developing projects and ideas that could contribute to the fight against the virus. The scope of the challenges addressed was broad, covering healthcare, the economy, education, and social well-being.

The significance of a diverse partner community is evident in making initiatives such as the EUvsVirus hackathon successful. EUvsVirus aimed to find solutions to pressing challenges spread over a whole continent. The hackathon required a collaborative model for partnership to fit the setup and purpose.

Following the EUvsVirus hackathon, a unique and pivotal phase unfolded in the form of a Matchathon. The post-hackathon event aimed to bridge the gap between innovators' needs and the opportunities provided by investors, corporates, public authorities (including hospitals and other contracting entities), academia, and research institutions. The Matchathon organized by the EU was a three-day online event organized from May 21 to May 28 2020 under the auspices of Commissioner Mariya Gabriel and the **European Innovation Council (EIC)**. This event aimed to enhance the development and application of innovative solutions to the challenges posed by the coronavirus. It successfully connected the 120 victorious teams from the hackathon with a diverse network of over 458 entities, including investors, corporations, public sector bodies, and educational and research institutions across 40 countries. Members of the Hack for Sweden project management team were involved in EUvsVirus, including Carolina Emanuelson as head of partnerships and Ann Molin as national curator for Sweden.

The European Commission, together with a dedicated multinational team of 600 volunteers, facilitated a remarkable 2,235 partnerships. These collaborations were not limited to financial support but also encompassed a broad spectrum of business acceleration services. Participants had access to mentoring, networking opportunities, advisory services, and incubators, among others, fostering a rich environment for innovation and growth.

This phase added a layer of complexity and opportunity, not only connecting promising ideas with potential support but also facilitating a collaborative network that extended beyond geographical boundaries.

Given that the EUvsVirus hackathon was a European initiative with winning teams from both within Europe and outside Europe, the partner engagement had a global dimension. This global reach expanded the scope for potential partners, involving organizations not only within Europe but also from other parts of the world. The diversity in geographical representation enriched the partner community, providing a broader spectrum of expertise, resources, and potential avenues for collaboration.

While the process of engaging and establishing a partner network had similarities to previous Swedish hackathons, such as Hack for Sweden 2019 and Hack the Crisis Sweden, there were notable distinctions. Being an EU-led initiative, the European Council wielded resources and influence on a scale previously unseen in national hackathons. Post-hackathon, the selected teams had the unique opportunity to pitch their solutions directly to a varied audience of potential partners, including investors, corporates, and public and private entities. This approach democratized the sourcing of support, allowing innovative solutions to find backing from a diverse set of stakeholders.

The recruitment of partner organizations for EUvsVirus had similarities to previous initiatives, utilizing existing networks and articulating a compelling vision for the potential outcomes. Describing the benefits of partnership and pitching ideas on how partner organizations could contribute with resources became a crucial aspect of the recruitment process. The emphasis was not just on securing partners but on creating a symbiotic relationship where each entity brought distinct resources and expertise to the table, contributing to the overall success and sustainability of the initiative.

In essence, the EUvsVirus initiative exemplified the evolving landscape of collaborative efforts on a global scale. The matchmaking aspect of the Matchathon and the global outreach for partner engagement added new dimensions to the collaborative model, demonstrating the adaptability and innovation required to address challenges on an international level. The diversity in the partner community was a key ingredient in forging a resilient and impactful response to the complex and evolving challenges posed by the COVID-19 pandemic.

Example 4 – Hack for Earth at Expo 2020 in Dubai

Our fourth and last example is the Hack for Earth at Expo 2020 hackathon in 2021. This is yet another example of how to build and engage your partner community on a global level to leverage a hackathon from a variety of perspectives. The Hack for Earth at Expo 2020 online hackathon, with organizations such as the United Nations, Amazon Web Services, AstraZeneca, and the Nordic Council of Ministers as official collaborative organizations in the partner community, went beyond the conventional scope of hackathons, aiming not only to be a global gathering of innovative minds but also a collaborative force addressing the United Nations' 17 SDGs. The success of this hackathon was not only reflected in the scale of participant recruitment but also in the strength and reputation of the 32 partner organizations involved.

The recruitment of partner organizations for Hack for Earth at Expo 2020 commenced almost a year before the actual hackathon, in the fall of 2020. This extended timeline was not merely a logistical necessity; it was a deliberate strategy to establish a network of partners who would serve as ambassadors for the international campaign **Dream for Earth**. This campaign sought to gather insights from around the globe, capturing the dreams and aspirations of both citizens around the world and ambassadors from the partner organizations. The information gathered through this campaign served as the foundation for crafting challenges that resonated with the real-world aspirations of people and organizations worldwide.

In the following figure, you can see a screenshot from `https://dreamforearth.com/`. We can see some of the Dream for Earth ambassadors from the different partner organizations sharing their dreams for the future in a video on the website. Alongside the official partner organizations' videos, there were ambassadors who were influencers on social media and children and youth representatives, showcasing the diversity of the campaign and the wide range of dreams.

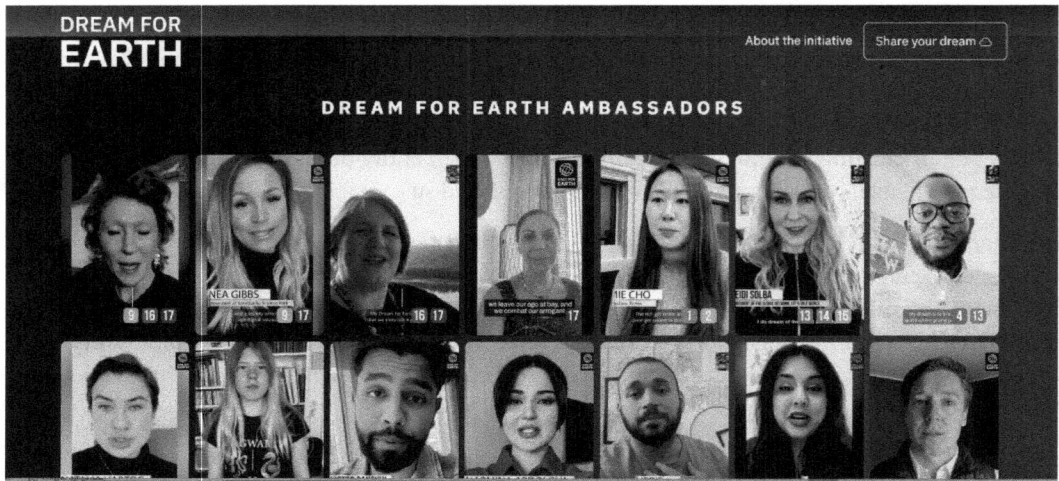

Figure 7.3 – Screenshot from dreamforearth.com, showing a few of the representatives from the 32 partner organizations in the Dream for Earth campaign, sharing their dream for the future in a video

The recruitment strategy for partner organizations was in this case multifaceted, involving an early engagement that went beyond the typical roles assigned to partners in the previous example of hackathons. These partners were not just collaborators; this time they were active participants in amplifying the initiative's message, acting as active ambassadors for the Dream for Earth campaign and sharing their own dreams for the future in a video on social media. Here we would like to mention partner organizations such as UNICEF Sweden, whose network with a younger generation was imperative to reach out to participants that had the potential to broaden the age perspective. To reach out to hackers in general, it was important to have this type of organization active in the campaign. There was also the non-profit organization Hackers Tribe, based in India, an example of the importance of having a mix of organizations acting as ambassadors. In total, there were 32 official organizations in the partner community, all providing different resources to the hackathon.

By leveraging their networks and spheres of influence, these partners, with their representatives, also became catalysts for global participation, encouraging individuals from their networks and individuals from all corners of the world to join the hackathon.

The partner community played a pivotal role in the hackathon, not only in the pre-hackathon phase Dream! but also during the hackathon itself. These partners were, as mentioned in the previous examples of hackathons, active contributors, offering lectures and workshops during the hackathon. These sessions served a dual purpose: first, they provided valuable information and insights to the participants, acting as a knowledge-sharing platform. Second, they played a role in inspiring and engaging the participants, infusing the hackathon with a sense of purpose and a deeper understanding of the global challenges the hackathon was addressing.

The Hack for Earth at Expo 2020 hackathon wasn't merely a technical competition; it was a collective effort to create tangible solutions with the potential to impact real-world issues. Partners, with their industry insights and global perspectives, played a critical role in shaping the narrative and providing participants with the necessary context to understand the broader implications of their innovations.

During the hackathon, the partner network with 32 organizations from all over the world became a dynamic source of expertise and inspiration. In most cases, the partner organizations provided mentors to the participants where they not only enriched the hackathon experience but also facilitated a direct exchange between participants and seasoned professionals, fostering a mentorship dynamic that extended beyond the hackathon's timeline. This showcases how partnership plays an important role in this innovation method.

A lot was learned through both establishing and managing the Hack for Earth partner community. Let's summarize what we have highlighted in this chapter and what to be aware of when building your partner community:

- To maximize the impact of a hackathon, it is in most cases crucial to establish partnerships with various types of organizations
- The diversity of organizations in your partner community will become a cornerstone of innovation for the participants of the hackathon
- Establishing and engaging with the partner community can offer substantial benefits throughout every stage of the hackathon, providing multiple resources
- From identifying potential collaborators to crafting enticing partner packages, the process is a strategic journey that shapes the success and sustainability of the hackathon ecosystem
- It's essential that your partner network aligns closely with the goals you've set for your hackathon

In conclusion, the Hack for Earth at Expo 2020 hackathon in 2021 exemplified a holistic and strategic approach to partner engagement strategy. The extended timeline for partner recruitment, the integration of partner organizations as ambassadors for a pre-hackathon campaign, and their active participation during the event underscored the transformative potential of a well-curated partner community.

The success of the hackathon was not just measured by the number of participants but by the depth of impact achieved through the collaborative efforts of a diverse and engaged partner network.

After diving into these examples of partner communities in hackathons, we will now move on to what you as a hackathon organizer can offer your potential partner organizations in your partner packages.

Value for partner organizations – communication, branding, and recruiting talent

Partner organizations are looking for what can provide them with value throughout the hackathon. Three of the most important values for a partner organization are, in our experience, communication, branding, and recruitment. The good news is that these important factors are very important to you as an organizer too, so there is a classic win-win situation to be harvested here.

Effective communication, strategic branding, and talent recruitment are pivotal aspects of orchestrating a successful hackathon. As the adage goes, *communication is key*, and in the context of hackathons, this holds tremendous significance. Your partner community plays a central role in amplifying the reach and impact of your event. Beyond financial resources or other valued contributions, partners bring with them valuable and influential brands as well as expansive networks that can significantly enhance the hackathon's visibility.

Encouraging partner organizations to actively brand and communicate their support for the initiative is a strategic move. This not only reinforces the credibility of your hackathon but also taps into the reputation and reach of these established brands. Partners becoming vocal advocates for the hackathon contribute to creating a positive narrative around the event, attracting attention from a wider audience.

Furthermore, providing your partners with relevant and well-thought-out communication messages, such as the reason behind their decision to support the hackathon, adds authenticity and purpose to the event. Whether driven by a commitment to innovation, community development, or a shared cause, these motivations resonate with potential participants and collaborators, creating a compelling narrative that extends beyond the confines of the hackathon itself.

The benefits of such communication efforts extend beyond mere brand promotion. A well-branded and articulated initiative becomes a magnet for talent. As your partner organizations actively communicate their involvement, they inadvertently showcase the hackathon as an attractive platform for skilled individuals to contribute with their expertise. This not only broadens the talent pool but also elevates the overall quality of participants, fostering a dynamic and competitive hackathon environment.

Moreover, the ripple effect of effective communication in the partner community cannot be overstated. When one reputable organization publicly supports and communicates its participation, it creates a domino effect. Other organizations, witnessing the endorsement and commitment of their peers, are more likely to feel secure and compelled to join the hackathon. This snowball effect is a powerful driver for expanding the partner community and, consequently, the overall success of the event.

In addition to ensuring effective communication messages, consider further amplifying your partners' involvement by promoting various aspects of their participation. This goes beyond just acknowledging their support; it involves showcasing their influence across different facets of the hackathon, thereby adding layers of authenticity and purpose to the event.

Highlight the expertise and eminence of your partner organizations' representatives serving as jury members. By showcasing the caliber of the jury, you not only underline the prestige of the evaluation process but also position your partners as contributors to the hackathon's overall success.

Emphasize the active involvement of professionals from partner organizations as mentors. Showcase their dedication to guiding and nurturing hackathon participants.

Communicate the specific resources contributed by partner organizations. Whether it's access to datasets, technical tools, infrastructure support, or funding opportunities, explicitly mention these contributions. This not only provides transparency but also positions partner organizations as enablers of innovation, showcasing their tangible impact on the development of groundbreaking solutions.

In conclusion, effective communication within the partner community is a force multiplier for a hackathon. Leveraging strong brands and an extensive network of partners, actively encouraging branding efforts, and articulating the reasons behind their support are all essential components of a successful hackathon.

This not only enhances the hackathon's visibility but also attracts top-tier talent and encourages more organizations to join the collaborative effort. It is through this synergy that a hackathon becomes not just an event but a dynamic ecosystem of innovation and collaboration.

Relevant resources offered by partner organizations

Harnessing the full potential of partner organizations in a hackathon involves strategically accessing a diverse range of resources that the hacker teams can use during the hackathon to create innovative solutions. By fostering collaborative relationships and understanding the multifaceted needs of hackathon participants, organizers can tap into a wealth of support from partner organizations. Here is a list of potential resources that organizations may possess, usually very valuable and appreciated by hackathon participants, that will ensure that the solutions created are significantly innovative:

- **Open data repositories**: Encourage partner organizations, especially those in the public sector, to provide access to open data repositories. Open data serves as a valuable resource for participants, enabling them to integrate real-world information into their solutions. This could include datasets related to demographics, environmental conditions, economic indicators, or any domain relevant to the hackathon's theme.

- **Technical resources and expertise**: Leverage the technical expertise within partner organizations to provide mentorship and guidance to hackathon participants. Technical resources can include specialized knowledge in areas such as software development, data science, and artificial intelligence. Engage technical teams from partner organizations to offer workshops, webinars, or one-on-one consultations to support participants in overcoming technical challenges.

- **Infrastructure support**: Access to robust infrastructure is crucial for participants working on resource-intensive projects. Partner organizations in the tech industry or cloud service providers can offer credits or access to their infrastructure services. This support ensures that participants have the necessary computing power, storage, and networking capabilities to develop and test their solutions effectively.

- **Funding opportunities**: Facilitate connections between hackathon participants and partner organizations that offer funding opportunities. Some partner organizations may have innovation funds, grants, or venture capital arms that align with the hackathon's themes. Encourage participants to pitch their ideas to these organizations for potential funding, enabling the transformation of innovative concepts into scalable and sustainable projects.

- **Network and industry connections**: Don't underestimate the importance of network connections. Encourage partner organizations to open up their network to create valuable networking opportunities for participants. Partner organizations can facilitate introductions to industry experts, potential collaborators, and mentors. Networking events, roundtable discussions, or virtual meet-and-greets organized by partners can provide participants with insights, guidance, and potential partnerships beyond the hackathon.

- **Access to incubator hubs and accelerators**: Many partner organizations, especially those in the start-up ecosystem, may have affiliations with incubator hubs or accelerators. These entities offer valuable support, including mentorship and workspace and business development resources. Collaborate with partner organizations to provide participants with access to these hubs, enhancing the potential for project development and long-term sustainability.

- **Credits for cloud services and software**: Partner organizations in the technology sector can contribute by offering credits for cloud services, software licenses, or other tools that participants may require. This not only reduces the financial burden on participants but also ensures they have access to cutting-edge technologies that can enhance the quality and scalability of their solutions.

- **Office space and co-working facilities**: In cases where physical presence is beneficial, partner organizations with office spaces or co-working facilities can offer participants a conducive environment for collaboration. Access to a workspace allows teams to work seamlessly, fostering creativity and collaboration during and after the hackathon.

- **Study trips**: Explore the possibility of study trips or immersive experiences facilitated by partner organizations. This could involve visits to industry-leading companies, research institutions, or relevant facilities. Immersive experiences provide participants with firsthand exposure to real-world applications, fostering inspiration and a deeper understanding of the industries they are innovating within.

- **Legal and intellectual property support**: Partner organizations with legal expertise can offer guidance on intellectual property matters, copyright issues, and legal frameworks surrounding project development. This support is particularly valuable for participants looking to protect their innovations and navigate legal considerations associated with their solutions.

- **Marketing and visibility**: Collaborate with partner organizations to amplify the visibility of the hackathon and the winning projects. Leverage the partner organizations' marketing channels, social media presence, and communication networks to showcase the innovative solutions developed. This not only provides recognition for participants but also promotes the partner organizations as advocates for innovation and collaboration.

Leveraging partner organizations effectively in a hackathon goes beyond their role as sponsors. With learnings from previous hackathons, engaging your partner organizations in providing mentors is essential to both the hackathon experience and the success of the hackathon.

But it is not only the hackathon organizers that will benefit from this collaboration. Working closely with the participants as mentors during the hackathon is an opportunity for the partner organizations as well. Hackathons bring together individuals with different skills and backgrounds. Providing mentors is a chance to network with other professionals and can lead to new collaborations beyond the hackathon event. Collaborating with participants can also spark fresh ideas and perspectives, enriching both parties' learning experiences. Moreover, being a mentor can be personally and professionally rewarding. Mentors often find satisfaction in helping others succeed and witnessing their growth throughout the event.

In conclusion, the success of a hackathon relies on the strategic utilization of partner organizations in accessing a diverse array of resources. By fostering strong relationships, understanding participant needs, and encouraging partners to contribute open data, technical expertise, infrastructure support, funding opportunities, and more, hackathon organizers can create an ecosystem where innovative solutions thrive. This collaborative approach not only benefits participants but also strengthens the partnerships between organizers and their diverse network of supporters.

Summary

In this chapter, you gained insights into the critical role a strong and robust partner community has in making your hackathon a success. We discussed the importance of a diverse approach, urging hackathon organizers to cast a wide net across industries and geographical regions when establishing the partner community. By fostering inclusive partnerships, you can tap into a variety of expertise and perspectives, enhancing the hackathon experience.

The chapter brought light to and emphasized the need for mutually beneficial collaborations and how to tailor pitches to showcase the value for potential partners. It also stressed the importance of post-hackathon engagement, highlighting how partners can benefit from the outcomes and fostering lasting partnerships for continued impact. Additionally, it suggested empowering partner organizations through strategic communication tools and recognition plans. Overall, this chapter provided a comprehensive guide to optimizing the process of finding and nurturing partner organizations for a successful hackathon.

With real-life examples of hackathons on a national and international level, the chapter included insights into using different strategies and approaches to crafting a partner community and how to align this with the vision and mission of the hackathon.

Overall, this chapter should have given you an understanding of how powerful a strong partnership community can be and that the success of a hackathon, in many ways, relies on strategic partnerships that provide access to resources and foster collaboration among diverse stakeholders.

In the following chapter, you will learn about communication and social media strategies to drive your hackathon. You will get deep insights into how to spread the word about your hackathon in external channels but also what social media channels work best and what factors are crucial for creating a good vibe and attracting more hackers, mentors, and partner organizations to your hackathon.

External Communication and Social Media Presence for Hackathon Success

Your hackathon is only as good as your ability to spread the word about it. This embodies the weight of communication and how vital it is for success. Effective communication serves as the bridge that connects your **hackathon** with your target audience, stakeholders, and the broader community. It enables you to convey the value and impact of your hackathon, mobilize support, and foster meaningful engagement.

In this chapter, we will dive deep into the significance of communication in the context of your hackathon. We will explore why communication plays a vital role in driving the success of your event and how it can be utilized strategically and effectively to achieve your goals. By mastering the art of communication, you will be equipped with a powerful tool to amplify your hackathon's impact and ensure its resonance with the intended audience.

Throughout this chapter, we will cover a range of essential topics that will empower you to harness the full potential of communication in your hackathon journey. These topics include the following:

- Communicating effectively to drive your hackathon
- Exploring the variety of social media platforms and their uses
- Exploring real-world examples
- Strategies to facilitate interaction via social media
- The importance of timing

Communicating effectively to drive your hackathon

The primary objective of external communication is to create the right atmosphere, feeling, and ambiance for participants, partners, **mentors**, **jury members**, and the interested public. How you communicate will shape the perception and mindset of your audience, thus influencing their engagement and anticipation as they enter the hackathon. It is crucial to evoke excitement, anticipation, and a sense of limitless possibilities, all while instilling confidence in the success of the hackathon.

Within the realm of external communication, there are several distinct sub-purposes:

- **Creating engagement with your existing community**: Effective communication allows you to cultivate and strengthen connections with your existing community. By engaging them through compelling content, updates, and interactive discussions, you can foster a sense of belonging, loyalty, and enthusiasm among your community members.

- **Inviting potential participants and mentors to join**: Your external communication should serve as a powerful invitation, attracting potential participants and mentors to join your hackathon. By showcasing the unique opportunities, benefits, and impact of participating in your event, you can entice individuals to become a part of your hackathon journey.

- **Inviting potential partner organizations to join:** Collaboration with **partner organizations** can greatly enhance the success and impact of your hackathon. Through targeted communication, you can effectively reach out to potential partners, highlighting the mutual benefits and value of their involvement. Building strong partnerships can provide access to resources, expertise, and a broader network, enriching the overall experience for participants and amplifying the hackathon's impact. It's important to keep in mind what your respective partner organizations would find valuable; this may differ if it's a corporate organization, a government entity, or a non-profit NGO. A few examples of smart ways to involve them is to invite partner organizations to provide mentors, jury members, open data, statistics, and reports to be used in the hackathon. In the process leading up to the hackathon, it may also be a good idea to invite your partner organizations to cocreate the **challenges** for the hackathon. This also serves as a key to engagement for partner organizations. If they have invested time and effort beforehand in creating the challenges, they will be more inclined to be actively involved in the results – that is, the hackathon itself. Partner organizations often find it valuable to contribute to the **acceleration program** afterward, with lectures, mentorships, and prize money. A partner organization can support the hackathon for a fee, but many non-profit organizations can give you value via their community and/or other assets (mentorships, jury members, statistics, reports, and so on).

- **Sharing deadlines and important information**: Timely and clear communication regarding deadlines, milestones, and essential information is crucial for participants and stakeholders. By effectively disseminating this information through various communication channels, you can ensure that everyone is well-informed and can actively participate in the hackathon with confidence and clarity.

- **Building your overall brand**: External communication plays a significant role in shaping and building your hackathon's brand. By consistently conveying your mission, values, and unique selling propositions, you can establish a distinct identity that resonates with your target audience. Building a strong brand presence enhances recognition and credibility and attracts the right participants, partners, and supporters. Choose a consistent voice and tonality in all your communication, be careful to choose brand guidelines and follow those, and, most important of all, convey a **sense of urgency** in your communication. Aim to convey a sense of urgency consistently, preferably focusing on one or more of the **sustainable development goals (SDGs)** connected to your organization's values. This way, the sense of urgency and context is clear to the audience.

The project management team responsible for social media management and content production plays a pivotal role in the success of your hackathon's external communication. *It is essential to empower the hackathon project management team with autonomy, and align them well with the purpose and goals of the hackathon so they can do their job independently.* The fast-paced hackathon structure demands that all team members have the authority to make independent decisions and that they feel the trust and power to do so. It is crucial that the project management team members feel they have the authority and knowledge to independently address questions and concerns raised through social media channels, minimizing the need for external assistance. This autonomy enables prompt and personalized communication, fostering a sense of connection and reliability.

It's vital that all project management team members have the authority to make independent decisions during the delivery of a hackathon, the fast-paced nature of a hackathon demands this. There is just no time to ask the Head Project Manager what to do, so autonomy is crucial for all team members. In the following image you can see the Hack for Earth project management team for the Hack for Earth global online hackathon at COP28 in Dubai, at the Closing Ceremony on December 3rd,2023. From left: Love Dager, Hackathon Manager, Silva Pilarv, Structure Manager, Mustafa Sherif, Community Manager, Ann Molin, Secretary General, Jacob Rosenholm, Head of Mentorship – they all of course had full autonomy to make decisions within their area of responsibility.

Figure 8.1 – Hack for Earth at COP28 project management team, on
location, in Dubai for the Prize Ceremony in December 2023

To ensure consistency and continuity in communication, it is recommended to have a minimal number of individuals monitoring social media channels, preferably assigning the same person to oversee one or more channels. This approach ensures a seamless flow of communication while maintaining consistency in tone, style, and messaging.

While the production of content, such as videos, posts, captions, images, and photos, can be outsourced to external agents, it is crucial to have the same individual handling **direct messages** (**DMs**) and similar channels. This fosters a relationship between your hackathon and its audience, nurturing engagement and building anticipation even before the hackathon commences.

By understanding the significance of external communication and effectively leveraging its power, you can create a vibrant and engaging environment for your hackathon. Through strategic and consistent communication, you will attract participants, mentors, partners, and supporters, building a strong foundation for success and amplifying the impact of your hackathon on a broader scale.

Exploring the variety of social media platforms and their uses

The channels of external communication are also suitable for different types of communication with different groups. The channels are also used differently and have different core groups of followers in different countries. Below is a short overview of the channels used in *Hack for Earth*, but, of course, more channels may be relevant for you and your hackathon, depending on your audience:

- **LinkedIn**: Targeted partner organizations, jury members, mentors, and participants to share updates and seek support

- **Instagram**: Focused on engaging participants through visual content and concise captions

- **Facebook**: Created event pages and groups to disseminate information and facilitate community-building

- **Twitter**: Enabled fast-paced updates, announcements, and resource sharing for participants

- **YouTube**: Utilized for hosting and sharing video content related to the hackathon

Additional channels may be relevant, depending on your hackathon's audience. Careful selection and utilization of these channels can effectively engage and communicate with your target groups.

In addition to social media channels, two other significant lines of communication should be considered: email and website. While these platforms may not fall under the umbrella of social media, they are still crucial components of a comprehensive communication strategy:

- **Email**: Participants, partner organizations, jury members, and mentors.

- **Website:** Facts, dates, and other important information relevant to all groups mentioned. This isn't a social media platform but one of the most important communication channels. A website mostly involves one-way communication, apart from the info email account that you must monitor regularly and efficiently – preferably with the same person so that the tonality and the voice are consistent over time.

It is essential to briefly mention email and websites, in this context, due to their interconnectedness with social media channels.

Email communication plays a vital role in engaging with your community and maintaining a direct line of contact. It allows for personalized and targeted messaging, enabling you to reach out to specific segments of your audience with relevant content. By integrating email campaigns with your social media efforts, you can amplify your message and reinforce the overall brand consistency. Coordinating the tonality and voice across all channels is key to presenting a cohesive and unified brand identity.

Similarly, your website serves as a central hub where visitors can access comprehensive information about your organization, initiatives, and events. It is a platform where you can showcase your achievements, provide in-depth resources, and foster deeper engagement with your community. Integrating your social media channels into your website allows visitors to seamlessly explore your online presence and encourages them to connect with you on different platforms. Maintaining consistent tonality and voice across your website and social media channels ensures a seamless user experience and reinforces your brand identity.

Recognizing the interconnectedness of these communication channels is essential. They collectively serve as your window to the community you are trying to engage with. Consistency in tonality and voice across all platforms is crucial for establishing brand cohesion and fostering a sense of familiarity and trust among your audience. By aligning your messaging and maintaining a unified approach, you can effectively leverage each channel's strengths and create a harmonious and impactful communication ecosystem.

To establish a strong and impactful presence on social media platforms, considerable time and effort must be devoted to developing a comprehensive strategy that outlines the intended message and purpose. Furthermore, maintaining an active and consistent presence is essential to achieving favorable outcomes. It is advisable to select a limited number of channels, perhaps two or three, to concentrate on and deliver content of exceptional value and significance. This approach is more effective than attempting to maintain a presence across multiple or all platforms simultaneously.

When determining which social media channels to participate in, it is crucial to always consider the target audience. There must be a compelling reason for followers to engage with your account on one platform and choose to follow you on another. Consequently, the content provided on different platforms must offer distinct value. If the content is identical across all channels, individuals may question why they should follow your account in multiple locations. Therefore, the content shared must offer unique benefits, catering to the specific interests and needs of each platform's audience.

It is essential to recognize that not all followers will necessarily follow all of your accounts on all platforms. However, both you and your followers must understand the potential reasons why this option exists and how it can bring value to each follower. By providing a clear rationale and highlighting the benefits of following multiple accounts on various platforms, you can foster greater engagement and loyalty among your audience.

Exploring real-world examples

As an example, the communication strategy of **Hack for Earth at Expo 2020** on LinkedIn primarily focused on engaging existing and potential partner organizations. These organizations were considered crucial in supporting the hackathon by providing valuable resources, such as data, and experts in the form of mentors and jury members. The communication efforts on LinkedIn aimed to establish and nurture relationships with these partners while providing them with relevant information about the hackathon. The United Nations, Amazon Web Services, Astra Zeneca, and The Nordic Council of Ministers were all official organizations who supported the Hack for Earth at the Expo 2020 hackathon, along with 28 more organizations worldwide.

Regular announcements were made on LinkedIn to attract jury members and mentors. These posts not only outlined the specific requirements and expectations for these roles but also highlighted the overall purpose and significance of the hackathon itself. Emphasis was placed on the hackathon's alignment with the United Nations SDGs, underscoring its commitment to addressing global challenges and making a tangible impact. By emphasizing the long-term vision and commitment to implementing the solutions generated during the hackathon, LinkedIn served as a platform for building credibility and inspiring potential partners to get involved.

Due to the nature of LinkedIn as a professional networking platform, the communication frequency was adjusted accordingly. With a slower-paced environment compared to other social media platforms, approximately one post per week was considered sufficient to maintain a consistent presence without overwhelming the audience. This allowed for thoughtful and well-crafted updates that resonated with the target audience.

In contrast, the communication strategy on Instagram for *Hack for Earth* at the Expo 2020 hackathon primarily targeted existing and potential participants, namely the hackers. Instagram provided a more dynamic and interactive platform to capture the attention of this audience. The content shared on Instagram included information about the hackathon itself but was delivered more frequently and engagingly.

To capture the attention of the Instagram audience, the posts were designed to be more visually captivating, utilizing short videos and other multimedia elements. The frequency of posts was higher compared to LinkedIn, to maintain a consistent presence and keep the audience engaged. Additionally, Instagram stories were utilized to provide a behind-the-scenes look into the project management team's activities. This approach allowed for more spontaneous and in-the-moment content, giving the audience a sense of involvement and immersion in the hackathon experience.

Interactivity was a key component of the Instagram strategy, with features such as polls, questions, and votes being incorporated regularly. These interactive elements encouraged followers to actively participate and share their opinions, fostering a sense of community and involvement. By leveraging these features, the organizers were able to gather valuable insights and feedback from the participants, further enhancing the overall experience of the hackathon.

To maximize the visibility and reach on Instagram, relevant hashtags such as *#hackathon*, *#hackforearth*, *#Expo2020*, and *#dreamforearth* were strategically chosen and incorporated into the posts. This ensured that the content reached a wider audience beyond the existing followers, increasing the chances of attracting potential participants and generating interest in the hackathon.

In conclusion, the communication strategies on LinkedIn and Instagram for *Hack for Earth* at the Expo 2020 hackathon were carefully tailored to the unique characteristics of each platform and the preferences of the target audience. By leveraging the strengths of these platforms, the organizers were able to effectively engage and inform both partner organizations and potential participants, ultimately contributing to the success of the hackathon.

Strategies to facilitate interaction via social media

Furthermore, it is essential to recognize that social media platforms are aptly named as they do just that – they focus on social interaction and dialogue, not just merely sending out information. Therefore, a successful social media strategy necessitates a reciprocal approach, whereby active and prompt engagement is prioritized. It is crucial to be present on each of the aforementioned social media channels, promptly responding to questions and actively interacting with the audience. In today's fast-paced digital landscape, individuals have come to expect swift responses, typically within a timeframe of 6 to 12 hours, if not sooner.

To meet these expectations, constant and rigorous monitoring of the channels is imperative. This entails a steadfast commitment to regularly check for any inquiries or interactions and promptly address them. By ensuring a timely and comprehensive response to all inquiries, you foster a sense of attentiveness and responsiveness, enhancing the overall user experience and maintaining a positive online reputation.

In addition to being responsive, it is crucial to cultivate an environment that encourages active participation and engagement from the audience. This can be achieved through the strategic implementation of communication techniques that invite the audience to actively partake in discussions, respond to polls, answer questions, and take on challenges. By incorporating these interactive elements, you foster a sense of community and involvement, which can significantly enhance user engagement and loyalty.

However, it is important to note that the success of such interaction lies not only in its implementation but also in the way it is executed. Responses should be personalized, inviting, and authentic, creating a sense of connection and rapport with the audience. Moreover, speed is of the essence as timely responses convey a sense of attentiveness and value to the audience, thereby further strengthening their engagement and loyalty.

To facilitate efficient and effective communication, it may be beneficial to turn on the social media notifications on the channels you are using. Some of these can be automated responses that ensure the person sending a request gets a reply instantly, but, of course, this does not mean that you can leave it at that – all requests on social media need to be addressed sooner or later by a real person on your staff who answers in a way that is respectful and knowledgeful – not just autogenerated. The autogenerated responses can, however, help automate certain aspects of engagement while ensuring that no inquiries or interactions go unnoticed.

A robust social media strategy necessitates active and prompt engagement with the audience. This requires constant monitoring of the channels, responding to inquiries promptly, and actively encouraging interaction through polls, questions, and challenges. By responding personally and swiftly, you foster engagement and build a positive reputation, ultimately maximizing the potential of social media as a platform for meaningful dialogue and community-building.

The three steps to implement your social media strategy

The following are the significant steps that can be taken to build your social media strategy.

Step 1

To implement a comprehensive social media strategy for your hackathon, the *first* step entails creating dedicated accounts on the various social media platforms you intend to utilize. However, this step may not be necessary if your organization already maintains accounts on the relevant platforms and you have decided to leverage these existing accounts for communicating the hackathon. This decision requires careful consideration as there are both advantages and disadvantages associated with each option.

Opting to utilize your organization's existing accounts offers the advantage of continuity and sustained engagement beyond the hackathon itself. By leveraging these established accounts, the followers gained during the hackathon can continue to receive updates, information, and communication regarding future events and initiatives. This seamless transition ensures that the audience remains connected with your organization, fostering a long-term relationship and facilitating ongoing communication and engagement.

However, it is also important to consider the nature and style of communication required for the hackathon. The hackathon may demand a distinct and unique approach, characterized by a more dynamic, frequent, and spontaneous communication style. This may not align well with the existing account of your organization, which may have a more formal or structured communication style in place. In such cases, creating a separate account dedicated solely to the hackathon can provide the necessary flexibility and freedom to adopt a more playful, innovative, and experimental communication approach that is synonymous with the spirit of a hackathon.

By establishing a separate account specifically for the hackathon, you can better cater to the specific communication needs and expectations of the hackathon participants and target audience. This dedicated account allows you to create a distinct brand identity for the hackathon, fostering an environment of creativity and collaboration. The ability to be more spontaneous and innovative in your communication efforts can contribute to enhanced user engagement as it aligns with the energy and dynamics associated with the hackathon experience.

The decision to create separate accounts or utilize existing organizational accounts for your hackathon's social media presence depends on various factors. While using existing accounts ensures continuity and long-term engagement, a dedicated hackathon account offers the opportunity for a more tailored and dynamic communication approach. Careful consideration must be given to the nature of the hackathon and the desired communication style to ensure optimal audience engagement and alignment with the hackathon's objectives.

Step 2

The *second* pivotal step in implementing an effective social media strategy revolves around establishing a cohesive **graphic profile** and a well-defined communication strategy. A cohesive graphic profile is what the hackathon needs to regulate its presence in all channels, not only social media, and this refers to the website, emails, and potential physical hackathon presence too. A cohesive graphic profile is usually referred to as brand guidelines in an organization. It is imperative to ensure consistency in the graphic profile across all utilized channels to facilitate immediate recognition by the target audience. Additionally, crafting a comprehensive communication strategy centered around a core message is indispensable in effectively engaging and resonating with the intended audience.

The **graphic profile** serves as a visual representation of the hackathon project and should be applied uniformly across all social media platforms employed. By maintaining consistency in the visual elements, such as logos, color schemes, typography, and overall design aesthetics, the audience can readily associate such visual cues with the hackathon project. This recognition fosters a sense of familiarity and trust, reinforcing the project's brand identity and increasing its visibility and impact.

In conjunction with the graphic profile, the development of a robust communication strategy is crucial for effectively conveying the hackathon project's purpose and value proposition to the target audience. Central to this strategy is formulating a compelling core message that instills a sense of urgency and importance surrounding the hackathon. Articulating a strong rationale for why the hackathon is of utmost significance at the moment and elucidating the broader value it brings across various dimensions are key elements in capturing the attention and engagement of the audience.

By effectively communicating the urgency and relevance of the hackathon, the communication strategy can elicit a strong call to action, motivating individuals to participate, support, or contribute to the event. This sense of urgency can be underscored by highlighting the pressing societal or environmental challenges that the hackathon aims to address, emphasizing the potential positive impact and transformative outcomes that can be achieved through collective efforts.

Furthermore, the communication strategy can be tailored to nurture a sense of excitement and anticipation surrounding the hackathon, employing various persuasive techniques such as **storytelling**, testimonials, or showcasing previous successful outcomes. By effectively conveying the value and benefits of participating in the hackathon, the communication strategy can inspire and mobilize individuals to align themselves with the project's mission and actively engage in its activities.

Establishing a consistent graphic profile and a well-crafted communication strategy form the crux of a successful social media strategy. Ensuring visual coherence across platforms enhances recognition and brand identity. Simultaneously, the communication strategy, driven by a compelling core message, effectively conveys the urgency and broader value of the hackathon, compelling the target audience to actively engage and contribute to the project's success.

Step 3

The *third* crucial step in implementing a successful social media strategy is forming a small yet proficient social media team to execute the devised plans. It is of paramount importance to entrust this team with the responsibility of improvising content and actively managing the social media accounts. To establish such an autonomous team, careful consideration must be given to selecting individuals who possess a desire to assume accountability and showcase a deep passion for effective communication.

In addition to identifying individuals who actively seek responsibility, fostering a high level of engagement within the hackathon project among the employees entrusted with managing the social media accounts is imperative. This engagement serves as a catalyst, igniting their commitment to the organization's purpose and overarching goals. Consequently, it is advisable to refrain from outsourcing this task to external entities as they may lack the same level of internal investment and fail to effectively convey the desired level of engagement to the target audience.

By opting for internal employees who are already aligned with the organization's mission, the trust placed in them to deliver the content is heightened. This trust is indispensable as it enables the social media team to adapt and respond swiftly to emerging opportunities or challenges in real time. However, these internal team members possess valuable insights into the organization's values, culture, and objectives, thereby facilitating the creation of content that resonates authentically with the intended audience.

The decision to build an internal social media team underscores the significance of cultivating a sense of ownership and dedication within the organization. By leveraging the existing knowledge, skills, and commitment of employees, the team can effectively represent the hackathon project and communicate its goals and achievements in a manner that aligns with the organization's overarching vision.

In conclusion, forming a dedicated social media team comprising passionate and responsible employees who are deeply engaged with the hackathon project is vital for the successful execution of the social media strategy. Internal employees, already immersed in the organization's purpose and goals, possess the necessary commitment and understanding to effectively communicate with the target audience. Therefore, relying on external agencies may compromise the level of engagement and authenticity conveyed through social media channels.

The nuances of various social media platforms

The following insights pertain to the specific dynamics of social media platforms, particularly those that have been utilized by *Hack for Earth*. It is important to note that numerous other platforms exist, such as TikTok and Snapchat, that may also be incorporated, depending on the target audience's preferences and usage patterns.

LinkedIn, being a professional business network, exhibits a distinctive communication pattern characterized by slower and less frequent interactions compared to other channels. Users on this platform are primarily engaged in professional networking and career development, resulting in a more deliberate and measured approach to communication.

Instagram, on the other hand, places a significant emphasis on visual content, particularly images and videos. Communication on Instagram tends to be more rapid and frequent, fostering a dynamic environment for engagement. To optimize visibility and reach the intended target audience, the utilization of hashtags becomes imperative as they play a vital role in enhancing algorithmic performance and content dissemination.

Facebook occupies a position that lies between the pace of Instagram and LinkedIn. It attracts a substantial number of hackers, making it an ideal platform for sharing content and engaging with like-minded individuals. Furthermore, Facebook harbors various groups dedicated to specific hacker interests, thereby providing an avenue for focused content sharing. It is worth noting that Facebook enjoys the status of being the largest social media platform in certain countries, thereby increasing its significance and potential reach.

By considering the distinctive characteristics of these platforms and tailoring the social media strategy accordingly, you can effectively leverage the strengths of each platform to engage with its target audience.

Another consideration – paid advertising

In addition to organic reach, organizations have the option to utilize paid advertising on social media platforms to target specific groups and amplify their message. This strategy involves allocating a budget to promote a selected post to a defined audience segment. By leveraging the advanced targeting capabilities offered by social media platforms, organizations can tailor their messaging to reach individuals who are most likely to be interested in their hackathon.

Paid advertising on social media offers several potential benefits for hackathon organizers. Firstly, it enables the expansion of reach beyond the existing follower base, allowing the hackathon to attract a larger pool of potential participants. By specifying demographic characteristics, interests, and behaviors, organizers can ensure that their advertisements are displayed to individuals who align with their target audience. This level of precision targeting can result in higher engagement and conversion rates, ultimately leading to increased participation in the hackathon.

However, hackathon organizers need to approach paid advertising on social media with caution and conduct thorough testing before committing significant resources. Conducting pilot campaigns on a small scale can provide valuable insights into the effectiveness of paid advertising for the specific hackathon. By carefully monitoring the performance of these initial campaigns, organizers can assess the **return on investment** (**ROI**) and determine whether the cost of paid advertising justifies the expected benefits.

It is advisable to establish clear objectives and **key performance indicators** (**KPIs**) before initiating paid advertising campaigns. These could include metrics such as reach, click-through rates, conversion rates, and cost per acquisition. By tracking and analyzing these performance indicators, organizers can evaluate the effectiveness and efficiency of their paid advertising efforts. This data-driven approach allows for informed decision-making and the optimization of future campaigns.

Furthermore, it is crucial to consider the budget allocated to paid advertising and balance it with other marketing and promotional activities. While paid advertising can be an effective tool for reaching a larger audience, it should be seen as part of a comprehensive marketing strategy that includes both organic and paid channels. Evaluating the cost-effectiveness and ROI of paid advertising in comparison to other marketing tactics, such as influencer partnerships, public relations efforts, or content marketing, can help organizers make informed decisions about resource allocation.

To maximize the impact of paid advertising, organizers should develop compelling and visually appealing content that resonates with the target audience. Advertisements should communicate the value proposition of the hackathon and highlight its unique features and benefits. A strong call to action should be incorporated to encourage interested individuals to take the desired action, such as registering for the hackathon or visiting the hackathon's website for more information.

In conclusion, leveraging paid advertising on social media platforms can be an effective strategy to expand the reach and attract more participants to a hackathon. However, organizers need to approach this tactic with caution and conduct small-scale testing to evaluate its efficacy before committing significant resources. By setting clear objectives, monitoring KPIs, and optimizing campaigns based on data-driven insights, organizers can make informed decisions about the allocation of resources and maximize the impact of their advertising efforts.

In this section, we covered how to use effective communication to drive your hackathon, how to build engagement with your existing community, how to invite potential participants, mentors, and partner organizations to join your hackathon, and the importance of building your brand through communication. We also explored the variety of social media platforms and their uses, shared valuable real-world examples of how this can be executed, and delved into strategies to facilitate interaction in social media. Finally, we demonstrated three important steps regarding how to implement your social media strategy: creating dedicated social media accounts for your hackathon, deciding on a graphic profile including brand guidelines, and shaping an autonomous and efficient but small project management team to handle the hackathons social media. As a final point, we discussed the nuances of various social media platforms and the topic of paid advertising.

If you have considered all these steps and executed the ones you deem relevant to your hackathon, you are ready to get started and launch your social media campaign. The next section will cover what to keep in mind when interacting with your audience to keep your existing community interested and what to do to grow your community, as well as give you a few real-world examples to clarify how this can be done.

Building your audience and hacker community

Better to get things out there that are okay fast than getting things out there that are perfect!

In the realm of social media, it is crucial to recognize the significance of establishing and maintaining an active and engaging online presence, particularly when it comes to promoting events such as hackathons. In this context, it is often more advantageous to consistently publish content that is satisfactory rather than striving for perfection in every post. This approach necessitates relinquishing a certain degree of control over the team responsible for managing your social media accounts, which can understandably pose a challenge. However, it is essential to embrace this necessary shift to cultivate the desired atmosphere and appeal that your hackathon requires.

When considering your social media presence, it is vital to understand that the overall impression and emotional impact conveyed by your posts are more significant than the pursuit of absolute correctness, flawless visuals, or optimal timing. While these elements certainly contribute to the overall quality of your content, they should not overshadow the importance of consistently delivering value and fostering a connection with your audience. However, there is one notable exception to this principle, and that pertains to spelling. Spelling errors, no matter how minor, can significantly detract from your brand's professionalism and credibility on social media platforms. Therefore, it is imperative to meticulously review your captions and content before publishing. It is worth noting that in the event of a spelling mistake being discovered after posting, there is no need to panic, as most social media platforms allow for post edits.

To create the desired buzz and excitement surrounding your hackathon, your social media accounts must consistently exhibit relevant and valuable content that captivates and entertains your audience. This requires a combination of unwavering commitment to social media delivery and a genuine willingness to listen and learn from your audience. As mentioned previously, social media is a dynamic platform that necessitates an acute awareness of audience preferences and expectations. It is crucial to recognize that social media is a two-way street, where engagement and responsiveness are paramount. If a post that you believe to be exceptional fails to resonate with your audience, it is essential to acknowledge that the audience's response is indicative of their preferences, and you need to reassess your approach.

To achieve success on social media, it is crucial to recognize that even if you perceive a post to be outstanding, if it gets minimal interaction in the form of likes and comments, it is necessary to confront reality and make adjustments accordingly. This process involves evaluating the performance of your posts and analyzing the underlying factors that contribute to their success or lack thereof. By closely examining the posts that resonate with your audience, and looking specifically at which posts gain the most likes, comments, and reshares, you can identify the common characteristics and elements that capture their attention and generate meaningful engagement. Armed with this knowledge of which of your posts gain the most interaction from your audience, you can then strive to replicate these successful aspects in future content, increasing the likelihood of achieving favorable outcomes.

It is important to remember that social media is a dynamic and ever-evolving landscape. What works today may not necessarily yield the same results tomorrow. Therefore, it is essential to continuously adapt and refine your social media strategy based on ongoing feedback, trends, and audience preferences. By embracing a mindset of constant learning and improvement, you can establish a thriving social media presence that effectively promotes your hackathon and cultivates a vibrant and engaged community around your event.

When it comes to achieving success on social media, several key elements can significantly impact your engagement and reach. We should carefully consider the following key elements:

- **Interactive competitions to generate buzz and excitement**: One effective strategy is to leverage the excitement and anticipation surrounding contests and competitions by announcing the winners through your social media platforms. Such announcements often generate high levels of interaction as individuals are eager to celebrate and congratulate the victors. Additionally, incorporating visually appealing elements such as trophies or cups into your posts can further enhance engagement as these images tend to captivate and invite a multitude of likes, comments, and shares.

In the following image you can see one of the photos from the **Hack for Earth at COP27** Prize Ceremony in Sharm-El-Sheikh, which received a lot of attention on social media, due to the Hack for Earth Cup as shown in the photograph. The photograph shows Ann Molin, Secretary General with the Hack for Earth Cup in the United Nations Climate Change Global Innovation Hub at COP27 in Sharm-El-Sheikh, Egypt in November 2022, just before the Prize Ceremony took place there.

Figure 8.2 – Prize Ceremony in Sharm-El-Sheikh

- **A personal and inviting language to engage your audience eloquently**: Language plays a crucial role in establishing a personal and relatable tone for your hackathon on social media. Don't shy away from using emotionally potent words such as *love* to express your enthusiasm for open data or any other relevant topic. By infusing your captions and content with genuine emotions, you create a more authentic and inviting atmosphere for your audience to connect with. It is important to strike a balance between being genuine and maintaining professionalism in your communication efforts.

- **Animations and videos to catch the attention of your followers instantly**: Video content holds immense power in capturing attention and driving engagement, particularly on platforms such as Instagram. However, it is essential to keep the videos concise and impactful. Long-form videos, exceeding one minute, should only be used when there are compelling reasons to do so. In general, aim to convey your message swiftly and effectively to ensure maximum viewer retention.

- **Captivating captions to get your message across in a concise mode**: When crafting captions for your social media posts, it is advisable to keep them short and focused. One common pitfall is making the text excessively long, which can lead to decreased audience engagement. Remember that attention spans are typically shorter on platforms such as LinkedIn, Facebook, Instagram, and TikTok. Therefore, the challenge lies in delivering your message succinctly and efficiently. Mastering the art of brevity is crucial to capturing your target audience's attention swiftly and effectively.

- **Hashtags to amplify the visibility and reach of your content**: By incorporating relevant and popular hashtags in your posts, you increase the chances of your content being discovered by individuals who are genuinely interested in your hackathon or its related topics. Careful selection and strategic use of hashtags can significantly enhance your social media presence and attract the right audience to your content. This is especially important for Instagram, where the right hashtags can play a huge difference in how many interactions you get. It's also a good idea to decide early on, a few must-have hashtags that you communicate to your audience. Remember to share these hashtags with your community so that everyone sharing your content uses the same hashtags.

- **Polls and questions to create a relationship with your followers**: To foster active engagement and encourage interaction with your social media accounts, consider utilizing features such as polls, questions, and voting – this can be done on Instagram or via Facebook stories. For example, you can invite followers to contribute with suggestions for challenges for the hackathon and choose which **challenge category** they are most interested in or what country or organization they are representing. These are only suggestions, and you can modify them to suit your hackathon's purpose. The voting and polls tools provide an easy and interactive way to connect with your audience, allowing them to express their opinions, share their perspectives, and actively participate in the conversation. By demonstrating a genuine interest in your audience's viewpoints and incorporating their feedback, you establish a stronger relationship with your followers. This fosters a sense of community and can ultimately contribute to the growth of your hackathon, attracting more participants, mentors, jury members, and partner organizations.

Leveraging the power of social media requires careful consideration of various elements. By announcing contest winners, utilizing engaging visuals, using emotionally potent language, incorporating concise videos and captions, employing strategic hashtags, and encouraging audience interaction, you can create a vibrant and impactful social media presence for your hackathon. Embracing the interactive nature of social media platforms can help you expand your audience, foster meaningful connections, and attract valuable stakeholders to make your hackathon a resounding success.

Building a strong community

Social media platforms offer a remarkable opportunity to cultivate and expand a vibrant community encompassing partners, hackers, mentors, and jury members. Leveraging this community allows organizers to generate the necessary content for both social media channels and the hackathon itself while concurrently developing a meaningful relationship with its members.

A critical aspect of harnessing the potential of social media is to incentivize individuals to share the produced content across their own social media channels, including both official organizational accounts and personal profiles. By encouraging such content sharing, organizers can significantly amplify their reach and exponentially grow their audience. However, it is important to acknowledge that motivating individuals to share content on social media entails navigating diverse and multifaceted motivators, which can present challenges in achieving widespread participation.

Moreover, the presence of organizers on social media platforms serves another purpose: fostering the formation of a robust community comprising various groups and entities involved in the hackathon. Ideally, this community-building process should commence before the hackathon commences. By establishing a sense of belonging and fostering a shared sense of purpose among community members, organizers can cultivate an environment characterized by collaboration and collective engagement. This feeling of unity and togetherness is of paramount importance as it permeates throughout the entire hackathon experience, contributing to a cohesive and impactful event.

To facilitate the cultivation of a thriving social media community, organizers should adopt effective strategies. This may involve implementing creative and compelling content formats that resonate with participants and resonate with their interests and motivations. Additionally, fostering open and inclusive communication channels through social media platforms can facilitate ongoing engagement, enabling organizers to actively listen to community feedback, address concerns, and foster dialogue among participants.

Furthermore, organizers can employ various techniques to incentivize content sharing on social media. These techniques may include offering exclusive rewards or recognition to individuals who actively participate in content dissemination, developing captivating and shareable content that aligns with the values and aspirations of the community, and fostering a sense of reciprocity by actively engaging with and promoting the content shared by community members. By employing these strategies, organizers can generate a sense of excitement and enthusiasm among participants, encouraging them to become active advocates for the hackathon and its broader objectives.

In conclusion, social media platforms provide valuable avenues for organizers to cultivate and nurture a robust community comprising diverse stakeholders. By harnessing the power of social media, organizers can generate the necessary content for both social media channels and the hackathon itself, while concurrently fostering a strong sense of community and shared purpose among participants. Employing effective strategies to incentivize content sharing and engagement, organizers can maximize their reach, grow their audience, and create an environment conducive to collaboration and co-creation throughout the entire hackathon experience. In the following sections, we'll explore some real-life examples where effective collaboration led to success.

Breaking down the Dream for Sweden campaign

The **Dream for Sweden** campaign, organized in 2019, exemplifies a strategic initiative undertaken by the **Hack for Sweden** community, comprising 50 government agencies and companies, to foster civic engagement and raise awareness about the annual *Hack for Sweden* hackathon. The primary objective of this nationwide campaign was to gather the aspirations and visions of Swedish citizens concerning the future of society. To achieve this, a dedicated website, www.dreamforsweden. com, was established as an interactive platform where individuals across the country could articulate their dreams for a prospective society through written submissions.

The campaign's central feature was an interactive map of Sweden, which showcased the collected dreams, enabling visitors to explore and draw inspiration from the diverse range of ideas. Each dream shared on the platform was carefully collected, analyzed, and ultimately utilized as the fundamental inspiration for the challenges posed during the subsequent *Hack for Sweden* 2019 hackathon.

To amplify the reach of the campaign, ambassadors were appointed from partner organizations within the *Hack for Sweden* community. These ambassadors, representing various government agencies and companies, contributed by recording videos in a professional studio setting. In these videos, they articulated their visions for a better future society in Sweden. The videos featuring the ambassadors' dreams were strategically integrated into the launch campaign, effectively broadening the campaign's impact to encompass the audiences associated with the partner organizations within the *Hack for Sweden* community.

The *Dream for Sweden* campaign stands as an exemplary demonstration of leveraging community engagement to generate content for social media platforms. It effectively involves citizens in the community, transforming them into active contributors and co-creators of content. This approach not only prepares individuals for the co-creation activities inherent in the hackathon but also fosters a sense of anticipation and enthusiasm within the community for the upcoming event. Furthermore, utilizing the campaign's outcomes as the foundation for the hackathon's challenges serves to enhance participation, co-creation, and contribution among the community members, further reinforcing their sense of involvement and ownership in the overall process.

Breaking down the Dream for Earth campaign

The **Dream for Earth** campaign, which was conducted in 2021, served as a global initiative that shared similarities with the *Dream for Sweden* campaign. However, it differed in terms of its extensive magnitude, broader scope, and the analysis of dreams shared by the public through the utilization of an AI tool. The campaign's outcomes were subsequently employed as the fundamental basis for the challenges presented in the *Hack for Earth* hackathon held at the Expo 2020 in Dubai.

The social media content generated for the campaign took the form of videos that showcased individuals' aspirations for the future. These videos were collaboratively created in partnership with ambassadors representing various partner organizations. To facilitate the campaign, a dedicated website, `www.dreamforearth.com`, was established, acting as a central hub where individuals could contribute by sharing their dreams for the future in the form of videos or text. Participants were able to connect their dreams to one or multiple **United Nations SDGs** and subsequently post them on the website. To know more about United Nations SDGs, go to the *Appendices*.

The campaign successfully amassed thousands of dreams from individuals across the globe, which were subsequently subjected to analysis using an AI tool. The analytical process aimed to gain insights into the geographical distribution of dreams as well as their alignment with specific SDGs. This comprehensive analysis provided valuable understanding regarding the global distribution of aspirations and how they correlated with the SDGs. Such insights not only informed the campaign's strategy but also played a crucial role in establishing the foundation for the challenges presented during the *Hack for Earth* hackathon.

Beyond its analytical significance, the *Dream for Earth* campaign also served to strengthen the *Hack for Earth* community. By incorporating dreams shared by ambassadors, the campaign effectively personalized its message, fostering a sense of connection and engagement among participants. Additionally, the campaign encouraged individuals visiting the website to share their video dreams on their social media platforms. To enhance the social media impact, participants were also allowed to vote for their favorite dreams. As an incentivizing element, the campaign offered a prize in the form of a trip to the **Expo 2020** in Dubai, including a visit to the United Nations pavilion at the world exhibition, for the winner of the voting process. The winner of the Dream for Earth campaign was Joseph Adedeji, a young man from Nigeria, gaining more than 20.000 likes for his dream of a just and fair world of equality and peace.

See the winning video dream by Joseph Adedeji here:

```
https://youtube.com/shorts/lxIQhlHy4CA?feature=shared
```

The *Dream for Earth* campaign serves as a prime example of how community-generated content can be leveraged to create significant social media impact for a hackathon. By harnessing the power of individuals' dreams and aspirations, the campaign successfully engaged a diverse range of participants, strengthened community bonds, and laid the groundwork for the subsequent hackathon challenges. It exemplifies the potential for utilizing user-generated content to amplify the reach and impact of a hackathon while fostering a sense of collective purpose and shared responsibility.

In the following image, you can see one of the social media posts from the Dream for Earth campaign, where we showcased the results of the campaign, highlighting the connection to the United Nations 17 Sustainable Development Goals.

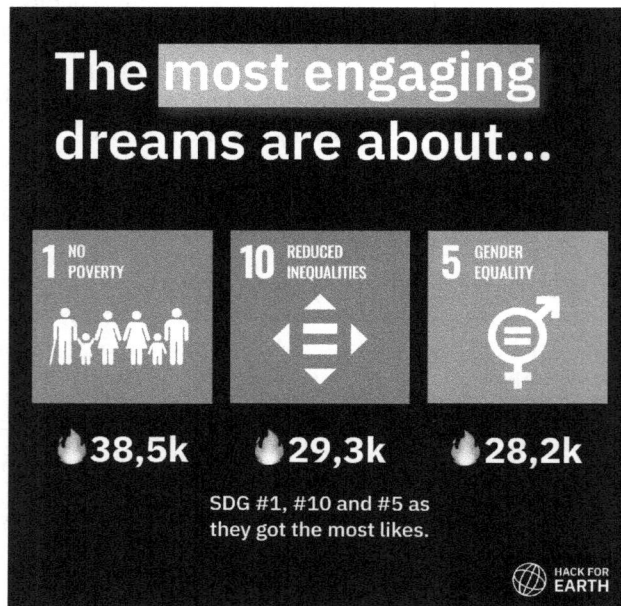

Figure 8.3 – Social media posts from the Dream for Earth campaign

After breaking down the Steam for Sweden and the Dream for Earth campaign, you should have a better understanding of how you can use interactive campaigns in social media to drive the communication for your hackathon.

The importance of timing

Timing is everything is an old saying we often resort to. Timing may not be absolutely everything, but it is extremely important if you want to create an impact with your external communication.

We have already covered the importance of a well-thought-through strategy for your external communication, where you outline why you are posting what, when, and where. To build a relationship with your audience and community, however, you need this strategy to be flexible and to exercise good timing.

This means that you need to be able to adapt to events happening in the world around you and pick up on events happening around you so that you can integrate them into your external communication. This gives your communication a dynamic, vibrant, alive feeling that people will react and respond to – and voilá, you are building a relationship with your audience.

For example, if your country wins the football World Cup, you could upload a congratulatory post or a football anecdote on your social media page the next day.

Of course, this type of communication requires a balance between what is tasteful and what will be perceived as being up to date, and what will not. It is good advice to stay away from anything political or religious, or even potentially offensive content.

Another aspect of timing is to communicate posts about an event when it happens or immediately after it has ended. In this day and age, you cannot communicate about an event long after it has happened – it feels hopelessly outdated. Think of your external communication as a newspaper or a news TV station – nobody is interested in yesterday's news. This is why timing is of utter importance, and this is especially important when it comes to announcing the winners of a hackathon. This has to be done immediately, within a few hours tops, after the prize ceremony.

Therefore, the key aspects of timing are proactiveness, responsiveness, and flexibility.

With these key aspects as guidelines, the communication of your hackathon in your external channels will have a good foundation to rely on.

Summary

In this chapter, we delved into the realm of external communication for hackathons and discovered how it can be leveraged to expand your audience and establish a profound connection with your community. We began by examining the distinctions between various social media platforms, unraveling their unique features and advantages. To illustrate our points, we drew upon the remarkable campaigns of *Dream for Sweden* and *Dream for Earth*, showcasing how they effectively utilized social media.

Moving forward, we explored the fundamentals of setting up social media accounts for your hackathon. We provided insights into the key considerations that must be taken into account when crafting a social media team capable of delivering on your hackathon objectives. The significance of assembling a team with diverse skill sets and a shared passion for the event was emphasized.

Additionally, we emphasized the pivotal role of timing in your hackathon's external communication strategy. The importance of strategic planning and synchronization with key milestones was underscored as it enables you to maximize engagement and impact. By carefully selecting the optimal moments to release announcements, updates, and calls to action, you can effectively capture the attention and interest of your target audience.

In conclusion, this chapter has equipped you with the knowledge and insights necessary to harness the power of external communication for your hackathon. By understanding the nuances of different social media platforms, building a robust social media team, and implementing strategic timing, you can propel your hackathon to new heights of success.

In the next chapter, we will dive into the realm of what happens after the confetti at the prize ceremony of the hackathon event has landed – *Build for Earth*, the acceleration program designed to make the winning solutions become a reality in record time.

Part 3:
Introduction to How to Build

Part 3 focuses on how to turn your hackathon solutions into reality by developing a customized acceleration program based on scientific principles and the proven experiences of innovation leaders. You will delve into the scientific foundations and rationale behind the *Build for Earth* acceleration program and gain insights from practical examples of successful hackathon winners who are currently thriving in the market. In this section, co-author, Dr. Kristofer Vernmark, has contributed with a chapter on the creation of the *Build for Earth* acceleration program.

This section has the following parts:

- *Chapter 9, Taking Citizen-driven Innovation to the Next Level*
- *Chapter 10, Converting Hackathon Results into Real Tools (by Kristofer Vernmark)*
- *Chapter 11, Build for Earth Learnings – How to Make a Startup a Success Fast*

9

Taking Citizen-Driven Innovation to the Next Level

The last part of the *Dream-Hack-Build* process is *Build*, where the solutions created in your **hackathon** are allowed to become real tools. Through our work with hackathon winners over the years, we have made many observations and learned a lot about what to do and what to avoid when supporting great solutions to come to life. After a hackathon, you need a plan on how to support the winners to become real tools to make an impact. This plan is often constructed as an **acceleration program;** that is, a set of lectures, workshops, interactive sessions, and assignments for the winning teams. The idea is to give the solutions created during the hackathon the best possible environment to evolve into hands-on tools that bring value to people and your organization as fast as possible. This entails supporting them in setting up a company or, if this is done within your organization, to give the solution the personnel and other resources it requires.

So, let's get started! We will cover the following topics in this chapter:

- The final step in citizen-driven innovation
- Traditional acceleration programs
- Why Build for Earth is unique
- Can't I just have a hackathon event and skip the acceleration program?
- Impact on the future
- About prize money
- Tracking winners

By the end of this book, you will have the knowledge you need to set up and execute your own in-house acceleration program customized for your winning solutions. This will ensure your hackathon results are given the best possible environment to grow into real tools and have an impact.

The final step in citizen-driven innovation

The belief that a great idea is nothing if it isn't made a reality underscores the critical distinction between conceptualization and implementation in the realm of innovation and progress. While the ideation phase represents a crucial starting point, it is the subsequent translation of those ideas into tangible actions, products, or outcomes that truly determines their value and impact. This concept encapsulates the fundamental truth that the mere existence of an innovative concept, no matter how brilliant or transformative, holds limited significance unless it is actively pursued, developed, and brought to fruition.

The process of bringing ideas to life involves a continuous cycle of learning, adaptation, and refinement. Rarely does a concept emerge fully formed and flawless; rather, it is through ongoing experimentation, iteration, and feedback that ideas evolve and improve over time. This iterative approach not only increases the likelihood of success but also fosters a culture of innovation that values agility, resilience, and a willingness to embrace failure as an essential part of the learning process. This is true for hackathon winners too!

Ultimately, the notion that a great idea is nothing if it isn't made a reality serves as a potent reminder of the transformative power of action and execution in driving meaningful change and progress – in **Build for Earth** and other settings as well. Everyone can have a great idea, but to execute this idea and make it a reality is what makes it have an impact on its surroundings and have a meaning other than just theoretical. This is true in innovation, but generally, this is a rule that transcends into all areas of life and business. It underscores the importance of moving beyond abstract theorizing or wishful thinking to actively engage with the messy, challenging work of implementation. By prioritizing action and commitment to turning ideas into tangible outcomes, we can unlock the full potential of innovation to shape a better future for all.

Citizen-driven innovation, at its core, embodies the fundamental belief that the entirety of a society's citizenry should be actively engaged in shaping and cultivating an environment conducive to collective well-being. This paradigm posits that a society stands to reap substantial benefits when its members participate actively in its co-creation. Central to this ethos is the notion that when individuals contribute directly to the creation of societal structures, systems, and initiatives, they inherently assume a heightened sense of accountability for the resultant outcomes. Furthermore, the collaborative act of co-creation fosters interpersonal connections and a sense of shared ownership, thereby mitigating tendencies toward discrimination, entrenched hierarchies, and isolated groupings within the social fabric.

Harnessing the principles of citizen-driven innovation presents organizations and individuals with an unparalleled opportunity to tap into a profoundly positive and transformative force. By embracing citizen involvement in innovation processes, entities can catalyze a synergistic relationship between stakeholders and the initiatives they support, fostering a sense of collective responsibility and solidarity. This inclusive approach not only amplifies the **diversity** of perspectives and expertise brought to bear on complex **challenges** but also cultivates a culture of collaboration that transcends traditional barriers, ultimately enriching both the organizational landscape and the broader societal tapestry. This is the essence of the **Dream! Hack! Build! method**.

The *Dream! Hack! Build!* method relies heavily on its final and pivotal stage – *Build for Earth*. This phase serves as the linchpin of the entire process, simultaneously embodying its most critical juncture and presenting its greatest challenges. Despite the inherent complexities, participating in and delivering this phase is an inherently exhilarating endeavor, marked by the promise of transformative impact and the excitement of overcoming obstacles.

After reaching the finish line

Once the excitement of the hackathon fades, there is a tendency to shift focus toward planning the next event, inadvertently relegating ideas generated to the sidelines. However, this would be a sorely missed opportunity. To truly capitalize on the momentum generated by the hackathon, it is essential to ensure that the ideas it spawns are not left to wither away but are instead nurtured and developed into actionable solutions – real tools bringing value to society.

While the grand finale of the hackathon may seem to be the announcement of winners at the prize ceremony, this should not mark the end of the journey. For the hackathon to be truly impactful, organizers must demonstrate a commitment to seeing ideas through to fruition. Neglecting this crucial phase risks reducing the hackathon to a mere spectacle, perpetuating the phenomenon known as **innovation theater** and undermining its credibility as a catalyst for meaningful change.

Moreover, it is important to recognize that success in the post-hackathon phase goes beyond the mere provision of financial incentives. While monetary rewards certainly have their place, they are only one piece of the puzzle. What is equally, if not more, important is providing innovators with the support, guidance, and resources they need to translate their ideas into tangible outcomes. Without this support, even the most well-intentioned initiatives are at risk of faltering.

In essence, the key to unlocking the full potential of the *Dream! Hack! Build!* method lies in its ability to shepherd ideas from conception to implementation, ensuring that they are not just lofty aspirations but tangible solutions that make a real difference in the world. By prioritizing the post-hackathon phase and providing innovators with the tools they need to succeed, organizers can ensure that the hackathon serves as more than just a flash in the pan – it becomes a springboard for lasting change and innovation.

The significance and impetus behind the *Build* component within the *Dream! Hack! Build!* process is multifaceted, reflecting both its pivotal role in demonstrating tangible outcomes from hackathons and its capacity to enhance organizational credibility and attract broader participation. This dual motivation underscores the imperative of not only showcasing action but also fostering meaningful innovation that aligns with organizational goals and societal needs. The following can be considered to ensure that hackathons deliver long-lasting results:

- Firstly, *the Build phase serves as a powerful demonstration of tangible outcomes* emerging from hackathons, thereby dispelling any perception of "innovation theater" and affirming the authenticity of the organization's commitment to driving substantive change. By showcasing real tools and solutions, organizers signal to prospective participants and stakeholders that their hackathons yield concrete results, motivating more individuals to engage with the process and reinforcing trust in the organization's ability to deliver on its promises.

- Moreover, the viability and effectiveness of the solutions generated during the *Build* phase hold intrinsic value for both the organization and society at large. These *solutions have the potential to not only address specific business challenges* but also contribute positively to broader social and environmental objectives. However, realizing this potential requires careful alignment between the challenges posed and the desired outcomes, a process that demands meticulous planning and consideration, as discussed in detail in *Chapter 4*.

- It is important to acknowledge, however, that the *outcomes of a hackathon are inherently unpredictable*, given the organic and collaborative nature of the process. Organizers must relinquish absolute control and trust in the creativity and ingenuity of participants to produce innovative solutions that may exceed initial expectations. While it may not be possible to dictate the precise solutions that emerge, organizers can influence the direction of the hackathon by defining clear jury criteria that reflect organizational priorities and values.

- The *selection of jury criteria serves as a strategic tool* for steering the outcome of the hackathon toward desired objectives. By delineating specific evaluation criteria, organizers provide participating teams with a framework for understanding the expectations and priorities of the judging panel. This not only clarifies the assessment process but also incentivizes teams to align their solutions with the organization's goals, thereby increasing the likelihood of generating impactful outcomes.

In essence, the *Build* phase of the *Dream! Hack! Build!* process represents a crucial juncture wherein the organization's commitment to action and innovation converges with the imperative of delivering tangible solutions that create value for both the business and society. By embracing the inherent unpredictability of the hackathon process while strategically shaping its trajectory through clear jury criteria, organizers can maximize the potential for generating innovative solutions that resonate with stakeholders and drive meaningful change.

In this chapter, we will go through the background to why you should invest in creating an acceleration program based on the *Build for Earth* paradigm, and why this is imperative to the entire process of *Dream! Hack! Build!* will be covered. Designing your own in-house acceleration program for your solutions will be introduced in a few easy steps, which will ensure that your winning solutions are given the best possible context to grow into real tools, capable of making an impact.

Traditional acceleration programs

Acceleration programs, incubation hubs, and similar educational platforms for start-up growth have emerged as significant players in the contemporary business landscape, with a global footprint spanning diverse regions. In a world where innovation is highly prized, these initiatives serve as fertile grounds for nurturing budding entrepreneurs and cultivating groundbreaking solutions poised to revolutionize industries. Investors are drawn to these programs, eager to identify and capitalize on the next disruptive innovation before it gains mainstream attention.

The comprehensive support offered by these programs encompasses a wide array of critical elements essential for start-up success. From strategic business planning and financial guidance to refining communication strategies, bolstering social media presence, and mastering the art of effective pitching, participants receive comprehensive assistance tailored to their specific needs and objectives. Despite the wealth of resources and expertise provided, however, the harsh reality remains: a significant percentage of start-ups fail within their first few years, with estimates suggesting that up to 90% may face this fate.

Unveiling the elusive formula that distinguishes the 10% of start-ups that thrive from the majority that falter has become the holy grail of entrepreneurial discourse. Numerous attempts have been made to decode this phenomenon, yet the answer proves elusive, reflecting the intricate and multifaceted nature of entrepreneurial success. To understand this better, you can read this article in Forbes magazine by Neil Patel: `https://packt.link/0FzN1`. Amid this complexity, one factor emerges as a prominent predictor of team success: **psychological safety**.

> **Note**
>
> Psychological safety, defined as the belief that one will not be punished or humiliated for speaking up with ideas, questions, concerns, or mistakes, transcends the realm of start-ups and permeates virtually any team-based endeavor. Research indicates that teams characterized by a climate of psychological safety exhibit higher levels of creativity, innovation, and performance. In the context of start-ups, where uncertainty, ambiguity, and risk are omnipresent, the presence of psychological safety assumes heightened significance, serving as a linchpin for fostering collaboration, risk-taking, and resilience.

Indeed, the correlation between psychological safety and team success underscores the importance of cultivating a supportive and inclusive environment within start-up ecosystems. By nurturing a culture where individuals feel empowered to voice their perspectives, challenge assumptions, and take calculated risks, organizations can harness the collective intelligence and creativity of their teams to navigate challenges and capitalize on opportunities effectively.

Moreover, the recognition of psychological safety as a critical determinant of start-up success underscores the imperative for programmatic interventions that prioritize not only technical expertise but also socio-emotional competencies. By integrating strategies for cultivating psychological safety into acceleration programs and incubation hubs, stakeholders can equip entrepreneurs with the tools and skills necessary to thrive in the dynamic and often unpredictable start-up landscape.

While the quest for entrepreneurial success may defy easy categorization, the presence of psychological safety emerges as a compelling factor that transcends industry boundaries and organizational contexts. By fostering an environment where individuals feel valued, respected, and supported, start-ups can unlock the full potential of their teams, driving innovation, resilience, and sustainable growth in the pursuit of transformative solutions. You can find out more about this in this article by Michael Schneider here: `https://protagonistconsulting.com/wp-content/uploads/2023/10/Google-Spent-2-Years-Studying-180-Teams.pdf`.

Google Aristotle research

Google spent 2 years studying 180 teams. The most successful ones shared these five traits:

- **Dependability**: Team members get things done on time and meet expectations
- **Structure and clarity**: High-performing teams have clear goals and well-defined roles within the group
- **Meaning**: The work has personal significance to each member
- **Impact**: The group believes their work is purposeful and positively impacts the greater good
- **Psychological safety**: The most important one, according to the research that Google did

Why Build for Earth is unique

The entire *Hack for Earth* process of *Dream! Hack! Build!* was born out of a trial-and-error mindset, testing our way forward to what works. In order to explain what makes the *Build for Earth* acceleration program unique, it's imperative to explain the background and context it was born out of.

When our team engaged in the government mission of **Hack for Sweden**, we embarked on a journey that not only exposed us to the intricacies of organizing hackathons but also shed light on a pervasive issue plaguing the innovation ecosystem: the lack of sustained support for winning solutions beyond the jury announcement. This phenomenon, prevalent across hackathons worldwide, raised profound questions about the efficacy and impact of these events, prompting us to reevaluate the underlying motivations for participation.

Exploring the challenges of making winning solutions come to life

While hackathons serve as catalysts for innovation and creativity, their true value lies in the realization of winning solutions into tangible tools that address pressing societal challenges. However, the discontinuation of support post-hackathon has left many brilliant ideas stranded in the ideation phase, unable to materialize into impactful solutions. This disconnect between ideation and implementation has struck at the core of the hackathon ethos, prompting us to question the purpose of our involvement in such endeavors.

Undeterred by the prevailing status quo, our team endeavored to rectify this deficiency by providing post-hackathon assistance to winning teams. Yet, our efforts unearthed a myriad of challenges, chief among them being the prevalence of internal team dynamics issues within winning teams. In addition to grappling with strategic direction, financial planning, and business model development, many winning teams struggled with interpersonal conflicts and communication breakdowns, further complicating the path to implementation.

Despite our best intentions, our attempts to support winning solutions were constrained by resource limitations, particularly the absence of dedicated funding for post-hackathon initiatives. As the mission of *Hack for Sweden* primarily focused on organizing an annual hackathon, securing additional resources for an acceleration program proved to be a formidable task, necessitating a creative approach to leveraging existing assets and personnel.

Nevertheless, our commitment to fostering innovation and driving meaningful impact remained unwavering. After assisting three cohorts of winning solutions emerging from *Hack for Sweden* hackathons, it became increasingly evident that a more structured and dedicated approach was necessary to bridge the gap between ideation and implementation. The complexity inherent in bringing solutions to fruition underscored the need for comprehensive support mechanisms that addressed not only technical challenges but also interpersonal dynamics and strategic planning.

Moreover, our interactions with thousands of hackers, both in-person and through online platforms, revealed a pervasive sentiment of skepticism toward hackathon organizers' intentions post-event. Many hackers expressed concerns that organizers either sought to exploit their solutions for personal gain or displayed indifference toward their fate after the hackathon concluded. This perception underscored the importance of transparency, accountability, and trust-building in fostering a collaborative and supportive innovation ecosystem.

In response to these challenges, our team resolved to take proactive measures to reshape the narrative surrounding hackathon participation and maximize the societal impact of winning solutions. This included advocating for the establishment of a more structured and robust post-hackathon support framework, dispelling misconceptions surrounding organizers' intentions, and fostering a culture of collaboration, transparency, and mutual respect within the innovation community. Our journey with *Hack for Sweden* served as a catalyst for change, inspiring us to redouble our efforts in driving innovation and creating positive social change through hackathons and similar initiatives.

The genesis of our endeavor stemmed from a realization of the glaring gap between hackathon participation and meaningful societal impact. Inspired by a commitment to drive innovation and effect positive change, our team conceived a visionary plan: to design and implement a high-quality acceleration program tailored to the unique needs of winning teams and their solutions. Grounded in both empirical research and real-world experience, our approach aimed to seamlessly integrate the critical element we identified as indispensable to team success: psychological safety.

Central to our vision was the creation of an environment dedicated to catalyzing the transformation of winning hackathon solutions into tangible tools that address pressing societal challenges. To achieve this ambitious goal, we embarked on a multifaceted journey that encompassed rigorous research, insightful interviews with international innovation leaders, and professional training in psychological safety.

Drawing upon a wealth of research on start-up success, we meticulously curated a repository of insights, strategies, and best practices gleaned from the experiences of successful entrepreneurs and industry experts. This comprehensive knowledge base served as the foundation upon which our acceleration program would be built, providing invaluable guidance and direction as we navigated the complexities of transforming innovative ideas into impactful solutions.

In parallel, we embarked on a journey of discovery, engaging in insightful conversations with international innovation leaders to glean firsthand insights into the keys to entrepreneurial success. These interviews provided invaluable perspectives on challenges, opportunities, and best practices shaping the innovation landscape, enriching our understanding of the multifaceted dynamics at play in the start-up ecosystem. More about these interviews will be covered in *Chapter 10*, by the creator behind the *Build for Earth* acceleration program, Dr. Kristofer Vernmark, and a full list of the experts interviewed can be found under *Build for Earth* in *Appendix B*.

However, our quest for excellence did not end there. Recognizing the pivotal role of psychological safety in fostering team cohesion, creativity, and performance, we made a strategic decision to incorporate professional training in this critical area into our acceleration program. Drawing upon cutting-edge research and practical insights from organizational psychology and leadership development, we designed a curriculum that equipped participants with the skills, tools, and techniques necessary to cultivate a culture of trust, openness, and collaboration within their teams.

By integrating these three pillars – research-driven insights, firsthand perspectives from industry leaders, and professional training in psychological safety – into our acceleration program, we aimed to create a holistic and impactful framework for nurturing winning hackathon solutions into real-world tools for societal good. Our approach represented a synthesis of scientific rigor, practical wisdom, and human-centered values, reflecting our unwavering commitment to driving innovation, fostering collaboration, and effecting positive change in the world.

In the next chapter, *Chapter 10*, Dr. Kristofer Vernmark will introduce the process of creation and the science of the *Build for Earth* acceleration program in detail, explaining how you can use the learnings of *Build for Earth* to create your own successful acceleration program for your hackathon winners.

Can't I just have a hackathon event and skip the acceleration program?

Indeed, the temptation to focus solely on organizing the hackathon event itself, without investing resources and effort into an acceleration program afterward, may be alluring. Budget constraints and other logistical considerations often prompt organizers to prioritize the event over post-hackathon support initiatives. However, as we will explore in this section, this approach is not only shortsighted but also undermines the long-term impact and sustainability of the hackathon endeavor.

Organizing a hackathon event of high quality requires substantial effort and meticulous planning to ensure a positive and enriching experience for all stakeholders involved – from hackers and **jury members** to **mentors** and partners. The logistics of securing venues, recruiting participants, coordinating mentors, and curating challenges demands careful attention to detail and a commitment to excellence. However, the true measure of success lies not only in the seamless execution of the event itself but also in the meaningful outcomes that result from it.

Despite the considerable investment of time, energy, and resources into organizing the hackathon event, it is imperative not to lose sight of the critical importance of post-hackathon engagement. Skipping the acceleration program in favor of focusing solely on the event risks squandering the momentum and enthusiasm generated during the hackathon, relegating winning solutions to a state of limbo without the necessary support and guidance to realize their full potential.

The acceleration program plays a pivotal role in bridging the gap between ideation and implementation, providing winning teams with the resources, mentorship, and support needed to transform their ideas into tangible solutions. By neglecting this crucial phase, organizers risk undermining the impact and relevance of the hackathon, perpetuating the perception of hackathons as mere one-off events rather than catalysts for sustained innovation and societal change.

Moreover, the acceleration program serves as a testament to the organizers' commitment to fostering a culture of innovation and entrepreneurship beyond the confines of the hackathon event. It signals a long-term investment in the success and growth of winning solutions, reflecting a genuine desire to effect positive change and make a meaningful impact in the world.

In essence, while organizing a hackathon event represents a significant undertaking in its own right, the true value and legacy of the endeavor lie in the ability to support and nurture winning solutions beyond the confines of the event itself. By prioritizing the acceleration program and committing to post-hackathon support initiatives, organizers can maximize the impact and sustainability of the hackathon, empowering winning teams to realize their full potential and drive meaningful change in society. The following points summarize why it's not a good idea to skip an acceleration program for your winning solutions:

- You will lose credibility with your audience. If you don't take care of the solutions after the hackathon, you will be the organizer who didn't take action on the great solutions that were created.

- The participants may feel you have used them for your event but that you don't take the outcome and the work they put into it seriously. If you did take it seriously, you would be mindful of the outcome and take action on it.

- You may have trouble getting people to sign up for another of your hackathons in the future. Why should I attend this if my effort and work will not have the chance to be taken forward?

- You risk looking like an organizer who is more interested in innovation theater than real action.

- The solutions created in the hackathon will not be given the best opportunity to develop into real tools.

The pros of having an acceleration program, by taking care of the winning solutions, are the following:

- You gain credibility by showing your employees, your audience, and hackathon participants that you execute, you take action, and you mean business. This helps in building the impression that you do not just talk like many others; you lead the way.

- Participants of the hackathon feel appreciated and valued and that you respect the effort they have put into the hackathon event.

- You will likely have more people wanting to sign up if you organize another hackathon in the future. Good hackathons travel by word of mouth.

- You will give the winning solutions the best possible environment to develop into real tools and might just see the birth of some really innovative solutions that are solving your organizational challenges.

- Your brand will be positively affected by you showing that you take action on the solutions and follow through on your dedication to making innovation happen.

From the aforementioned points, it is fairly evident that it is a smart and efficient investment to follow through with an acceleration program for your winning solutions after hosting a hackathon event. The exact structure can vary; the most important thing is that it has the overall aim of giving the solutions the best possible environment to develop into real tools for impact. Examples and hands-on ideas on how this can be done will be discussed next.

Impact on the future

Anyone can have a great idea, and most people probably will sometime in their lifetime. The only thing that matters, however, is execution.

This encapsulates a profound truth in the world of innovation. It underscores the critical importance of turning conceptual brilliance into tangible outcomes through effective execution. Nowhere is this principle more relevant than in the context of hackathons, where creative energy abounds and ideas flow freely.

In this light, an acceleration program emerges as the linchpin in the journey from hackathon ideation to impactful implementation. It serves as the conduit through which the seeds of innovation planted during the hackathon event are nurtured and cultivated into actionable solutions with real-world significance. By providing winning teams with the necessary support, resources, and guidance, the acceleration program ensures that the momentum generated during the hackathon is sustained and translated into tangible results.

Far from being an optional addendum to the hackathon experience, the acceleration program represents the culmination of the *Dream! Hack! Build!* process. It signifies a commitment to not just ideate but to execute – to transform lofty visions into concrete realities that make a tangible difference in people's lives. In this sense, it sets organizers apart as champions of action-oriented innovation, distinguished by their unwavering dedication to turning ideas into impact.

The decision to invest in an acceleration program speaks volumes about an organizer's ethos and values. It reflects a deep-seated belief in the transformative power of innovation and a commitment to nurturing the next generation of changemakers. By providing winning teams with the tools, resources, and support they need to succeed, organizers demonstrate their commitment to fostering a culture of entrepreneurship and driving positive change in society.

The acceleration program also serves as a testament to the enduring legacy of the hackathon experience. It ensures that the energy, creativity, and passion ignited during the event are not merely fleeting sparks but rather seeds planted for future growth and impact. By harnessing the collective ingenuity of participants and guiding them through the process of implementation, organizers pave the way for a future where innovation thrives and transformative ideas become reality.

In essence, the decision to incorporate an acceleration program into the hackathon experience is not just a strategic choice – it's a statement of purpose. It signals a commitment to turning ideas into action, dreams into reality, and aspirations into achievements. In a world where innovation is the currency of progress, the acceleration program is the key that unlocks the door to a brighter, more impactful future.

Organizing an acceleration program in-house does not have to be rocket science, but there are a few things to keep in mind to get it right:

- Workshops on relevant topics (pitch technique, business planning, decision making, finance, partnerships, specific topics for solutions development, and so on)
- Guest lecturers to provide teams with expertise on relevant topics
- Mandatory attendance for a minimum of two people from every team during all workshops
- Focus on creating psychological safety in teams
- Leadership development for the team leader
- **Pitch for Earth** (explained further next) event at the end
- Restrain from giving winning teams their prize money at the beginning

When considering the optimal duration for the acceleration program, it is recommended to allocate a period ranging from 3 to 6 months, a timeframe that can be tailored based on available budgetary resources. Striking the right balance is paramount; the program should be neither too brief nor overly protracted. A **sense of urgency** is essential to drive progress, prompting teams to showcase tangible results within a reasonable timeframe. To facilitate this, we advocate for the inclusion of a culminating event– *Pitch for Earth* –which serves as a platform for winning teams to present the progress made in realizing their solutions into tangible tools.

The *Pitch for Earth* event, ideally held at the conclusion of the acceleration program, serves as a powerful motivator for teams to demonstrate the fruits of their labor. The prospect of presenting their accomplishments before an audience serves as a compelling impetus for action, instilling a sense of accountability and driving teams to strive for excellence. While the composition of the audience is significant, with potential investors among the attendees, the primary focus remains on showcasing tangible outcomes and progress.

The choice of venue for the *Pitch for Earth* event can vary, ranging from a standalone event organized specifically for this purpose to integration within an existing external conference or similar gathering. Leveraging an established platform not only enhances visibility but also provides an opportunity for broader dissemination of winning solutions to a diverse audience.

In terms of workshop facilitation, prioritizing expertise and credibility is paramount. While workshops can be conducted by experts within the organizing organization, certain components demand specialized knowledge and skill sets. In particular, sessions on psychological safety and leadership development necessitate the involvement of licensed psychologists and experts in group psychology. This non-negotiable requirement ensures the maintenance of high standards and the delivery of expected results.

By integrating these elements into the acceleration program, organizers can create a comprehensive and impactful framework for supporting winning solutions from ideation to implementation. The structured timeline, culminating in the *Pitch for Earth* event, provides a roadmap for teams to navigate the complexities of execution while instilling a sense of purpose and accountability. Through strategic collaboration and leveraging specialized expertise, organizers can maximize the potential of the acceleration program, driving meaningful outcomes and fostering a culture of innovation and impact.

About prize money

The inclusion of prize money in hackathons serves as a double-edged sword, wielding significant influence in both attracting participants and igniting motivation among competing teams. However, the timing and manner in which prize money is dispersed can profoundly impact the outcomes and sustainability of the hackathon experience. While immediate gratification may seem appealing, particularly in the aftermath of an intense and demanding hackathon event, the premature dispersal of prize money without accompanying support mechanisms can have detrimental consequences.

Dispersing prize money directly after the conclusion of the hackathon event, devoid of any structured support or guidance, is a practice that we caution against. This approach risks fostering a short-sighted mindset among winning teams, who may hastily expend the funds without strategic foresight or long-term planning. Without the benefit of ongoing mentorship, training, or access to resources, teams may inadvertently allocate the prize money to suboptimal endeavors or fail to capitalize on the full potential of their solutions.

In contrast, we advocate for a more deliberate and strategic approach to prize money dispersal, one that aligns with the overarching objectives of the acceleration program. By disbursing prize money at the conclusion of the acceleration program, organizers provide winning teams with a vital opportunity to leverage their newfound skills, knowledge, and expertise to make informed decisions about resource allocation.

This delayed dispersal of prize money serves as a tangible incentive for teams to actively engage with the acceleration program, knowing that their efforts will be rewarded upon successful completion. Moreover, it underscores the organizers' commitment to supporting teams beyond the confines of the hackathon event, providing a structured pathway for continued growth and development.

By synchronizing the dispersal of prize money with the culmination of the acceleration program, organizers purposefully align financial incentives with programmatic objectives. This integrated approach not only empowers winning teams to make strategic decisions about resource allocation but also reinforces the value of ongoing support and mentorship throughout the journey from ideation to implementation.

Furthermore, by coupling prize money and **seed funding** with the structured support of the acceleration program, organizers create a more sustainable and impactful framework for nurturing innovation and driving positive change. The combined impact of financial incentives and structured support mechanisms ensures that winning teams are equipped with the tools, resources, and guidance needed to maximize the potential of their solutions and have a meaningful impact on the world.

Here is a photo of the winning team *Daresay* with their giant cardboard prize checks with the sums of 30.000 SEK and 50.000 SEK, taken at the award ceremony at *Hack for Sweden 2019*. Team *Daresay* won the *Health* category award and was also chosen by the head jury to win the best-in-show *Hack for Sweden* award. In total, team *Daresay* won 80.000 SEK in prize money.

Figure 9.1 – The winning team Daresay with their prize checks at
the award ceremony at Hack for Sweden 2019

Tracking winners

Example 1 – BrightAct

BrightAct was the winner of *Hack the Crisis Sweden* in April 2020 and also the **EUvsVirus** hackathon in May 2020. The two founders of *BrightAct* met at the *Hack the Crisis Sweden* online hackathon in April 2020. Soon realizing the potential of their innovative winning solution, Elinor Samuelson and Sofie Wahlström quit their day jobs shortly thereafter to focus on developing the business of *BrightAct* full-time. Today, only 3 years later, *BrightAct* is establishing itself in several countries in Europe and on its way to establishing itself in other parts of the world too. They have won several prizes for their innovative systemic approach to a longstanding and worldwide issue. *BrightAct* is a great example of a winning hackathon solution that has come to the market fast. Here are some facts about it:

- *BrightAct* is a digital matching tool to connect people seeking help with support organizations to help victims of domestic violence
- Victims of domestic violence can get in touch with everything from aid organizations, emergency services, social services, and lawyers to municipalities, county administrations, regions, and employers – everyone who provides some type of support for people who need to get out of a harmful relationship
- *BrightAct* has won a multitude of international recognition, winning several hackathons and prizes
- In only a few months' time, they set up their first pilot in a municipality in Sweden
- 3 years later, they are present in several countries in Europe and expanding to more parts of the world

Example 2 – Recy-Block

Recy-Block (renamed during the acceleration program to *Zelij*) was the winner of *Hack for Earth* at **Expo 2020**, a global online hackathon in 2021. The founder Saif Eddine Laalej has made astounding progress in a very short time with the solution and now works full-time with his company. *Zelij Invent* is present with factories in several countries in the Middle East, apart from Morocco where it was founded and has its headquarters. Here's a summary of the company's achievements:

- *Recy-Block* winner of *Hack for Earth* at *Expo 2020*
- Won out of competition from 1,471 teams from 121 countries
- Set up production in their factory in Morocco within 3 months
- Got a major investment from a foundation (10 million USD) within 6 months
- Now present with production in several countries in the Middle East

Zelij Invent is an impressive example of a hackathon winner making its way to the market in a short period of time. It's a pioneering venture within the realm of green technology, offering a transformative solution aimed at addressing the pressing issue of plastic waste while simultaneously advancing sustainable construction practices. *Zelij Innovations* has emerged as a trailblazer in the field, leveraging cutting-edge research and innovation to develop an innovative formula capable of converting plastic waste into durable paving blocks and traditional floor tiles.

At the heart of *Zelij*'s groundbreaking technology lies an ingenious formula that blends 80% reclaimed plastic waste with 20% eco-friendly materials, resulting in construction materials that boast unparalleled sustainability credentials. This unique composition not only mitigates the environmental impact of plastic waste but also delivers a more cost-effective alternative to conventional construction materials. By harnessing the inherent properties of plastic waste and augmenting them with eco-friendly additives, *Zelij* has succeeded in creating a versatile raw material that can be shaped and molded to suit a myriad of applications.

Central to *Zelij*'s approach is its commitment to innovation and sustainability, driving the development of products that not only meet stringent environmental standards but also deliver tangible benefits to end users. By repurposing plastic waste into valuable construction materials, *Zelij* not only diverts harmful materials from landfills but also contributes to the conservation of natural resources and the reduction of carbon emissions associated with traditional manufacturing processes.

Zelij's technology offers a wide range of design possibilities, enabling architects, designers, and construction professionals to unleash their creativity and create aesthetically pleasing and environmentally sustainable structures. Whether used for outdoor paving projects or interior flooring installations, *Zelij*'s products offer a compelling blend of durability, versatility, and sustainability, making them an ideal choice for eco-conscious consumers and businesses alike.

This hackathon winner represents a paradigm shift in the way we approach construction materials, offering a viable and scalable solution to the global plastic waste crisis. Through its innovative technology and unwavering commitment to sustainability, *Zelij* is paving the way for a more environmentally conscious and socially responsible built environment, one where waste is transformed into opportunity and sustainability is synonymous with progress.

Summary

In this chapter, we have delved into the critical importance of implementing an acceleration program following the culmination of a hackathon event. Central to our discussion is the recognition that ideas, no matter how innovative or promising, hold little value if they remain dormant and unrealized. Therefore, the essence of citizen-driven innovation lies not merely in ideation but in the proactive pursuit of execution and tangible outcomes.

Throughout the chapter, we have underscored the pivotal role of action-oriented strategies in driving the transformation of ideas into impactful solutions. By organizing and implementing an acceleration program, hackathon organizers can provide winning teams with the necessary support, resources, and guidance to navigate the complex journey from concept to realization. This includes facilitating access to mentorship, funding opportunities, and technical assistance, all of which are essential components in the journey toward bringing ideas to fruition.

We have also elucidated the *Build for Earth* approach as a unique and innovative framework for acceleration programs. Unlike traditional models, which may prioritize financial incentives or market potential, the *Build for Earth* approach places a strong emphasis on psychological safety. By fostering an environment of trust, collaboration, and support, this approach empowers participants to take calculated risks, explore bold ideas, and confront challenges with resilience and creativity.

In illustrating the efficacy of the *Build for Earth* approach, we have provided compelling examples of winning solutions from our hackathons that have successfully transitioned into tangible, market-ready tools. These case studies serve as tangible evidence of the transformative power of acceleration programs in driving real-world impact and innovation.

We have conducted a comparative analysis of traditional acceleration programs, highlighting the unique strengths and advantages of the *Build for Earth* framework. While conventional programs may focus primarily on commercial viability or scalability, the *Build for Earth* approach prioritizes holistic outcomes, including social impact, sustainability, and ethical considerations.

Hence, this chapter serves as a comprehensive guide to the essential role of acceleration programs in realizing the full potential of citizen-driven innovation. By embracing the *Build for Earth* approach and prioritizing psychological safety, hackathon organizers can empower participants to embark on transformative journeys of ideation, collaboration, and execution, ultimately driving positive change and innovation in society.

In the forthcoming chapter authored by Dr. Kristofer Vernmark, you will delve deeper into the background, dynamics, and scientific principles underpinning the *Build for Earth* framework. Dr. Vernmark will provide valuable insights into how these principles can be applied in the context of acceleration programs, offering practical guidance for organizers.

Converting Hackathon Results into Real Tools

By Kristofer Vernmark

In this chapter, you will learn more about the **Build for Earth acceleration program**, how it was created, and what is important to consider when aiming to create high-performing, innovative teams. We will cover important aspects of innovation and why some start-ups fail while others succeed, with an extra focus on teamwork, **psychological safety**, and **transformational leadership**, working together toward creating impactful real-world solutions. We will also address why **diversity,** task conflict, a shared vision, and individual motivation are important aspects when working to foster innovation.

In this chapter, we will cover the following topics:

- Creating an acceleration program – Build for Earth
- The importance of psychological safety in teams
- Transformational leadership
- Working with virtual teams in digital settings
- Content and themes in Build for Earth
- Voices from participants
- Setting up your own acceleration program

By the end of this chapter, you will have learned how to go from a great idea to building something tangible, by forming a great team and unlocking the potential in human behavior. You will also have concrete knowledge about what to include in an acceleration program within your organizational setting.

Creating an acceleration program – Build for Earth

The Build for Earth program was created out of the need to support the winning solutions of Hack for Earth hackathons in taking the next step in realizing their solutions after the competition was over and winners had been declared. Out of this need, and the vision of the Hack for Earth Foundation's founder, Ann Molin, the Build for Earth acceleration program was created by Dr. Kristofer Vernmark and first delivered to the winners of the Hack for Earth hackathon at **Expo 2020** in Dubai in the spring of 2022. The aim of the acceleration program was to, in a short period of time (six months), create autonomous teams with value-driven team members that would continue to grow and realize their ideas into tangible tools on the market.

The content and structure of the program was created by using four main sources of input:

- Research and real-world data on start-up failure and success.
- Interviews with innovation experts and successful entrepreneurs.
- Conclusions and learnings from earlier hackathons.

Published research and real-world data, dialogues with innovation experts, input from previous hackathon winners, and our own experiences all pointed in a clear direction – a great team is the most crucial aspect when aiming to take on the difficult task of turning an innovative idea into something tangible and thereby achieving real impact. This is even more so the case when working with citizen-driven innovation where teams can constitute a diverse set of people from different parts of the world, with sometimes only the shared vision of wanting to achieve impact. Build for Earth program participants are usually not experienced serial entrepreneurs and we have not focused on individual characteristics and personality traits connected to being an entrepreneur, as has been the case with other acceleration programs. Instead, the goal of Build for Earth is to invite anyone to innovate and potentially contribute to a better world, giving everyone the opportunity to be a change-maker. We know that diversity is the mother of innovation, but it also comes with a cost, increasing the risk of conflict and misunderstandings. Based on this insight and research showing that **psychological safety** within the group correlates with improved performance, learning, and work satisfaction, a strong focus on team collaboration and psychological safety was integrated into the program. The assumption was that a value-driven and supportive team, with a **transformational leadership**, can attain the necessary skills and knowledge on how to become a successful start-up, such as creating a workable business model, understanding product-to-market fit, involving stakeholders, creating important partnerships, and measuring progress toward impact.

The following targets were set for the teams to have achieved by the end of the acceleration program:

- An autonomous team with the right skill set, a high degree of psychological safety, and a transformative leadership within the team

- Knowledge and skills for a resilient startup life and building the foundation for a start-up company and understanding what it takes to realize a great idea with an appropriate business model

- A well-defined, easily communicable, and deliverable product and/or service that is presented in the form of a **Minimal Viable Product** (MVP), prototype, and/or proof of concept

- The integration of a sustainability mindset and associated behaviors into the team and measurable indicators of a sustainable service/product

- Supportive partnerships and collaborations, knowledge of suitable financing options, and ongoing interaction with potential end users and customers

Since our hackathon-winning teams were often in the pre-start-up phase, the overarching goal was to help potential change-makers go from innovation to impact by creating resilient and collaborative individuals and teams, providing support and resources along the way, and focusing on what we consider the most important aspect of this process – a team that can learn from its experience and mistakes.

The importance of psychological safety in teams

Talent wins games, but teamwork and intelligence win championships.

– Michael Jordan

When a start-up is successful, we often credit it to the lone genius and brilliant founder; however, the majority of new ventures are founded and led by teams, rather than by individuals. The power of teamwork cannot be underestimated as it can bring out the best in each individual under the right circumstances and therefore has the potential to become more than the sum of its parts.

A team is usually defined as a highly interdependent group of people working toward a common goal. Teams plan their work, solve problems, make decisions, and review their progress together, among many other things. The difference between a working group and a team is that team members need each other to get their work done; they are dependent upon each other. One can say that a group becomes a team when shared goals and effective methods to accomplish these goals are in place. Teams vary in their size, physical distance (e.g., virtual versus in-person meetings), purpose, experience, competencies among team members, and surrounding context, among many other factors. Research from the famous group and organizational psychology professor Susan Wheelan shows that members of high-performance teams feel involved, committed, and valued, producing a higher quality of work than members of low-performing teams.

In 2012, Google wanted to find out more about why certain teams were successful and some were not. They called it Project Aristotle, based on the quote "the whole is greater than the sum of its parts." A total of 180 teams were examined and variables such as personality traits, educational backgrounds, demographics, and team dynamics were measured. The highest-performing teams turned out to experience a high degree of *dependability* (e.g., team members believe that teammates will follow through with their tasks on time), *structure and clarity* (e.g., the team has clear roles and goals, and team members feel that the team has an effective decision-making process), *meaning* (e.g., team members think that the work they do for the team is meaningful and personally important), and *impact* (e.g., team members understand how their work contributes to the larger goals of the organization and believe their work matters and creates change). These are all important aspects of a highly functioning team, but the most important mechanism for an effective team, underpinning all other aspects, turned out to be another group phenomenon – **psychological safety**.

These findings confirmed the notion that coming together and using the skills, experiences, and personal attributes that exist in a team is crucial for success. You are no better than how you perform as a group, and a diverse team that uses this diversity to its advantage is more innovative, as team members tend to attend and follow each other's actions.

Interestingly, interviews with failed start-ups summarized by Failory and data from Autopsy show the same thing, that *almost 1 in 5 failures are due to problems within the team*. Such team factors can result in conflict between team members, conflict between founders, and not having the right competence and team composition. It can also result in individual burnout among team members and founders because of the daunting and emotionally draining nature of entrepreneurship and start-up life, all contributing to start-up failure.

That is why it is so important to focus on the team in your acceleration program. Without a great team, there is no perseverance and realized innovation.

Since **citizen-driven innovation** creates an open space for anyone to participate in a hackathon, the newly created teams participating in our Build for Earth programs have mainly held together based on these premises:

- An interest in hackathons, innovation, sustainability, and collaboration (working in a team)
- An innovative idea
- A shared vision of a better and more sustainable world if their idea is realized

In a way, this is quite a loose base for forming a team, but it is based on maybe the most important aspect of long-lasting commitment – a shared vision of a better tomorrow.

Before we move on to why the secret to team performance and learning is about how the team works together, and not the individuals that are in it, we want you to think about this question.

> **Question**
>
> How do you go about assembling a team? Think about the choices you make to include team members and how you follow up and measure successful teamwork within your organization. Are you creating teams based on the right premises for successful teams or is there room for improvement?

How to create psychological safety

The Project Aristotle study by Google did not stumble across something new. The term psychological safety was coined by Edgar Schein in the 1960s and the concept has been developed and extensively studied by Professor Amy Edmondson at Harvard University Business School for over three decades.

Psychological safety can be defined as the experience of confidence within a team that you can speak freely and be yourself without the fear of being rejected, embarrassed, or punished, creating a team climate of interpersonal trust and mutual respect that is focused on inclusion and achieving a common goal. People's beliefs about each other in a team are closely connected to how willing they are to engage in behavior where the outcome is uncertain and take an interpersonal risk. Having a high degree of psychological safety in a team can lead to increased learning, higher performance, and more engaged team members.

> **Five steps for innovative breakthrough**
>
> Psychological safety is one of the most important aspects of innovative teams. In her book Teaming to Innovate, Professor Edmondson declares the five steps necessary for innovative breakthrough:
>
> **Aim high**: Create a shared vision and long-term goal that will motivate the team.
>
> **Team up**: Create a team with clear goals, the right skills, and competencies, but most of all, a team climate that is defined by psychological safety and supportive leadership.
>
> **Fail well**: Plan for failure and aim for *intelligent* failures within your team.
>
> **Learn fast**: The essence of an innovative team is to use failures to learn. Mistakes and failures can be great opportunities if that is the mindset of your team.
>
> **Repeat**: Visions, teamwork, failure, and learning are not one-time things that you do and move on. You constantly have to remind yourself and continue the hard work.

We have attempted to integrate these aspects into the acceleration program. One example is letting teams work with creating their own **Theory of Change** (**ToC**), explicitly defining long-term goals and a shared vision before moving on to other topics. Another example is letting each team member state their motivation for being part of Build for Earth before it starts and providing sessions on psychological safety and transformational leadership early on.

It is important to clarify that psychological safety is not about avoiding conflict and always being "nice" to each other. It is about addressing difficult issues and focusing on the task-oriented aspects of conflict instead of getting caught up in conflicts spurred by strong emotions and personal attacks.

The first steps of psychological safety are actually quite simple: be genuinely interested in other people's opinions and feelings, make sure everyone is invited to participate in discussions, ask more questions than you give answers, communicate in a clear way that you have been listening, be open and share relevant information with team members, ask for feedback, and encourage learning from your own and other's mistakes. If you begin measuring these behaviors in your team, you will probably find room for improvement within your team.

Hackers at the Hack for Earth hackathons are provided with three short exercises to prompt participating teams to think and address the teamwork aspect of innovation at an early stage. These exercises are as follows:

Before you start (15 minutes)

Begin with setting the ground rules for how you interact and collaborate within your team by answering these three questions together and writing them down as a team agreement. This can be even more important in digital and hybrid forms of teamwork.

How do we make sure that everyone's opinion is heard and respected?

What is each person's specific strength, contribution to, and role within this team?

Who is the appointed team leader and what mandate does that person have?

Learning during the hackathon (5-10 minutes)

Evaluate and learn continuously to make sure you are on the right track, using the **After Action Review (AAR)** method. After you have finished a specific task, stop and ask yourself these three questions in the team. Share your answers with each other. Learn and move on.

What was the goal of what we set out to do?

What did we as a group do good that took us towards that goal?

What can we do differently next time?

Handling conflicts (15 minutes)

Are your conflicts task-related and about different opinions on how to solve a problem or move forward with your solution? Or are they more directed towards personal attributes and "not liking" each other? Allow task conflict but quickly address relationship conflicts, as they will have a negative effect on the performance of the group. Tackle the conflict by discussing personal feelings about observable behaviors in the group that are affecting the team's ability to function. Do not allow accusations, judgmental opinions about individuals, and the critique of personal attributes. And answer the most important question:

What is needed right now from the team and the individuals to restore psychological safety in the group and continue to collaborate successfully?

The reason for introducing the **After Action Review** (**AAR**) debriefing tool early on is that psychological safety is closely related to learning. The AAR can be used to improve teamwork and has been shown to have quite a remarkable effect on performance, improving effectiveness by up to 25%.

Psychological safety is something we experience and do as a group. We can talk about it all we want, but it is the behaviors in the team that define the degree of psychological safety in the team. In Build for Earth 2024, all teams have scheduled team sessions during the acceleration program that just focus on how the team works together. These sessions are aimed at both experiential and cognitive learning. As psychological safety can be trained in a plethora of ways, there are endless possibilities. In the *Appendix*, you will find the agenda for the first team session so that you can try this yourself in your own team.

Amy Edmondson has stated seven questions that work as a way of measuring the degree of psychological safety. The questions are to be answered by all members of the team. The scale goes from *Strongly disagree* to *Strongly agree* on a five-point scale (1-5). Questions 1 and 4 are inverted:

- Q1: If you make a mistake on this team, it is often held against you
- Q2: Members of this team are able to bring up problems and tough issues
- Q3: People in this team sometimes reject others for being different
- Q4: It is safe to take a risk on this team
- Q5: It is difficult to ask other members of this team for help
- Q6: No one on this team would deliberately act in a way that undermines my efforts
- Q7: Working with members of this team, my unique skills and talents are valued and utilized

These questions have been used in research to measure psychological safety, but they can also be used before and after working with psychological safety in a group to see if there has been any improvement over time. And, to achieve that, one of the most important aspects is the behavior and influence of team leadership, which we will discuss in the next section.

Transformational leadership

Leadership can come in all different styles and forms. It can be formal or informal. It can be a one-person job or a shared task. We have all had experiences with both good and bad bosses that have affected our mood in the morning before going to work. Great leadership has been shown to lead to positive emotions in team members, a higher sense of pride, better outcomes in the workplace, and higher job satisfaction. On the other hand, destructive leadership can lead to the opposite, creating a stressful work environment and insecure team members.

Psychological safety demands a certain type of supportive leadership that sets the stage for those types of behaviors, such as talking about mistakes, inviting the participation of all group members, and aiming to create high-quality relationships within the team and with external parties. A leader who wants to help create psychological safety goes from "having the answers" to "setting the direction."

A well-known and studied leadership model is the **full-range leadership model**, developed and defined by leadership and organizational behavior professors Bernard Bass and Bruce Avolio. Their model includes different types of transactional leadership, such as laissez-faire and contingent reward styles, and transformational leadership. Over 30 years of research have shown that both transactional and transformational leadership can positively predict a variety of performance outcomes, including individual, group, and organizational variables, with transformational leadership having the strongest effect on follower satisfaction and performance.

Transformational leadership is measured firstly by the extent of influence on the followers and their feeling of trust, admiration, loyalty, and respect for the leader. The transformational leader offers followers something more than just working for self-gain; they provide an inspiring mission and vision that gives them a shared identity, aligning the interests and values of individual team members with those of the whole team. A transformational leader enhances commitment, involvement, and performance, all aspects that are crucial to moving from innovation to impact.

The four aspects of transformational leadership

Idealized influence: Be a role model and create trust within the team

Inspirational motivation: Motivate and inspire your team, making everyone part of a shared vision

Individualized consideration: Pay attention to individual needs and show that you care about every member of the team

Intellectual stimulation: Challenge and stimulate team members, encouraging creativity

---

It is not easy being a leader. The experience of leadership positions and formal education have varied greatly when it comes to team leads in the Build for Earth program. We have had team leads who have been on multiple start-up journeys, excelling in their leadership skills and knowledge, but a more common situation has been the need to guide those who have limited experience and education, maybe even finding themselves in a formal leadership position for the first time, struggling to be comfortable in this new role. This comes with big challenges, of course, but we would not want it to be any other way. It is very much in line with the concept of citizen-driven innovation, not only inviting those who are already experts in innovation and leadership but also contributing to building new leaders that develop their competency and confidence during the acceleration program. There are also indications that transformational leaders are better at accepting and adapting to cultural diversity, which is crucial when leading a team with different nationalities and cultural backgrounds.

As transformational leadership includes being a role model and inspiring others, we have also made it our job to try to act in that way in our interactions with teams and team leads – always encouraging, always reminding them of their visions and long term goals, always supporting, but also setting boundaries and stimulating their own development when needed. It sounds easier than it is, and of course, we constantly fail at this task, but at least it is something we can remind ourselves of to get back on track.

> **Note**
>
> A team lead can work with transformational leadership behaviors, but remember that the team lead is influenced by the context and the experience of other leaders in the same organization. If you are the one who initiated the team or are supporting its members, remember that you are also a role model who influences the behaviors of the team lead, and in the end, the behaviors of the whole team!

As research has shown that transformational leadership can be trained, part of the Build for Earth program has been specific leadership sessions with team leads. We have tried different versions, such as support on demand and scheduled sessions, and different content in these sessions, with transformational leadership skills being addressed during the sessions. Time has always been an issue, as there is usually a limited amount of time for leadership support. Also, we have had to adapt each session to the needs of the specific team lead and the level of knowledge and skills. A student with experience in leading their fellow classmates in group projects at school needs a very different approach than the serial entrepreneur with tons of experience and an already elaborated view of leadership.

We also invite you to think of leadership not only as the act of a single person but as something that can be adapted by the whole team.

> **Shared leadership in new teams**
>
> In start-ups and new venture teams, there can often be a lack of clear titles, thereby leading to team members alternating in leadership. Shared leadership has in some studies been shown to account for up to 15% of the variance in firm performance, making it an interesting aspect of leadership.

A recently added feature has been to target leadership skills and work through challenges in a specific group stage using the integrated model of group development by Professor Susan Wheelan. Teams in the Build for Earth program usually move from phase I (*forming*) to phase II (*storming*) during the acceleration program. As leaders are often confronted in phase II and conflicts increase, specific leadership behaviors can be needed to set the rules and roles of a functioning and collaborating team in this phase to move on to the next phases of *norming* and *performing*, the more productive stages of a working group. We have seen this in many teams, where members are very positive and speak of their team as the best they have ever been in when the acceleration program starts, but when struggles begin, team members start to mistrust, criticize, and put the leadership to the test. It is a critical phase where the team can shatter at worst but hopefully evolve into a more effective constellation of team members. That is why in our latest version of Build for Earth we have targeted **challenges** within the team that lead to frustration and potential conflict in both team and leadership sessions 1 to 2 months into the program.

Working with virtual teams in digital settings

A virtual team can be defined as a geographically dispersed team that relies on technology as its primary tool of communication. In reality, many teams are hybrid, combining in-person and digital communication, in both team meetings and team communication between meetings. Leadership within a digital context has been studied, but there is a lack of knowledge of how transformational leadership and other leadership styles fit within the advancement of new technologies.

The Build for Earth program gathers individuals and teams from all over the world. In the first program, team members from 18 countries across 5 continents participated, and in the ongoing Build for Earth 2024, 19 nationalities across 5 continents are represented in the acceleration program. Creating a program that is dependent on meeting each other in person was never an option from a practical and sustainability perspective. The Build for Earth program was intended to be predominantly digital from the start, working in communication channels such as Zoom, Google Meet, Discord, and WhatsApp, and using other software solutions, such as Google Drive and Gmail, to share material and information. All meetings with the teams during the acceleration program, whether it be teamwork sessions, lectures, workshops, on-demand meetings, or pitch sessions, have been digital.

A digital deliverance leads to certain advantages and challenges that are specific to virtual work environments. As we have stated, getting to know each other on a personal level in a team is an important aspect of psychological safety. This is, of course, possible in a virtual setting, but the lack of face-to-face contact and spontaneous communication can lead to difficulties in establishing trust and high-quality relationships. It demands a more structured way of communicating and planning that ensures all team members are included in the conversations. We have experienced this firsthand, as we met up in Dubai with the team leads in the first cohort of Build for Earth and created personal relationships with them, as they also did with us and other team leads. The second time around, because of time and resource constraints, we were unable to do this, which created a bit more distance between us and the team leads. In the Build for Earth 2024 acceleration program, we decided to make sure we quickly created personal bonds with team leads and team members, starting off the Build for Earth program with online team and leadership sessions with a focus on sharing appropriate personal information and communicating a shared vision together with all teams.

Note

In their study from 2022, Lechner and Mortlock interviewed 16 virtual team members and leaders to find out about their experience of working with psychological safety in virtual teams. In this study, three concrete actions were identified to address the connection as human beings in digital settings:

Demonstrate a genuine interest in your fellow team members

Share appropriate personal information with each other

Create new experiences together

Using virtual teams and digital tools for communication gives the possibility of having teams with members from all parts of the world, but it also means you have to consider time zones, different digital resources, digital literacy, cultural differences, and other potential barriers to success. Our main struggle when working with teams from all over the world has been the lack of infrastructure and stable internet connection in certain parts of the world, as some participants have resided in countries that have low internet access and unstable power sources. The consequence of this is participants not being able to attend virtual sessions, not having enough bandwidth to have their cameras on, abysmal sound quality that makes it difficult or impossible to make out what is being said, connection issues leading to sessions starting later than scheduled, and participants disconnecting and re-connecting during sessions. And technical issues are, of course, not limited to certain parts of the world. Even participants with great bandwidth, new hardware, and updated software in the most developed countries when it comes to digital infrastructure can experience technology failings at times.

With that said, you get used to it. Accepting virtual challenges and discussing the parameters for collaborating this way can be one way of minimizing frustration with technology. We have learned that technological struggles can be frustrating, but they can also be less of a barrier than you think. People are quite tolerant when it comes to small delays in meetings and minor technical difficulties, especially if that is what they experience and expect in their everyday digital world. Virtual meetings can be done without the camera on (no different from a phone call!) and sessions can be recorded for team members to catch up on afterward if disconnected or if technical difficulties hinder participation.

Our recommendations to address technical difficulties in diverse virtual teams are as follows:

- Examine the preconditions, for example, access to hardware and software, digital literacy, and stability in internet connection, and try to solve these issues in advance.

- Lower your expectations and accept digital challenges if you are working in teams with members in settings with unstable digital conditions. If you are accustomed to stable connectivity, remember that your situation may not be the norm for everyone.

- Use solutions that consume less bandwidth and do not require the newest software and devices.

- Continuously make sure that participants feel involved by including them in the conversation and welcoming them when they return from disconnecting.

- If the majority cannot use their camera, have the entire team turn off their cameras.

Being truly inclusive means working through technological challenges and being creative. The digital gap cannot be the excluding factor in creating a diverse team. With that in place and a plan to handle difficulties, we are one step closer to providing online workshops, meetings, and working material in an acceleration program.

Content and themes in Build for Earth

The Build for Earth program was created together with global experts from business areas of innovation, start-up, entrepreneurship, sustainability, and psychology, and some of these experts have also contributed as lecturers during the Build for Earth program. To mention a few here, we interviewed Marie Claire Maxwell, Dr. Rafat Malik, Maya Moukbel, and Annie Lindmark (full list in the *Appendices*). These experts' experiences and learnings from successful innovation endeavors were crucial to the development of the acceleration program. The content was carefully selected to provide an optimal setup for the participating teams with the aim of fast-forwarding the development of the teams and their solutions into actual products and services for sustainability.

To choose what to include and prioritize in the Build for Earth acceleration program, we also turned to science. Data on start-ups and new venture teams is not the most encouraging read, as data show that 92% of all start-ups fail within three years. But as we know, failure is an opportunity for learning, and if the reasons for most failures could be learned and addressed early on during an acceleration program, it could prepare and create resilience in the team at an early stage in their start-up journey.

One way to learn more about start-up failure is to interview and gather data on those who have failed, learning from post-mortem reports. An analysis of 300 failed tech start-ups by Autopsy showed that the most common reason for failure was not having the right team. Interviews with representatives from start-up failures by Failory showed that the most common reasons for failure were lack of product-market fit, marketing problems, team problems, finance problems, tech problems, operational problems, and legal problems. Lack of product-market fit accounted for 34% of failures in their dataset, making it the most common reason for failure. Other research studies, also using post-mortem data, have found that the most common reasons for startup failure are a lack of or the wrong business model, together with a lack of business development, with the latter being closely related to managerial actions. As data from different sources shows somewhat different but overlapping reasons for start-up failure, and that an acceleration needs to have a clear focus, our strategy was to make sure to include the most important themes that could lead to a successful impact.

We have given a short description of the different themes in Build for Earth later in this chapter. As we stated the importance of team and leadership perspectives earlier, as well as that the right business model and product-market fit are crucial, we also want to explain the inclusion of two other themes and considerations regarding the delivery of the acceleration program.

To make sure that innovating teams do not spend time on creating solutions or services that are not wanted by or fit for the market, ToC can be used as a planning and evaluation tool. The ToC model uses backward mapping and begins the acceleration journey by pulling the hand break and pausing for a moment to fully understand the problem at hand and the potential pathway to successful impact. It includes mapping out the long-term goal and intended impact, the context and environment the problem exists within, key assumptions about preconditions and how change will come about, and which stakeholders can influence the dissemination of the service or product. ToC is commonly used for planning and evaluation in sustainability and social change settings and comes in many different forms and shapes. It is a collaborative process that should include the whole team and relevant stakeholders.

Another aspect of start-up life and innovative teams is how to create structures for decision-making within the team, use efficient models for the development of services and products, and utilize conflict to develop as a team. Research shows us that constructive task conflict mediates the relationship with innovative work behavior and that it is moderated by psychological safety within the team. Therefore, we decided to add a theme about how to make better decisions within the team and introduce the team to working methods and concepts such as an agile mindset and using the Sprint method. We also included a specific workshop on human-centered design. The reason for not choosing only one specific method and delving into it was because of the diverse needs of the teams as they have had ideas spawning from digital products, educational services, manufacturing processes, construction materials, and much more.

The workshop content has been delivered differently in the Build for Earth programs so far. The first time it was delivered through scheduled live video lectures and workshops that were recorded and made available for all teams afterward. The second time around it was delivered as digital material made available at the start of the acceleration program (using adapted versions of the recorded sessions in the first program). In Build for Earth 2024, we used live video lectures and workshops again but shared materials and assignments early in the program. Our experience so far is that providing the acceleration program in the form of only digital resources with limited interaction such as online lecturers and workshops had a negative impact on motivation, leading to teams not working with assignments and an uncertainty of what material the team actually had worked with during the acceleration program.

In the following image, you can see the lecturers of the Build for Earth acceleration program in 2024, guiding the eight winning solutions from the Hack for Earth hackathon at COP28 in Dubai.

Figure 10.1 – Lecturers of the Build for Earth 2024 acceleration program

Assignments are provided for each theme, as it is crucial for the teams to not only listen, experience, and learn but also actively work with each aspect of the acceleration program. A parallel can be drawn to **Cognitive Behavioral Therapy (CBT)**, the most researched psychotherapy method, where we know that there is no change without the use of homework and a clear structure of change in behavior. Assignments are worked through by the teams and feedback is provided by the head of the Build for Earth team or the specific lecturer at times.

Extra resources in the form of links to online material and courses, research articles, exercises, and more have been provided for all teams, with the purpose of creating an opportunity for those team members who further want to increase their knowledge and skills in the different themes to do so. Leadership sessions have been provided on demand or in a scheduled fashion and monthly team sessions specifically focusing on psychological safety have been integrated into later versions of the Build for Earth program. Mentorship has also been an integral part of the whole hackathon process, including the Build for Earth program, where participating teams have been provided with a list of **mentors** that they can reach out to, many of them mentors who were also available during the hackathon.

Halfway through the program, the teams participating in Build for Earth at Expo 2020 attended the **Pitch for Earth** event, where they presented their progress during the first three months of the acceleration program. A jury consisting of five high-level experts in specific areas within sustainability and innovation provided feedback and determined a winner of this event. The Pitch for Earth concept can be used as a way for the teams to summarize and reflect on their progress during the acceleration program, and to practice their communication skills at the same time.

Description of themes and content

We have made slight changes to the original themes of the Build for Earth acceleration program at Expo 2020, which are described as follows, but no major changes. They can be used in the specific order they are presented in, starting with *Clarify the concept*, or in an adapted order based on the specific needs of the team. In the Build for Earth 2024 program, we started off with a specific psychological safety session with each team, instead of doing a session on this topic with all teams together.

Clarify the concept – using the theory of change

A starting point for the development of any innovative solution is to reassess whether you as a team have understood the problem you are trying to solve correctly. The most common reason for failing as a start-up is having misunderstood the market and the needs for your product/service. Once that is done, it is also important to set up a road map toward your vision with a long-term goal and checkpoints along the way. Lastly, including stakeholders in this process is crucial for success.

In this workshop, psychologist Kristofer Vernmark presents the ToC model, a widely used method within social change projects, and how to use it within teams.

Assignment: Creating a Theory of Change for your team

Prioritize and plan – make better decisions

Great teams also know how to make great decisions, when to pivot, and how to develop a useful product or service. Having a structured way of working together in a team makes working together smoother and decreases the risk of misunderstandings and role diffusion.

In this workshop, psychologist David Brohede addresses three key aspects of making better decisions as a sustainability start-up – *Think like a scientist*, *Allow task conflict in your team*, and *Prototype with real people*.

Assignment: Exercise on making better decisions in the team

Optimize the team – psychological safety and transformational leadership

Google's Project Aristotle showed that the most important factor for a successful team is the level of psychological safety. This is a concept with a strong research foundation and can be taught to teams to improve their collaboration and learning. Forming a start-up means setting the culture for how individuals work together, which will affect every step along the way. It is crucial to create an environment that accepts, and even encourages, failing and learning from mistakes. This type of group climate also demands transformational leadership, with leaders who are role models and challenge the team in a positive way.

In this workshop, psychologist Kristofer Vernmark presents the concept of psychological safety and how it can be increased and emphasized in a team setting. Concrete behavioral recommendations and exercises are introduced. The concept of transformational leadership within the full-range leadership model is also presented.

Assignment: Start using the After Action Review (AAR)

Business and market

A solution that is to be implemented within a market economy cannot do without a profound understanding of the market and an achievable business model. A good way to plan out a business model is using the business canvas model, which includes important aspects such as value propositions, customers, and system change. As every team has sustainability as a key value, this must be integrated into the business model as well. Also, the teams must learn that their business model will most probably take different forms along the way, adjusting to the market, product development, and new information available.

In this workshop, EVP head of Europe and MEA at Hitachi Energy Johan Söderström shares his experience of working with business models for 30+ years at ABB and Hitachi Energy.

Assignment: Fill out the Sustainability Business Model Canvas

Partnership, social media, and presentation

Learning how to communicate and create relationships in your business is vital for success. Mastering social media channels, having a relevant digital presence, and nailing your elevator pitch are key ingredients to any endeavor in business. How you tell your story to stakeholders, investors, and potential partners is imperative.

No great idea can survive in a vacuum – the importance of partnerships is crucial. Finding the right partner organizations is very important for the future of an innovative solution, and sometimes innovators overlook this important part.

In this four-part workshop series, Secretary General Ann Molin, Erik Nilsson, and Oscar Mörke address the art of partnership and social media strategy, TikTok influencer Rasmus Häggkvist presents different social media options and how to use them depending on the purpose, and Evangelia Daskalakis from TEDx Stockholm introduces how to use storytelling as a tool when creating a powerful pitch.

Assignment: Start creating a partnership and social media plan

Data collection and measuring impact

Sustainability is all about measuring what you do. To achieve impact, it has to be measured, and not just the product or service; the team behind the work has to be a role model for sustainability. Data is crucial for the testing of prototypes and MVPs, no matter whether it is the properties of a specific product or the opinions of potential users. There are models to collect data and to align your start-up with the United Nations SDGs.

In this workshop, co-author of the yearly Sustainable Development Report issued by the United Nations Sustainable Development Solutions Network, Finn Woelm, introduces the work on a global level with the SDGs and how progress is measured with relevant data. Finn explains different alternatives to align as a team with the SDGs and how to measure sustainability impact with a data-driven method.

Assignment: Investigate presented options for measuring sustainability

Financing

Without resources and financing, it would be impossible for a team to realize their solution in the long run. Choosing carefully how to finance the development of a new product or service is an important decision. It is crucial to understand the financing opportunities available and the differences between these options.

Dr. Rafat Malik introduces teams to the basics of financing and how venture capitalists and business angels think and act when investing. The terminology of start-up financing is introduced to the teams.

Assignment: Create a one-pager on financing preferences

Growing as a start-up

A great idea and innovation has to be formalized to continue to grow. This could mean creating a new venture company and defining equity/shares in that company or deciding to become a non-profit organization.

Serial entrepreneur Mikael Ahlström and business expert Marie Claire Maxwell share their experience of entrepreneurial success and failure from three perspectives: how to handle risk, life as an entrepreneur, and what challenges arise when formalizing as a start-up.

Assignment: Three things that would make me leave the team

Voices from participants

We have gathered participants from all over the world, reaching change-makers from five continents, coming from different countries and cultures, having a variety of religious beliefs, and speaking many languages. Diversity in our teams is of the utmost importance, which is why it has been a specific jury criterion when picking the winning teams to participate in Build for Earth. We are proud to say that we have achieved this diversity of gender, age, and cultural background so far, probably making it one of the most diverse acceleration programs to this date.

Build for Earth – Hack for Earth at Expo 2020
• 7 teams • 42% women • 18 nationalities
Build for Earth at COP27
• 7 teams • 51% women • 14 nationalities
Build for Earth 2024
• 8 teams • 55% women • 19 nationalities

Figure 10.2 – Gender, age, and cultural diversity in the three Build for
Earth acceleration programs that have been organized so far

Another interesting aspect of diversity is that our teams have been made up of team members from many different nationalities within the same team. Since we had this diverse set of teams and individuals, it was important to learn early on how participants experienced being part of our acceleration program. As part of the program, the teams in the first cohort were asked to provide feedback at different points in time:

- Preparatory survey for all teams that addressed needs and motivation to participate in the program
- Halfway evaluation survey
- Survey at the end of the acceleration program, evaluating all parts of Build for Earth
- Team lead evaluation of their progress during Build for Earth

Our survey on the first cohort of Build for Earth participants showed the following:

- **100%** would recommend the Build for Earth program to other teams
- **92%** were satisfied or very satisfied with the Build for Earth program as a whole
- **85%** were satisfied or very satisfied with the support provided during the program and also believe that Build for Earth has been adapted to their specific needs

- **All** team leads were satisfied or very satisfied with the usefulness of the specific team lead meetings during Build For Earth
- **5 out of 6** team leads were satisfied or very satisfied with the leadership support that was provided
- **5 out of 6** team leads were satisfied or very satisfied with the help provided to create successful partnerships
- **95%** on average said that the workshops were relevant to their team
- Workshops had an average **4.4 out of 5** rating when participants were asked how interesting the workshops were

We also let participants describe their own experiences of participating in the acceleration program.

> **Quotes from the survey**
>
> "I loved the workshops and the evolution or growth of our solutions throughout the period and the idea of thinking about more aspects you would not have normally considered such as psychology."
>
> "All the sessions were well-planned. Especially, the ones on ideation, finance, growth, and partnerships were cool enough. I enjoyed the emphasis you put on implementing the knowledge and takeaways. And another great thing was the leadership sessions where I could express my vulnerabilities and seek help & concrete advice."
>
> "Every knowledge and lesson shared by the Foundation under the Build for Earth Program has impacted me personally and the team as a whole. It gives us knowledge and the motivation to go further in creating, planning and developing a concrete solution."
>
> "Feeling a bit nostalgic to bid farewell to this! However, I do hope to have Hack for Earth team with us along our journey, the way you have showed care and support in a down-to-Earth directly impactful level. It felt inclusive, accessible, and most importantly, like a family with the other teams as well. I am happy to build relationships that are for a lifetime! I couldn't receive more!"

The positive response from participating team members in this evaluation showed us that we were at least on the right path to achieving what we set out to do.

Development of the program over time has included an increased focus on individuals and teams, including an even greater focus on psychological safety early on and making it an ongoing integrated part of the program from start to end. Another learning is that providing the workshops in a pre-recorded video format made compliance harder, leading to the decision to, with Build for Earth 2024, once again add "live" workshops and increase the interaction with participants during the whole program.

Setting up your own acceleration program

The Build for Earth program took six months to create and is continuously developing. Preparatory work included reading up on scientific findings, searching for real-world data, interviewing experts, setting up the structure and content, and communicating with subject experts to participate in the acceleration program. What to include and exclude in an acceleration program is not an easy choice, as there are many important considerations to make when it comes to succeeding with the task of going from innovation to an actual solution. We know from research and real-life that success is not dependent on a single factor. Along the way, we have added extra material and workshops to adapt to the needs of participating teams, such as how to use human-centered design and understand customer perspectives. We have also made sure to include participants from earlier cohorts, presenting their perspectives on participating in the acceleration program, as well as their progress and struggles so far.

If you are in the process of creating your own acceleration program, feel free to be inspired by the content in the Build for Earth program, remembering that it is only one way of delivering help to innovative teams. It is also a child of its context guided by the aim of citizen-driven innovation, diversity, sustainability, and transformative change. Build for Earth could be considered a pre-start-up acceleration program with many teams in the very early stages, working as a team but not having formed a company together and usually not having external funding; this is something that we have considered when setting up the program. Depending on the setting, the stage of the teams, funding options, and many other factors, the content and provision of an acceleration program will vary.

We have had our share of struggles, that is for sure. Most acceleration programs do. Diversity is great for innovation, but it also means challenges, and we have had cohorts with team members from all over the world, all continents included, living in different time zones, having full-time jobs, being affected by war, and speaking different languages within the team. The cultural diversity has been a challenge but more so an opportunity to learn and take steps toward borderless innovation. Also, it is fascinating how cultural barriers can be overcome by focusing on what are inherently shared human perspectives, as well as ensuring psychological safety in groups. When setting up your acceleration program, remember to aim for and utilize diversity, such as gender, age, nationality, cultural background, experience, and competence, but also plan for how to handle its implications when doing teamwork.

And don't forget the boring stuff. A big part of delivering an acceleration program is a great structure and clear expectations, including defining the roles and tasks in your own organization. We have had teams prepare for the start of the acceleration program by reading the instructions, making material available in advance, and answering online questionnaires about motivation and psychological safety in the group. Even so, motivation can be lacking at times, and it is important to constantly tap into the reasons for not being accountable as a team and team member, as they can vary significantly.

So, have you run into a problem that you cannot seem to fix? Have you realized that your organization has a lot of great ideas that no one seems to build upon? Do you want to see how far you can move an innovative idea toward an actual product or service? The starting point is defining what you want to achieve with your acceleration program. Build for Earth has the vision of anyone being able to make their idea come to life to create a more sustainable planet. It also promotes building teams and relationships while building your solutions. The more people who get involved in innovating and building, the faster we can reach our goals. The transformative purpose would be millions of people not only participating in hackathons but also taking the time and effort to realize their dreams. What is your vision and long-term goal?

We have shared the building blocks, our insights and experience so far, questions we have asked ourselves along the way, and the structure and material used in the Build for Earth program. Feel free to be inspired, use, and share your ideas to create your own acceleration program. And use the necessary expertise to guide you along the way.

If you want to dive deeper into the world of psychological safety, transformational leadership, start-up success and failure, and other things we have mentioned in this chapter, see the *Reference* section for references and further reading.

Summary

In this chapter, you learned how the Build for Earth program was created and first delivered for the participants of the Hack for Earth Expo 2020 hackathon, and how it has developed since. We have tried to be transparent regarding all the choices we made along the way to make it easier for you to reflect on how you would want to set up your own acceleration program.

We have tried our best and made mistakes along the way. Of course, if we knew the magic formula for instant success, we would have used it. But then again, we might not have learned that much along the way without our mistakes. Or, in the words of Professor Edmondson – *fail well, learn fast, repeat.*

The focus on psychological safety and transformational leadership came out of reading up on innovation and start-up failure and the input we received, as we combined it with our background in psychology and the belief in human behavior as a powerful tool for change. We combined this perspective with targeting specific knowledge and behaviors that are needed to move from innovation to impact, such as using ToC, creating a sustainable business model, involving stakeholders, and considering relevant financing options.

We hope reading this chapter has provided you with an interesting and hands-on experience of what it is like to take on the task of moving from innovation to an impactful product or solution.

References

The following are some sources that were used in the development and description of the Build for Earth program described in this chapter.

Scientific publications

Al-Ghazali, B. M. & Afsar, B. (2021). Investigating the mechanism linking task conflict with employees' innovative work behavior. *Int J Confl Manage* 32, 599–625.

Avolio, B. J., Sosik, J. J., Kahai, S. S., & Baker, B. (2014). E-leadership: Re-examining transformations in leadership source and transmission. *The Leadership Quarterly*, 25(1), 105–131.

Camuffo, A., Cordova, A., Gambardella, A., & Spina, C. (2020). A scientific approach to entrepreneurial decision making: Evidence from a randomized control trial. *Management Science, 66*(2), 564–586.

Bass, B. M. (1999). Two Decades of Research and Development in Transformational Leadership. *European Journal of Work and Organizational Psychology*, 8(1), 9–32.

Cantamessa, M., Gatteschi, V., Perboli, G., & Rosano, M. (2018). Startups' roads to failure. *Sustainability*, 10(7), 2346.

Colby, D., Collins, E., & Taplin, D. (2013). *Theory of change technical papers: A series of papers to support the development of theories of change based on practice in the field.* Technical Report. Center for Human Environments, New York. 23 pp.

Edmondson, A. (1999). *Psychological Safety and Learning Behavior in Work Teams. Administrative Science Quarterly,* 44(2), 350–383. https://doi.org/10.2307/2666999.

Edmondson, A. C. & Lei, Z. (2014). Psychological safety: The history, renaissance, and future of an interpersonal construct. *Annual review of organizational psychology and organizational behavior,* 1(1), 23–43.

Klotz, A. C., Hmieleski, K. M., Bradley, B. H., & Busenitz, L. W. (2014). New venture teams: A review of the literature and roadmap for future research. *Journal of management*, 40(1), 226–255.

Lechner, A. & Mortlock, J. T. (2022). How to create psychological safety in virtual teams. *Organ Dyn* 51, 100849.

Newman, A., Donohue, R., & Eva, N. (2017). Psychological safety: A systematic review of the literature. *Human Resource Management Review*, 27(3), 521–535.

Sachs, J., Kroll, C., Lafortune, G., Fuller, G., & Woelm, F. (2021). Sustainable Development Report 2021. Cambridge: Cambridge University Press.

Tannenbaum, S. I. & Cerasoli, C. P. (2013). Do Team and Individual Debriefs Enhance Performance? A Meta-Analysis. *Human Factors,* 55(1), 231–245.

Zineldin, M. (2017). Transformational leadership behavior, emotions, and outcomes: Health psychology perspective in the workplace, *Journal of Workplace Behavioral Health*, 32:1, 14–25.

Books

Avolio, B. J. & Bass, B. M. (Eds.). (2001). *Developing Potential Across a Full Range of Leadership TM: Cases on Transactional and Transformational Leadership* (1st ed.). Psychology Press.

Bass, B. M. & Avolio, B. J. (Eds.). (1994). *Improving organizational effectiveness through transformational leadership.* Thousand Oaks, CA: Sage Publications.

Bass, B. M. & Riggio, R. E. (2006). *Transformational leadership* (2nd ed.). Lawrence Erlbaum Associates Publishers.

Edmondson, A. C. (2013). *Teaming to innovate.* Jossey-Bass.

Edmondson, A. C. (2018*). The fearless organization: Creating psychological safety in the workplace for learning, innovation, and growth.* John Wiley & Sons.

Wheelan, S. (2005). *Group processes a developmental perspective.* 2nd ed. Allyn and Bacon, Boston, MA.

```
https://packt.link/XAMBM
```

Web pages

```
https://www.nytimes.com/2016/02/28/magazine/what-google-learned-
from-its-quest-to-build-the-perfect-team.html
```

```
https://www.failory.com/blog/startup-failure-rate
```

```
https://www.getautopsy.com/research/top-startup-failure-reasons
```

11

Build for Earth Learnings – How to Make a Startup a Success Fast

In this chapter, we will summarize the takeaways from **Build for Earth** winners. We will distill a handful of key ingredients that are imperative for the success of **hackathon** winners for solutions that come from hackathons and make the journey into a thriving start-up. We will share the start-up journeys of three winners from our hackathons and solutions that are now on the market: RecyBlock, Coronafree, and BrightAct.

In this chapter, we will cover the following main topics:

- General takeaways of successful hackathon winners
- Recy-Block, winner of Hack for Earth at Expo 2020 – example 1
- BrightAct, the winner of Hack the Crisis Sweden and EUvsVirus in 2020 – example 2
- Coronafree, the winner of Hack the Crisis Sweden in 2020 – example 3
- Key factors for the success of hackathon winners

The general takeaways shared in this chapter from hackathon winners include insights from notable solutions such as Recy-Block from Hack for Earth in Expo 2020 BrightAct from Hack the Crisis Sweden and **EUvsVirus** in 2020, and Coronafree, also from Hack the Crisis Sweden in 2020. These examples of winners, who we have supported after they won their respective hackathons, illuminate the path to success, highlighting key factors that contribute to the prosperity of start-ups. Through the course of this chapter, you will gain an understanding of what makes a winning solution successful and how you can foster an environment that nurtures these victorious initiatives.

General takeaways from successful hackathon winners

Making great ideas come to life is no easy task. That is why not all people do it.

On our way from working with **Hack for Sweden**, via Hack the Crisis, EuvsVirus, and Hack for Earth, we have learned a lot of hard lessons together with our winning solutions and made these learnings part of our strengths. In this chapter, we will summarize these takeaways with you so that you can cut to the chase, so to speak, and get right to what works instantly without having to make all the hard lessons we did. This will hopefully save you both time and money on your journey to making your hackathon winners a reality.

We will also share three real-world examples of hackathon winners who are now registered companies and have their tools on the market. Finally, we will share the key factors of hackathon winners' success, summarized and distilled from our work with hackathon winners from 2018 until 2024.

The crux of making a solution from a hackathon come to life lies in several factors that are unique to solutions from hackathons. The power of a hackathon is that it creates solutions to difficult **challenges** in a very short time by bringing people with different backgrounds and competencies together. The challenge is that after the hackathon, the team is often at the beginning of its team-building journey if they met at the hackathon, which means that they are not working optimally as a team yet. Trust and effectiveness in a team take time to build, and this is especially true for virtual teams. The solution was also created really quickly, and it often needs quite a lot of work before it is ready to launch.

So, the question is: how do you handle these two challenges in the best possible way, supporting the team and its solution in a way that encourages them and facilitates the realization of the solution quickly?

In this chapter, we will give you three examples of hackathon winners we have supported in different ways over the years. You will learn what was important to make them come to life as hackathon winners, and at the end, we will also list a few of the key things we have learned that are important for start-up success for hackathon winners.

Example 1 – Recy-Block, winner of Hack for Earth at Expo 2020 in Dubai, 2021

Recy-Block is the winner of Hack for Earth at Expo 2020 in Dubai, in the Sustainable Society **challenge category,** and Recy-Block was the winner from 1,800 teams from 121 countries. The team leader and founder of Recy-Block is Saif Edine Laalej, based in Morocco. Recy-Block is an innovative solution that combines the principles of sustainable development with cutting-edge technology to address pressing challenges in Africa. The solution aims to revolutionize the construction industry by introducing sustainable and affordable building materials, paving the way for a more environmentally conscious and inclusive future.

Recy-Block is today the main product of the Zelij Invent brand. Its mission is to support the eco-responsible transition of economic actors, especially in recycling and upcycling linked to the construction sector, through the activities of awareness, eco-planning, and recovery of non-organic waste.

Zelij Invent is committed to advocating for and implementing practices that align with responsible consumption and production, emphasizing the importance of sustainability in both our lifestyles and economic activities. The organization places a strong emphasis on the development of sustainable cities and communities, recognizing the critical role urban environments play in shaping the future of our planet. By focusing on creating environmentally friendly, socially inclusive, and economically viable spaces, Zelij Invent aims to contribute to the resilience and sustainability of urban areas. Additionally, Zelij Invent is dedicated to addressing the pressing challenges of climate change. Through innovative solutions and strategic initiatives, the organization seeks to mitigate the impacts of climate change and support global efforts towards environmental sustainability. This holistic approach underscores Zelij Invent's commitment to fostering a more sustainable and equitable world.

Rethinking construction practices

Recognizing the urgent need for sustainable alternatives in the construction sector, the founders of Recy-Block embarked on a mission to transform traditional practices. Research tells us that conventional building materials often contribute to deforestation, produce excessive carbon emissions, and lack affordability in Africa and worldwide.

The team behind Recy-Block crafted a cold production process, addressing multiple facets of climate. The solution seamlessly intertwines environmental, economic, and societal benefits. By recycling plastic waste into construction materials, the Recy-Block solution mitigates the environmental toll of waste accumulation while directly impacting vulnerable ragpickers, providing them with dignified employment and vitalizing their communities. Furthermore, the innovation of Recy-Block drastically reduces sand consumption in construction, a pivotal adaptation measure.

This curbing of sand use not only preserves fragile ecosystems but also diminishes pressures on coastal areas, battling erosion, a dire climate-induced threat. The Recy-Block solution champions green construction, which, in turn, reduces carbon-intensive concrete demand. This approach exemplifies holistic climate action by minimizing greenhouse gas emissions. It is a testament to Recy-Block's comprehensive understanding of climate change's interconnected challenges.

Introducing Recy-Block

Recy-Block is a versatile and eco-friendly building material.

The team behind Recy-Blocks started in Morocco, where they have been implementing an initiative aimed at actualizing the construction industry from being the most polluting and exhaustive sector to being an ethically sustainable sector using plastic waste upcycling solutions. The team behind Recy-Blocks has developed a new formula based on 50% plastic waste and a whole new cost-effective production process. The first product is a hollow recycled block that can be used in all the same ways as hollow concrete blocks but has better characteristics. The Recy-Block hollow block is eco-friendly and five times harder and more durable than hollow concrete blocks with a 550 PSI compressive strength. These materials took the construction sector to the next level. Using the Recy-Block bricks, the contractors use 38% less cement and accelerate the building process by up to 40%.

Zelij Invent is committed to advocating for and implementing practices that align with responsible consumption and production, emphasizing the importance of sustainability in both our lifestyles and economic activities. The organization places a strong emphasis on the development of sustainable cities and communities, recognizing the critical role urban environments play in shaping the future of our planet. By focusing on creating environmentally friendly, socially inclusive, and economically viable spaces, Zelij Invent aims to contribute to the resilience and sustainability of urban areas. Additionally, Zelij Invent is dedicated to addressing the pressing challenges of climate change. Through innovative solutions and strategic initiatives, the organization seeks to mitigate the impacts of climate change and support global efforts towards environmental sustainability. This holistic approach underscores Zelij Invent's commitment to fostering a more sustainable and equitable world.

In conclusion, Zelij Invent's multifaceted approach to sustainable development and climate change resilience reflects a profound commitment to not just the present but the future of our planet. Through their relentless pursuit of innovative practices, sustainable urban development, and climate action, they not only champion environmental stewardship but also pave the way for a more sustainable, inclusive, and thriving global community. Zelij Invent's efforts underscore the imperative of collective action and the power of dedicated organizations to effect meaningful change, setting a laudable example for others to follow in the quest for a sustainable future.

Collaboration

Recy-Block recognizes that addressing complex challenges requires collaboration. To amplify the impact of the solution, they actively engage with various stakeholders, including local communities, governments, architects, and construction companies. By fostering partnerships, Recy-Block promotes knowledge sharing, gathers diverse perspectives, and ensures the successful integration of Recy-Block into existing construction practices.

Enhancing local capacity

Empowering local communities is at the heart of the Recy-Block initiative. They prioritize training and skill development programs to equip individuals with the knowledge and expertise to produce, handle, and install our products. By enhancing local capacity, Recy-Block creates employment opportunities and stimulates economic growth while fostering a sense of ownership and sustainability within communities.

Demonstrating affordability and accessibility

Affordability is a crucial factor in ensuring widespread adoption of sustainable building materials. Through efficient production processes and strategic partnerships, the Recy-Block team has achieved a cost-effective solution that is accessible to a wide range of construction projects, including affordable housing, schools, and community infrastructure. The Recy-Block product's affordability enhances inclusivity and ensures that sustainable construction practices are accessible to all.

Showcasing the environmental impact

Zelij Invent takes pride in its commitment to environmental stewardship. By using recycled materials as the primary source for our Recy-Blocks, we significantly reduce the demand for virgin resources and divert waste from landfills. Using our solution, we can rid our environment of over 4.5 Kg of plastic waste per block, spare 8.2 kg per block of CO_2 emissions, and offer an affordable construction product that has the following properties:

- Self-locking blocks (Lego format) on all four sides that are easy to install
- 30*15 cm construction blocks of Class CII according to the classification of the international standard

Having successfully demonstrated the viability and benefits of the solution, the focus is on scaling the adoption of the Recy-Block solution across Africa. Through strategic partnerships, Zelij Invent aims to establish production facilities in key regions, ensuring a steady supply of materials and promoting local economic growth. By expanding their reach, they aim to catalyze a paradigm shift towards sustainable construction practices throughout the African continent and beyond.

Next milestone

Although this process has several advantages on the market, the team behind Recy-Block has identified various factors that hinder its duplication and development, for instance, the heavy investment in industrialization and especially the supply of plastic waste between the communities of ragpickers.

This is why the team behind Recy-Block has started to relocate their solution through Block units, 28 m2, which allows them to upcycle plastic waste at the source. Each Block is a delocalized recovery unit that allows the team to treat and transform plastic into construction products, either bricks, paving stones, or tiles, according to the needs of the local community. Each Block will recover at least 15 tons of waste per month and thus create three direct job opportunities and more than 250 indirect beneficiaries. The cost of installing a Block unit varies between 17,000 and 35,000 Euros.

By the end of 2024, the goal is to implement four Blocks that will serve as pilot tests for the launch of mass duplication to achieve the goal of 3 million tons of plastic waste recovery in 2025.

This first example of a winner of a Hack for Earth global hackathon, created during an online hackathon in 2021, shows that citizen-driven innovation with hackathons can produce real solutions that go to market in a relatively short amount of time. After entering the Build for Earth **acceleration program** in January 2022, Recy-Block was on the market in Morocco within 6 months. The publicity they gained for winning Hack for Earth opened even more doors for Recy-Block, and they got major investments early on. What set them apart was a strong but small and well-functioning team, a solution that was easily communicated with its tangible nature. Recy-Block also knew how to build their network with **storytelling** as they were building their brand.

In *Figure 11.1*, you can see the first prototype of the Recy-Block solution, introduced by team leader and founder Saif Edine Laalej at the Award Ceremony of Hack for Earth at Expo 2020 in Dubai, on December 15, 2021.

Figure 11.1 – First prototype of the Recy-Block solution

The innovative blocks boast a durability that surpasses cement by five times, with a lifespan extending beyond 100 years.

Designed similarly to Lego pieces, these plastic blocks easily interlock, significantly reducing the need for cement and further diminishing the overall carbon footprint. The material is ready for construction as soon as it cools down.

Constructing a house with these bricks leads to a 30% reduction in energy consumption compared to traditional homes of equivalent size. The bricks stand out for their robustness, virtually eliminating the breakage issue seen in approximately 10% of cement products during transit. In contrast, less than 1% of Recy-Block's bricks suffer any damage during transportation. For more information on Recy-Block, see the Zelij Invent website: `https://zelijinvent.com/`.

Example 2 – BrightAct, winner of Hack the Crisis Sweden in 2020

BrightAct was one of the winners of the hackathon Hack the Crisis Sweden in 2020, where 7,500 participants competed in teams from 91 countries.

BrightAct connects domestic violence help-seekers with support to shorten the road to support and reclaims autonomy for victims and their children. The background to the story of BrightAct started back in early 2020 when the COVID-19 pandemic hit the world. The soon-to-be founder of BrightAct, Sofie Wahlström, was working with digitalization for the public sector in Sweden and was hired to automate the process of subsistence allowance for a municipality. She realized the people looking for support from the municipality did not know where to turn or find help. She started sketching the idea that later became BrightAct.

At Hack the Crisis Sweden in April 2020, the idea later known as BrightAct was launched. This is where the founder Sofie Wahlström found her first teammates who would continue the development of the platform with her. The team at the start consisted of Elinor Samuelsson, Hassan Nazar, and Philip Andersson.

Having found a winning concept, at every subsequent hackathon BrightAct joined, they found more teammates who wanted to work with them to make sure that they together could create a safer world for domestic violence victims.

Now BrightAct had the designer, the public sector specialist, the full stack specialist, a winning concept, and the team to realize the idea.

BrightAct soon came to realize that they were on a winning streak; they won every hackathon they entered. They soon entered the pan-European hackathon EUvsVirus, where BrightAct won out of 22,000 participants, which resulted in quality support from the EU Innovation Council and their team of experts, and they were contacted by people and organizations from around the world who wanted to work with them. BrightAct won prizes and awards and was invited to talk at conferences and events globally.

BrightAct had found its secret sauce, which made building a support platform easier and a very positive experience. They were invited by Hack for Earth Foundation to join the Award Ceremony of Hack for Earth at the world exhibition Expo 2020 in Dubai to introduce the BrightAct solution in the United Nations' pavilion and to coach the winners of Hack for Earth at Expo 2020 on how to scale their new solution and make it as successful as BrightAct.

BrightAct company was founded by Sofie Wahlström to make sure the product could flourish and to secure a solid business model that could scale globally.

The why

The question of necessity frequently arises within the start-up community, and the imperative for BrightAct's existence is unquestionably clear. Globally, one in three women falls victim to domestic violence, a statistic that is alarmingly paralleled by the fact that one in six men is also affected. Initial findings from an extensive EU-wide survey conducted by the European **Agency for Fundamental Rights (FRA)** on 42,000 women, published in 2014, revealed several critical insights: notably, four out of five women did not seek help from services such as healthcare, social services, or victim support following severe incidents of violence by non-partners. Those who did seek help predominantly turned to medical services. Additionally, two out of five women were unaware of any laws or political initiatives designed to protect them in instances of domestic violence, with half being oblivious to any preventative measures. Furthermore, over three-quarters believe violence against women is a common issue in their country, and approximately half have avoided certain public or private spaces due to fear of physical or sexual assault.

The team behind BrightAct's investigation into the global issue of domestic violence, driven by human need, revealed the enormity of the problem, far exceeding initial assumptions. Starting the research in Sweden—a country known for its robust social support and structures, and considered a leader in social work—the team behind BrightAct recognized the need for improvement even there. Through comprehensive research, including interviews with victims and representatives from the public sector and NGOs, the team behind BrightAct gained profound insights into the pervasive nature of domestic violence, underscoring the critical need for solutions such as BrightAct.

What's happening?

BrightAct is developing its service in eight countries and is adjusting its services to make sure that the platform is considering all needs.

BrightAct has received many awards for its work in Sweden, such as IT-woman of the Year, Digital Inspirations of the Year, Young Idea of the Year, and Founder of the Year.

This has created a lot of publicity and, consequently, BrightAct is well known to a wide range of people in the industry globally. This has helped them to find collaborations and support for their solution.

The capital they have received is from winning multiple hackathons and receiving awards and grants. BrightAct has also received funding from the Swedish innovation agency, Vinnova, with the purpose of building and scaling its solution.

Now what?

In 2024, BrightAct is building a chat to make sure that support always is available and safe to receive. BrightAct is scaling in Sweden, and soon BrightAct will go into the European market.

The plan is to release the chat during the autumn of 2024 and to scale organically with the chat to go where BrightAct is needed.

The story of BrightAct from a winning solution in Hack the Crisis Sweden to a multiple award-winning solution on the market is yet another proof that real tools for the good of society can be born out of hackathons. Even though BrightAct did not have the well-rounded support of the Build for Earth acceleration program, they managed to develop their solution and take it to market within only a few months. BrightAct got support from us in the Hack the Crisis project management team after the hackathon in the form of introductions to potential partner organizations and stakeholders, and we also supported them by inviting them to pitch their solution on stage during the Award Ceremony of Hack for Earth at Expo 2020 in Dubai. What sets BrightAct apart is a combination of a great novel solution that also has an acute **sense of urgency**, making it obvious to all that this solution needs to come to the market soon, and it also has team members with large amounts of grit and resilience.

Here is a diagram that describes the functionality of the BrightAct solution, showing the basic traits of BrightAct as it is seen by a potential user:

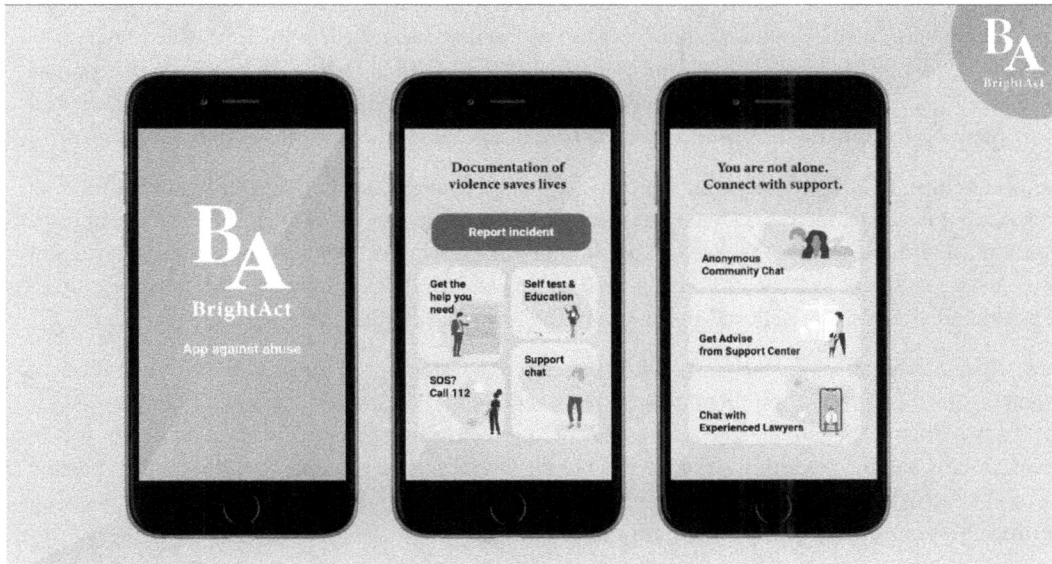

Figure 11.2 – Functionality of the BrightAct solution

For more information on BrightAct see their website: `https://www.brightact.nu/`

Example 3 – Coronafree, winner of Hack the Crisis Sweden in 2020

Another winner of the Hack the Crisis Sweden hackathon that came to market soon after the hackathon ended is Coronafree. This innovative solution won the competition of 7,500 participants from 91 countries. The team leaders behind the Coronafree solution are Jonathan Söderström, CEO and Co-founder of Giddir AB, and Ulf Löfström, Founder and COO of Giddir AB. In the early tumultuous days of COVID-19, as the world grappled with an unprecedented health crisis, an idea took root at Giddir AB, as a new start-up with a small innovative team in the HealthTech space. Recognizing the imperative need to rekindle air travel safely, the team at Giddir AB foresaw the potential of a digital health certificate based on PCR or antigen quick tests that could be digitally authenticated. This idea became an opportunity that guided them toward creating an MVP for their platform, already in the developmental phase, to address this urgent global problem. Their participation and subsequent victory at the Hack The Crisis Sweden hackathon in April 2020 was not just a win but a further validation of the solution, catapulting them into the development phase of what would soon be known as Coronafree.

Building Coronafree was an endeavor that transcended mere coding and software development; it was about crafting a solution that streamlined the cumbersome process for care providers in conducting mass testing and issuing health certificates. The solution wasn't just a digital repository for patients to access their health certificates but a comprehensive test management system that integrated seamlessly with labs, streamlining the way mass sampling for PCR and quick tests were handled. This period of intense development was characterized by forging strong alliances with labs, care providers, and government bodies, laying the groundwork for the successful market introduction of Coronafree.

Upon launching in 2020, Coronafree quickly captivated the market, drawing in customer interest and fostering new partnerships. During its lifespan, Coronafree processed over 250,000 patient tests, extending its services beyond the Swedish borders and making international strides. This achievement wasn't just a testament to the technology and flexible platform but to the trust and collaboration of the healthcare market that believed in the vision the team behind Coronafree had.

Today, Coronafree stands for the teams who created it as a testament to innovation born out of crisis. Leveraging the success and insights gained, the team at Giddir AB has evolved its solution into a modern SaaS/PaaS platform that streamlines the collection and communication of health data between care providers, labs, radiology clinics, and patients. Giddir works and serves leading industry players such as Unilabs, Synlab, Evidia, Abbott, and Funmed in the Swedish and European markets, processing hundreds of thousands of patient tests and exams annually.

As Giddir AB continues to grow and innovate, Coronafree remains a cornerstone of the journey, a symbol of turning adversity into opportunity, and a reminder that every successful journey starts with a group of individuals with an idea.

Coronafree is an example of a solution born in an online hackathon, with an acute sense of urgency. It is also easy to understand, and at the time of its creation, it was obvious to all of society that it needed to come to market immediately. The market fit was perfect. The team behind the Coronoafree solution was strong, and they had good problem-solving strategies and a strong drive to solve challenges and move forward. Coronafree did not have the support of the Build for Earth acceleration program, since this solution was created in Hack the Crisis Sweden. However, the Hack the Crisis project management team gave support in terms of connections to potential stakeholders, government entities, and partner organizations.

The following image shows the Coronafree app, as it looked in the year 2020. The headline **Friskhetsintyg** is in Swedish and means Certificate of Health. This app came to market soon after the hackathon, showing that society and citizens can work together to solve big societal challenges under extreme circumstances like the COVID-19 pandemic.

Figure 11.3 – The Coronafree app

The Coronafree app was a certificate of health created by Ulf Löfström, Jonathan Söderström, and Stefan Loorits during the Swedish Government's official hackathon to fight the effects of the Covid-19 pandemic, Hack the Crisis Sweden, in April 2020.

The three examples we've provided from hackathon winners, which are all on the market today and providing value for people and the planet, are proof that it is possible to create citizen-driven innovation and benefits for our future with hackathons as a tool. As these three examples from our hackathon winners also showcase in their stories, their journey from a winning solution to a working tool on the market has not been without struggles, challenges, and setbacks.

The stories of these winners, who have journeyed from conceptual victories to practical, marketable tools, encapsulate more than just success; they embody the resilience and determination required to navigate the arduous path laden with obstacles, adversity, and unforeseen hurdles. Despite these difficulties, these visionaries have managed to persevere and flourish. This resilience can be attributed to several critical key factors that have been instrumental in their journey – a combination of resources, support systems, and strategic insights that have equipped them to confront and conquer their challenges.

In the next section, we delve deeper into these pivotal elements. We aim to dissect and understand the cornerstone components that contribute to start-up triumphs, drawing from the experiences that have been critical in aiding our teams' ascendance. By listing the key factors for start-up success, we aspire to uncover the underlying principles that can serve as a beacon for future innovators on their own paths to making a difference.

Key factors for the success of hackathon winners

Throughout our journey of working with hackathon winners, it has become abundantly clear that certain factors significantly amplify their chances of transforming a winning concept into a thriving start-up. The process of evolving from an award-winning idea at a hackathon to establishing a successful enterprise is intricate and fraught with potential pitfalls. It demands a keen comprehension of pivotal elements that can either catalyze success or precipitate failure. In the following detailed exploration, we draw upon our wealth of experiences, including the accounts of the four illustrative examples previously mentioned, to delve into these crucial components that have repeatedly proven to be instrumental in the success of these emerging businesses.

Grit, resilience, and relevant competence

Success post-hackathon is far from guaranteed, even for the most ingenious ideas. It demands a mix of unwavering commitment and a strong ability to adapt. The leap from concept to execution is vast; we find the winners often need much more guidance and hands-on support than we first anticipated when we started supporting teams after our hackathons. Grit and resilience to challenges and setbacks, a mindset of not giving up, and seeing things through in the face of adversity, are key personality traits for hackathon winners who are making their solutions come to life. In our experience, we see that the solutions that are on the market today have team members with a great deal of these personality traits: grit and resilience.

It's also not a given that you are great at making an idea come to life into a real tool, just because you were great at creating it during the hackathon.

Theoretical and practical are two different things, and the skills needed to create a business are something else entirely other than participating in a hackathon. This is good to keep in mind when creating the team that shall take the solution to market:

- What competence does the solution need to be realized?
- At what time in the realization process is which competence needed?

These questions are most relevant to ask yourself as a winning team leader of a hackathon, and this is one of the first tasks in the Build for Earth acceleration program, mapping out what competence this solution needs and what competencies are already in the team. How much time do the team members who are to work with the realization of the solution have to dedicate to working with the solution? Is this enough time or does the solution need more to come to market in a reasonable timeline?

These are important tasks for our winning teams when they enter the Build for Earth acceleration program.

Sense of urgency

Articulating why your solution matters at this very moment in time is paramount. Winners must not only possess a compelling solution but also be able to communicate its importance. It's essential to frame your innovation within the context of current market needs and societal challenges. Being able to concisely express the pressing need for your solution is vital for grabbing attention and making a strong case for the immediate adoption and support of your start-up.

Important questions to ask yourself as a start-up are as follows:

- Why is your solution so important?
- Why is it important in the grander scheme of things that your solution becomes a real tool for people and/or the planet to use?
- What will happen if your solution does NOT come to the market/become a reality?

If you can master how to communicate these three topics you have already the first step ready for a great one- or two-sentence pitch too. In our experience, these are the key questions all team members must know how to answer when interacting with potential partner organizations, investors, and customers.

Storytelling and communication

Storytelling is the very fabric of human connection and the foundation of humanity. A compelling story to tell about your start-up's origin, the synergy within your team, and the obstacles you've faced is invaluable for interacting successfully with customers, partner organizations, and employees. It humanizes your brand and allows others to see the heart and soul behind the logo. Be sure to not shy away from disclosing the challenges you've faced; it's often through adversity that the most compelling stories are born.

And another important fact to keep in mind: *People may not remember what you said, but they will remember how you made them feel*—and this is the key to really successful storytelling.

The art of communication extends beyond the transmission of information; it's about connection and impression. How you interact through storytelling with potential investors, partners, and customers can leave a lasting impact that lays the foundation for investments and growth. The aim is to be memorable for the right reasons – ensuring that every communication reflects the passion, professionalism, and potential of your start-up.

In our experience, we have noticed that teams who have effective storytelling established early on about how they formed their idea and how they met, and who share this in social media and other environments such as conferences, have a better chance at forming valuable relationships with partner organizations and investors.

Pitch technique

Crafting an impactful **pitch** is essential in the business arena. It's the compact narrative of your start-up's mission and vision. It should be concise enough to be conveyed in one or a maximum of two sentences. This brevity is critical in a business environment, where attention spans are short and opportunities pass swiftly. A stellar pitch can be the deciding factor in catching an investor's interest versus a moment of potential slipping away. Besides the one- or two-sentence pitch, you need a longer one too, of course, for when you have one-on-one meetings with investors. The one- or two-sentence pitch is essentially you giving the person a reason to continue talking to you.

In many instances, the opportunity to make a memorable first impression is fleeting. A less-than-impressive initial encounter can set a tone that's challenging to recalibrate; business seldom grants second chances. First impressions hold considerable weight, and if they're squandered, attempting to revisit the opportunity later—even with a more polished presentation—may be futile. The moment is gone, and with it, the initial perception solidifies, often irrevocably.

As you prepare for a pitch meeting with potential investors, bear in mind the significance of this initial interaction. While you and your team are not expected to have an exhaustive answer for every question, it is imperative to clearly articulate the core concept of your solution and underscore the pressing need for its entry into the market. It is this clarity and sense of urgency that can ignite the interest of potential backers and set the stage for a successful partnership.

Pitch technique is a skill we let all teams practice extensively at Build for Earth, in seminars and workshops with individual assessments. The pivotal event is the Pitch for Earth event, where the teams pitch their solutions live to a selected audience of investors, partner organizations, and venture capitalists.

A great team

Chapter 10 delves deeply into the critical elements essential for the success of a start-up, pinpointing the cultivation of a robust team culture as a fundamental cornerstone. This culture is underpinned by **psychological safety**, a concept that allows team members to contribute and innovate without fear of censure or reprisal. It is this secure foundation that enables teams to navigate through the volatile phases of start-up development with confidence and resilience.

In parallel, the significance of assembling a team composed of individuals with the requisite competencies cannot be overstated. The richness of skills within a team acts as the propulsion system for a start-up's journey from inception to market presence. It is this blend of talent and expertise that potential investors scrutinize meticulously. They are not just investing in an idea but in the people behind it, assessing whether the team possesses the diverse capabilities needed to surmount the multifaceted challenges of bringing a product to market.

Beyond the essential mix of team culture and skill sets, leadership stands as the keystone in this arch of success. Great leadership is more than direction and decision-making; it's about inspiring a shared vision, cultivating a collaborative environment, and guiding the team through the inevitable maelstrom of start-up growth with a steady hand. It involves recognizing and nurturing each team member's strengths, fostering a united front where each individual feels valued and integral to the team's collective mission.

Each of these facets—psychological safety, skill **diversity**, and strong leadership—does not operate in isolation. Instead, they weave together to form a resilient framework that supports and elevates a start-up. As elucidated in *Chapter 10*, start-ups that carefully nurture these aspects are often the ones that thrive, transforming promising ideas into tangible, market-ready solutions that resonate with investors and consumers alike. This chapter not only outlines these principles but provides an in-depth exploration of how they manifest in the real-world success stories of our hackathon winners, setting a blueprint for aspiring entrepreneurs to follow.

Team building and leadership are key elements in the Build for Earth acceleration program, and are of course practiced already before the hackathon when the participants start forming their competing teams. In our experience, we notice that the teams who have managed to create a good team structure, with a high level of psychological safety and a culture where team members feel safe to express their opinions and their ideas are more successful than other teams.

Networking

Whatever your business revolves around, there will be people in that business. And you will need to have great relationships with the people in your business to thrive.

The profound value of networking in the entrepreneurial journey cannot be overstressed; it is often the network one cultivates that emerges as a pivotal asset in the voyage from start-up inception to market success. In the bustling tapestry of modern business, engaging with your network must be both active and sincere, extending across the digital realm and into the physical spaces where ideas converge and flourish.

To effectively harness the power of your network, every new encounter should be approached with a spirit of genuine curiosity. This is absolutely key. Whether online or in person, seek to understand each individual's work and their unique perspectives. This understanding equips you with the insight to position your solution in a resonant manner, aligning with their values and interests, thereby enhancing its appeal.

Remember, each conversation holds the potential to unlock doors to uncharted opportunities. This could manifest in diverse forms, from a mentorship that guides your strategic decisions to a partnership that elevates your business offering. The art of networking thrives not only through platforms such as LinkedIn but also within the vibrant hubs of conferences, workshops, and industry summits. These gatherings are fertile grounds for initiating and nurturing relationships that could be instrumental in catapulting your venture to new heights.

Networking, when executed with strategic finesse and authentic engagement, has the potential to create a much-needed supportive ecosystem around your start-up. It is through these interconnections that entrepreneurs gain access to critical resources, advice, and the collaborative potential necessary to navigate the competitive landscape of business. Building a broad, dynamic network is thus an indispensable strategy for any visionary seeking to leave an indelible mark in the world of innovation.

This is something we encourage our hackathon contestants to consider from the very start of the hackathon journey. We encourage the participants to connect with people actively in the hackathon and build their network strategically from there. We tell them to add other participants, **mentors**, and representatives of relevant partner organizations in the hackathon platforms (such as Discord) and through LinkedIn or other social media channels. We also encourage them to have their profile updated with relevant and accurate information, so people get an updated version of their competence and work. The teams that have been actively connecting with relevant actors in the hackathon community from the start are more successful in creating partnerships and getting investments than other teams, which goes to show that networking is an important factor in start-up success.

Branding

Crafting a potent **brand identity** should be a foundational step at the very inception of your startup journey. The elements that make up your brand — your logo, company name, and the overarching aesthetic — are far from superficial embellishments. They embody the core values, mission, and spirit of your company, serving as a visual manifesto of what you stand for.

A compelling brand identity acts as your business's signature, setting the tone for all interactions and communications with your audience. It's through this visual vocabulary that stakeholders, from clients to investors, come to recognize and differentiate your company in a crowded marketplace.

Invest in creating a cohesive and well-thought-out brand aesthetic that resonates across all materials. This includes business cards that leave a lasting impression, a professionally designed website that serves as your digital storefront, coherent email accounts that assure recipients of your team's professionalism, and social media profiles that consistently echo your brand's voice. Each of these elements plays a critical role in building a narrative around your business that speaks of reliability, quality, and professionalism.

In a world where first impressions are pivotal, your brand's visual and communicative consistency can be the deciding factor for potential clients or partners. It's a signal that your company pays attention to detail and values the perception it projects. Such coherence in branding not only fosters recognition but also engenders trust, paving the way for your start-up to establish itself as a formidable presence in the industry.

The teams who have a compelling brand identity from the start in Build for Earth have an easier job of getting their message across to make potential partner organizations and investors interested in meeting with them, so this is another aspect we put effort into in our acceleration program.

Embracing incompleteness

In the dynamic world of start-ups, it is common for early ventures to be in a constant state of evolution. Waiting for the perfect product to be ready before going public can be a major misstep. Embracing transparency about your developmental stage can open important doors to valuable feedback, bolster support, and might even spark new collaborations. When faced with questions that challenge your current knowledge, honesty is your best policy. Show your fierce determination to resolve uncertainties. The start-up ecosystem thrives on mutual support and collaboration, brimming with experienced professionals and organizations eager to contribute their knowledge to promising newcomers.

Hence, it's vital to recognize that you aren't expected to have all the solutions at your fingertips. Fear of not having all the answers should not prevent you from showcasing your project, even in its preliminary stages. Concealing your idea until you feel it's flawless may prevent you from accessing the resources that could propel your progress ahead.

If a question arises that stumps you, it's perfectly acceptable to acknowledge that you're actively seeking answers. Furthermore, use this as an opportunity to engage: inquire if the person you're speaking with might have the insight to tackle the issue, or perhaps they can connect you with someone who does. Often, the key to overcoming challenges lies in casting a wide net within your network to find the necessary expertise.

Remember, the community is particularly receptive to supporting innovative start-ups, especially those emerging as victors from hackathons – everyone is constantly looking for the next innovative solution that will become the future unicorn they are looking for. These companies and investors are often on the lookout to assist ventures that show exceptional promise and a forward-thinking mindset.

We actively encourage our winning teams to trust the innovative idea behind their solution, even though they may not have all the answers yet. After we equip them with the one- or two-sentence pitch, it's crucial that the teams dare go out to network and meet with their audience and community and engage actively with them. In our experience this is essential to start-up success, the answers to the issues they may be experiencing are often to be found in the network.

Key takeaways

These insights, borne out of our extensive experience with hackathon winners, are not exhaustive but serve as a guide to those embarking on the journey of transforming a hackathon solution into a thriving startup. Each start-up's journey will be unique, but these elements are the common denominators in the stories that we have had the opportunity to follow in our work with making great ideas come to life – the three mentioned here and the rest of the solutions that have emerged as winners from our hackathons from 2018-2024.

Embarking on the transformative path from a hackathon victor to a thriving start-up is a journey rife with learning curves and insights. While the experiences shared here, drawn from our extensive history of working alongside hackathon winners, are not all-encompassing, they provide a blueprint for aspirants on a similar quest. The trajectory of each start-up is inherently distinct, marked by its unique challenges and milestones. Yet, amidst this diversity, certain elements remain consistently influential – the strategies, philosophies, and pieces of wisdom that have become apparent to us through our committed efforts in nurturing groundbreaking ideas into fruition.

These guideposts illuminate a path trodden by those who have dared to dream and then relentlessly pursued those dreams into the market. They shed light on the indispensable value of teamwork, the art of perfecting a pitch, the strength found in community and networking, and the boldness required to showcase an idea before it reaches perfection. The landscape of start-up success is complex and multifaceted, and these observations serve as navigational aids for navigating its terrain. For those poised to embark on this expedition, these insights are the beacons that can guide your way through the exhilarating – and often tumultuous – waters of bringing a hackathon solution to life as a sustainable, market-worthy enterprise.

Summary

This chapter offers an in-depth exploration of the complex, often arduous paths that three hackathon-winning teams have traveled to bring their innovative solutions to the marketplace. By delving into these real-world examples, we've extracted crucial lessons and chronicled the sometimes-daunting odysseys these trailblazers endured to breathe life into their creations. These narratives are not just stories of success but are also profound learning experiences that encapsulate the essence of entrepreneurial tenacity and resilience.

The collective wisdom drawn from the three case studies and our rich experience in fostering hackathon winners' growth is now distilled into a comprehensive blueprint. This blueprint provides a set of strategic dos and don'ts, offering a valuable toolkit for others aspiring to replicate such success. It's a roadmap designed to help bypass common pitfalls and steer directly towards strategies proven to work, enabling new entrepreneurs to benefit from the hindsight of their predecessors without undergoing the same trials.

Despite the spotlight on successful transitions from concept to market, it's important to recognize that numerous solutions did not experience such fortunate outcomes. Their absence from the commercial landscape serves as a stark reminder of the daunting challenges inherent in this process and the intense labor that success demands. Yet, failure to commercialize is not the sole measure of a hackathon's value.

Beyond the development and launch of solutions, hackathons foster rich, invaluable connections among their participants. The value of networks created within the hackathon's crucible—connections between team members, interactions with mentors, exchanges with **jury members**, and collaborations with partner organizations—can be profoundly transformative and have great value in other areas. These relationships, often built on the foundational stones of mutual trust and respect, have the potential to outlive the hackathon itself and become catalysts for significant business opportunities in the future.

For organizing entities, particularly within large, multifaceted corporations where interdepartmental communication may falter, hackathons offer a unique convergence point. They break down silos, encourage cross-pollination of ideas, and spur cohesive collaboration. The shared endeavor of addressing a collective challenge unites participants in a way that daily operations may not, fostering a spirit of unity and cooperation that can refresh and invigorate corporate culture. While winners' success is important, this aspect is not to be overlooked.

This chapter also offered a list of the important factors for hackathon success that we have noted through our years of supporting winning teams after the hackathon ended. This is not to be understood as a definitive list, but it is rather to be seen as a collection of observations of what is successful so far.

In conclusion, the Dream! Hack! Build! method stands as a testament to the power of citizen-driven innovation with hackathons, transforming the collective ingenuity of individuals into tangible solutions that shape the future. Hackathons are not just mere events; they are exponential incubators for innovative ideas, where the dreams of today become the innovations of tomorrow. Through the Dream! Hack! Build! method, we are providing a democratization of innovation, as people from all walks of life contribute their unique perspectives to solve real-world problems. This book has not only chronicled a journey of creativity and collaboration but has also laid down a blueprint for how you can continue this vital work. May every reader feel empowered to dream big, hack with purpose, and build for a brighter future, where citizen-driven innovation is not just an ideal, but the standard.

Appendix A

In *Appendix A*, we cover two important topics that are relevant to the overall understanding of this book: the United Nations and its **17 Sustainable Development Goals (17 SDGs)** and their respective purposes. The 17 SDGs are the very foundation of the work we do at Hack for Earth, so it's important for you as a reader to have an overview of them:

1. **United Nations:** The United Nations (UN) is an international organization established on October 24, 1945, in the aftermath of World War II. It aims to promote peace, security, and cooperation among nations. Its founding charter articulates a commitment to upholding international law, providing humanitarian aid, protecting human rights, and promoting sustainable development. The UN functions through a system of intergovernmental agencies and bodies, with the General Assembly, the Security Council, the International Court of Justice, and the UN Secretariat being its primary components. It serves as a global forum for its 193 member states (as of 2023) to discuss and work together on a wide array of international issues.

2. **17 SDGs:** The 17 SDGs are a universal call to action to end poverty, protect the planet, and ensure that all people enjoy peace and prosperity by 2030. Adopted by all United Nations Member States in 2015, these goals are part of the 2030 Agenda for Sustainable Development. The goals are found at `https://sdgs.un.org/goals` and are as follows:

   - **No poverty**: End poverty in all its forms everywhere.

   - **Zero hunger**: End hunger, achieve food security and improved nutrition, and promote sustainable agriculture.

   - **Good health and well-being**: Ensure healthy lives and promote well-being for all at all ages.

   - **Quality education**: Ensure inclusive and equitable quality education and promote lifelong learning opportunities for all.

   - **Gender equality**: Achieve gender equality and empower all women and girls.

   - **Clean water and sanitation**: Ensure availability and sustainable management of water and sanitation for all.

   - **Affordable and clean energy**: Ensure access to affordable, reliable, sustainable, and modern energy for all.

   - **Decent work and economic growth**: Promote sustained, inclusive, and sustainable economic growth, full and productive employment, and decent work for all.

- **Industry, innovation, and infrastructure**: Build resilient infrastructure, promote inclusive and sustainable industrialization, and foster innovation.

- **Reduced inequality**: Reduce inequality within and among countries.

- **Sustainable cities and communities**: Make cities and human settlements inclusive, safe, resilient, and sustainable.

- **Responsible consumption and production**: Ensure sustainable consumption and production patterns.

- **Climate action**: Take urgent action to combat climate change and its impacts.

- **Life below water**: Conserve and sustainably use the oceans, seas, and marine resources for sustainable development.

- **Life on land**: Protect, restore, and promote sustainable use of terrestrial ecosystems, manage forests sustainably, combat desertification, and halt and reverse land degradation and biodiversity loss.

- **Peace, justice, and strong institutions**: Promote peaceful and inclusive societies for sustainable development, provide access to justice for all, and build effective, accountable, and inclusive institutions at all levels.

- **Partnerships for the goals**: Strengthen the means of implementation and revitalize the global partnership for sustainable development.

The most recent report on the progress of the SDGs issued by the UN can be found here: `https://packt.link/908qR`.

Appendix B

In *Appendix B*, we provide descriptions and details on important Hack for Earth hackathons and other events, concepts, and phenomena that are relevant to your overall understanding of this book:

1. **Build for Earth**: A uniquely tailored acceleration program, drawing upon a foundation of science, interviews with innovation experts, and the extensive experience of the Hack for Earth team it was crafted by Dr. Kristofer Vernmark in 2021. It represents the culminating component of the innovative **Dream! Hack! Build!** methodology specifically designed to ensure that the most promising ideas born out of the hackathons are not only conceptualized but are fully realized and functional. At the heart of Build for Earth is a commitment to see the winning solutions evolve into practical tools that can make a significant difference to our planet.

   Beyond just the creation of these tools, the Build for Earth program is designed to be comprehensive, offering a suite of modules that are critical for the journey of a solution from concept to market. These modules are not just about business acumen; they are about ensuring that these solutions are sustainable, scalable, and, most importantly, have a lasting impact on our future. The program aims to equip participants with the knowledge, skills, and networks necessary to navigate the complexities of bringing a product to life.

   The global innovation experts who have contributed to the structure of the Build for Earth acceleration program, by providing their valuable expertise in a series of interviews conducted by Dr. Vernmark, are:

   - Hoa Ly, CEO at Nuroe / Cogmed

   - Mikael Ahlström, CEO & Founder Sproutpark

   - Marie Claire Maxwell, Manager Export Promotion MEA & Americas, Business Sweden

   - Olle Lundin, Founder & CEO Swedish Jobtech

   - Jens Nordberg, Innovation Behavior Specialist and Co-Founder at Pollen.

   - Hans Alveros, Founder Brainspot Innovation

   - Laila Pawlak, Founder & CEO Rehumanize Institute

   - Fredrik Livheim, Research and Content Strategist at 29k

   - Jakob Andrén, Head of Assessment at Aon EMEA

   - Marjan Mohsenin, Co-Founder, Sales & Client Strategic Lead at FutrCoLab

   - Rafat Malik, Executive Chairman at IME Pension Fund

- Maya Moukbel, Senior researcher, Ericsson
- Alexandra Björk, Event Manager GoWest – Nordic Venture Capital Forum
- Annie Lindmark, Program Director at Vinnova – Swedish Innovation Agency
- Brighton Kaoma, Global Director UN Sustainable Development Solutions Network
- Edurne Gil de San Vicente, Program Director Water Alliance, UAE
- Elinor Samuelsson & Sofie Wahlström, Founders of BrightAct
- Nils Söderström , Board Member & Founder RenBloc
- PJ Mistry, Unilever Foundry Strategy & Operations Lead
- Charlotte Kalin, Director Public Affairs & Sustainability The Coca-Cola Company
- Mattias Weinhandl, Angel investor, owner of Boards on Fire and partowner Airmee
- Stefan Swartling Peterson, Professor of Global Transformations for Health at Karolinska Institutet and Health Specialist UNICEF Sweden

2. **Dream for Earth**: This was a significant global initiative in 2020 that aimed to gather insights from people worldwide about their visions for a sustainable future. The central hub of this movement was the `dreamforearth.com` website, a platform where individuals could express their hopes and ideas through videos or texts. Participants had the option to link their visions to up to five of the United Nations' SDGs, highlighting the aspects they found most pressing and pertinent.

The collective aspirations gathered through the Dream for Earth campaign served a dual purpose. First, they laid the groundwork for the challenges addressed at the Hack for Earth hackathon held at the world exhibition **Expo 2020** in Dubai. This ensured that the hackathon's challenges were deeply rooted in the global citizenry's real-world concerns and aspirations for a sustainable future. Second, the campaign acted as a digital tapestry of global dreams, with the website featuring a virtual Earth adorned with dreams submitted by people from over 100 countries. Visitors to the site could explore this mosaic of dreams, gaining insight into the shared and diverse wishes for our planet's future.

The Dream for Earth AI analysis was performed by Hack for Earth partner organization Kairos Future. Kairos Future is a consultancy and research firm that specializes in strategic foresight and future studies. It assists organizations in navigating complex futures through trend analysis, scenario planning, and strategy development. By combining data-driven research with expert analysis, Kairos Future helps clients identify opportunities, mitigate risks, and drive innovation. The firm leverages a global network of experts and advanced methodologies to provide actionable insights and transformative solutions for sustainable growth and was a strategic partner organization for the global hackathon Hack for Earth at Expo 2020.

The Dream for Earth analysis performed by Kairos Future delves into the dreams shared by individuals globally as part of the open Dream for Earth initiative. Analyzing a total of 1,056 dreams from 61 countries, this research scrutinizes submissions posted on dreamforearth.com between May 17th and August 28th, 2021. Dreams submitted in video format were transcribed into text to facilitate a comprehensive analysis. Utilizing natural language processing techniques, the content of these dreams was examined to identify thematic and narrative patterns by clustering dreams with similar content. Furthermore, an analysis of metadata, particularly focusing on the location and category of each dream, was conducted to uncover the geographic and thematic focuses of the dreams shared.

The next figures show a world map and three graphs showing the results of the Dream for Earth analysis, the geographic distribution of the dreams, and age group of people sharing dreams, the number of dreams per SDG, and the distribution of categories by region. To view the graphs in color, you can visit this link: https://packt.link/k0b5Z.

The following world map shows the 61 countries from where dreams were submitted in the Dream for Earth campaign, running from May 17th to August 28th, 2021; a little over three months' time:

The geograpic distribution of the dreams

Dreams were submitted from **61** countries

Powered by Bing
© Australian Bureau of Statistics, GeoNames, Microsoft, Navinfo, TomTom, Wikipedia

Countres from which dreams were shared are highlighted in blue.

dcipher
analytics

Figure 13.1 – World map showing the countries from where dreams
were submitted in the Dream for Earth campaign

In the following figure, you can see the distribution of dreams by region and age group, showing that the majority of dreams were submitted from countries in the Middle East (47%) and the majority of dreams were shared by young people under the age of 15 (53%).

Region and age group of people sharing dreams

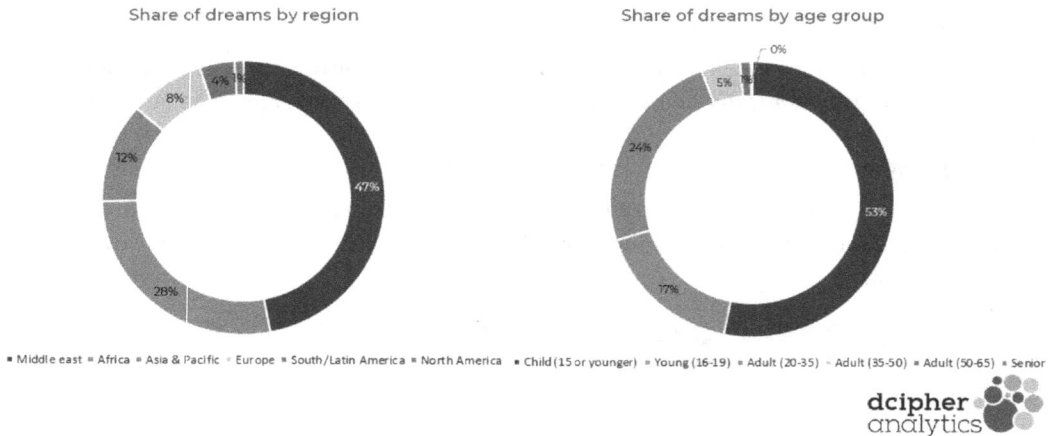

Share of dreams by region   Share of dreams by age group

- Middle east ■ Africa ■ Asia & Pacific ■ Europe ■ South/Latin America ■ North America   ■ Child (15 or younger)   ■ Young (16-19) ■ Adult (20-35) ■ Adult (35-50) ■ Adult (50-65) ■ Senior

Figure 13.2 – Image showing the distribution of dreams in regards to regions in the world and age groups.

The Dream for Earth website gave people the option to connect their dreams to up to five of the in total 17 SDGs. The following graph shows the number of dreams per SDG, and the SDG that had the most dreams attached to it was the third SDG: good health and well-being. This is followed by the fourth SDG, quality education, and the first SDG, no poverty. Visitors to the Dream for Earth website could also vote for the best dream, and the number of likes in the following graph shows that dreams connected to the first SDG (no poverty), fifth SDG (gender equality), and tenth SDG (reduced inequalities) got the most likes.

Number of dreams per SDG

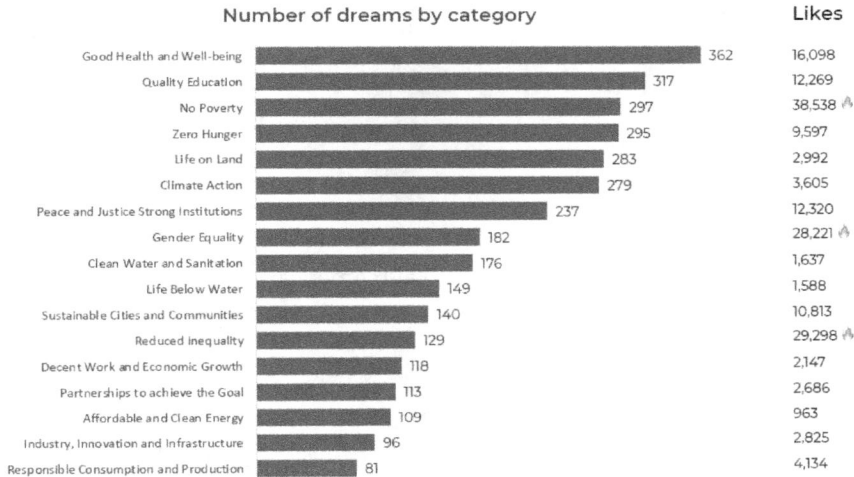

Number of dreams by category

Category	Number	Likes
Good Health and Well-being	362	16,098
Quality Education	317	12,269
No Poverty	297	38,538
Zero Hunger	295	9,597
Life on Land	283	2,992
Climate Action	279	3,605
Peace and Justice Strong Institutions	237	12,320
Gender Equality	182	28,221
Clean Water and Sanitation	176	1,637
Life Below Water	149	1,588
Sustainable Cities and Communities	140	10,813
Reduced Inequality	129	29,298
Decent Work and Economic Growth	118	2,147
Partnerships to achieve the Goal	113	2,686
Affordable and Clean Energy	109	963
Industry, Innovation and Infrastructure	96	2,825
Responsible Consumption and Production	81	4,134

Dreams can relate to more than one goal, so overlap between goals exists.

dcipher
analytics

Figure 13.3 – Image showing the number of dreams per SDG

In the following graph, you can see the distribution of dreams connected to the SDGs by region. Segment width reflects an SDG's share of dreams, height indicates an SDG's overrepresentation in a region compared to other regions, and the central circle indicates the number of dreams compared to other regions. The 17 SDGs are listed on the far right and color-coded:

Distribution of categories by region

How to read the charts: Segment width reflects goal's share of dreams; height indicates goal's overrepresentation in a region compared to other regions; the central circle indicates number of dreams compared to other regions.

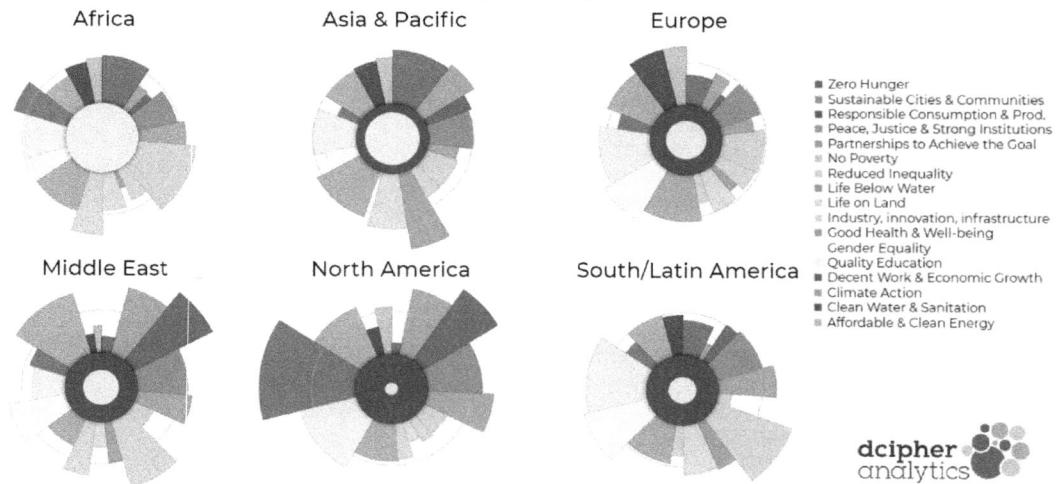

Africa

Asia & Pacific

Europe

- Zero Hunger
- Sustainable Cities & Communities
- Responsible Consumption & Prod.
- Peace, Justice & Strong Institutions
- Partnerships to Achieve the Goal
- No Poverty
- Reduced Inequality
- Life Below Water
- Life on Land
- Industry, innovation, infrastructure
- Good Health & Well-being
- Gender Equality
- Quality Education
- Decent Work & Economic Growth
- Climate Action
- Clean Water & Sanitation
- Affordable & Clean Energy

Middle East

North America

South/Latin America

dcipher
analytics

Figure 13.4 – Image showing the distribution of dreams connected to SDGs by region

More in-depth information on the Dream for Earth analysis for readers who may be interested in diving deeper into the analysis and connections to the SDGs can be found at this link: https://packt.link/k0b5Z.

3. **Dream for Sweden**: This was a national campaign aimed at engaging Swedes in envisioning their future society by the year 2045. Tied to the Hack for Sweden hackathon in 2019 and commissioned by the Swedish government through the Ministry of Infrastructure, it sought to crowdsource inspiration for the hackathon's challenges by tapping into the collective aspirations of citizens. The campaign revolved around the Dream for Sweden website, a platform where individuals could submit their visions for a better future in short text. This initiative transformed the abstract concept of future societal improvements into a tangible collection of ideas, represented visually on a map shaped like Sweden on the website. Each submission not only contributed to a collective dream but also served as potential fodder for hackathon challenges, ensuring the event addressed real, citizen-driven concerns.

This approach made the Dream for Sweden campaign a critical bridge between the public's aspirations and practical innovation. By leveraging the power of collective imagination, it positioned the Hack for Sweden hackathon as a direct response to the citizens' dreams, aligning technological and social innovation efforts with the shared goals of Swedish society. The campaign exemplified how engaging citizens in dialogue about the future could yield actionable insights and foster a sense of community and shared purpose, ultimately steering public initiatives and technological developments toward the common good.

With the campaign visited by over 110,000 people, approximately 80% of the dreams were related to the environment, highlighting unity around the most urgent and important challenges participants of the hackathon needed to solve. With six areas that were considered to be mature in terms of data, the dreams were compressed and thematized. This served as a foundation for creating the challenges in collaboration with the Hack for Sweden partner community, consisting of 88 partner organizations from the public and private sectors.

More information on Dream for Sweden can be found here:

`https://etablera.co/dream-for-sweden`

This is what the Dream for Sweden website looked like:

`https://upbeat-meninsky-6f8ebb.netlify.app/`

4. **Hack for Sweden**: Hack for Sweden is an itinerant initiative by the Swedish Government, where the task of organizing the hackathon moves from government agency to government agency every two years. During 2018-2019 the Hack for Sweden government mission was with the Swedish Employment Service, and from 2020 the government mission of Hack for Sweden is with the Swedish Government Agency for Digital Government (DIGG).

The government mission of Hack for Sweden is to engage Swedish government agencies, private sector companies, academia, and individuals to collectively use open data to address challenges that benefit Sweden and its citizens through a hackathon. This is done through an open hackathon event where participants use open data published by several Swedish government agencies to create solutions and applications that can improve public services, enhance transparency, and solve societal issues. The first Hack for Sweden hackathon took place in Stockholm in 2014. The connection to the authors of this book is: Ann Molin was appointed Head Project Manager of Hack for Sweden in 2018, and was in charge of Hack for Sweden during the years 2018–2019. At Hack for Sweden 2019, Love Dager was the hackathon manager and Carolina Emanuelson was the Partner Manager.

Participants in Hack for Sweden hackathons typically include developers, designers, entrepreneurs, and problem solvers who are interested in leveraging open data for the public good. The event encourages the development of new ideas and solutions in various areas such as health, education, environmental sustainability, and public administration.

Hack for Sweden serves as a platform for fostering collaboration between the public and private sectors and the general public, showcasing the potential of open data to drive innovation and create value for society. It highlights the importance of making government data accessible and usable to encourage civic engagement, stimulate economic growth, and address societal challenges through technology and creativity.

> **Note**
>
> Here's the link to the Hack for Sweden final report to the Swedish Government for further reading. Please note: the document in the link is in the Swedish language: `https://packt.link/3oCad`. To read in English, you can visit this link: `https://packt.link/AMxUf`.

5. **EUvsVirus** The EUvsVirus hackathon was a pan-European online event organized by the European Commission in partnership with member states and other stakeholders that took place in April 2020. This initiative was part of the European Union's collective efforts to combat the COVID-19 pandemic. Ann Molin was National Curator for Sweden and Carolina Emanuelson was Partner Manager for the EU commissions' initiative EUvsVirus.

    The hackathon aimed to connect civil society, innovators, partners, and investors across Europe in order to develop innovative solutions for coronavirus-related challenges. The EUvsVirus event brought together 22 thousand participants who collaborated on a variety of projects, addressing issues such as healthcare, business continuity, social and political cohesion, remote working and education, digital finance, and more. The hackathon supported the whole lifecycle of the solution development, from ideation to prototyping and deployment, with a follow-up two-day conference for all winners called "Matchathon", where the winning solutions were matched with investors and government entities.

    As a result, the EUvsVirus hackathon not only generated immediate technological solutions to help tackle the crisis but also fostered a community of European innovators and set the stage for long-term cooperation among EU member states in addressing the pandemic's challenges. This event was a testament to the EU's commitment to using collective intelligence and open innovation to solve complex problems.

6. **Expo 2020**: The most recent world exhibition was Expo 2020 in Dubai. The Expo 2020 was postponed by one year due to the Covid-19 pandemic; it was supposed to take place on the year 2020. When the event was postponed, the organizers decided to keep the name Expo 2020, even though the world exhibition opened in the year 2021. Expo 2020 was themed "Connecting Minds, Creating the Future" and was sub-themed "Opportunity, Mobility, and Sustainability" – areas seen as key to creating a better future. The event sought to inspire by showcasing the best examples of collaboration, innovation, and cooperation from around the world. With 192 participating countries and various organizations, NGOs, and businesses taking part, the Expo provided a rich tapestry of cultural experiences and insightful discussions on technology, the environment, and cutting-edge global issues. It aimed to inspire action through collaboration and innovation, acknowledging the interconnectedness of our world and the need for a renewed collective approach to its challenges.

7. **Hack for Earth at Expo 2020 (in 2021)**: The global online hackathon at Expo 2020 was organized by the Hack for Earth Foundation in collaboration with the United Nations. Amazon Web Services, The Nordic Council of Ministers, and Astra Zeneca as the main collaborating organizations in November, 2021. In total, Hack for Earth at Expo 2020 had 32 organisations as collaborating and/or supporting partner organizations. 1784 teams from 121 countries participated in the two-week-long hackathon. Seven winning solutions were selected by the jury in the seven challenge categories based on the SDGs and created in collaboration with the UN: Water, Partnership, Sustainable Society, Human Rights, Education, Environment, and Health. The seven winners concluded the very first Build for Earth 6-month acceleration program in the spring of 2022. More information about this is available at `hackforearth.com`.

8. **Hack for Earth at COP27 (in 2022):** The global online hackathon Hack for Earth at COP27 was organized in collaboration with the UN Climate Change Global Innovation Hub, UN World Food Programme Innovation Accelerator, UNICEF Office of Innovation, UNICEF, UNEP, World Bank Youth Summit, SIDA, Radiant Earth Foundation, Empire Partner Foundation and more. The 27th UN high level climate conference, the COP27, was held in Sharm-El-Sheikh in Egypt in November 2022. 1864 teams from 125 countriees participated in the 72 hour global online hackathon in November 2022, and the seven winning teams were selected by the jury to enter the Build for Earth acceleration program in the spring of 2023. More info about this is available at `hackforearth.com`.

9. **Hack for Earth at COP28 (in 2023):** The global online hackathon Hack for Earth at COP28 was proud to introduce Ericsson as a co-organizing company, and the hackathon was also organized in collaboration with UNICEF Office of Innovation and Junior Achievement Worldwide. In addition, MIT Climate Change and Energy Prize joined as a partner organization. 1200 teams from 112 countries participated in the 72-hour hackathon and the jury selected 8 winning teams in the 8 challenge categories: Water, Cities, Partnership, Environment, Transport, Education, Food, and Energy. The eight winning teams entered the Build for Earth acceleration program in the spring of 2024. More in about this is available at at `hackforearth.com`.

10. **Hack the Crisis movement:** The Hack the Crisis movement refers to a series of hackathons that were initiated as a response to various challenges posed by the COVID-19 pandemic. These events were organized globally with the aim of rapidly developing technological solutions to help manage and mitigate aspects of the crisis. The movement began in Estonia in March 2020 and quickly spread to other countries, becoming a worldwide initiative.

    The online Hack the Crisis hackathons focused on immediate issues related to the pandemic, such as healthcare, mental health, saving businesses, education during lockdowns, economic stability, and the resilience of societies. This movement is characterized by its community-driven approach, bringing together volunteers and organizations across public and private sectors. It represents a grassroots effort to use technology and innovation for social good, leveraging the collective skills of participants to create impactful solutions in a short period of time.

    The outcomes of the Hack the Crisis movement have been significant and varied across the globe. Many of the hackathons produced innovative solutions that were swiftly implemented to tackle immediate problems arising from the pandemic. In Estonia, for instance, one of the notable results was an app designed to connect volunteers with those in need of assistance, effectively organizing community support efforts. Other hackathons yielded tools for health monitoring, platforms for remote education and fighting domestic violence, and solutions to support disrupted businesses.

Beyond specific products and services, Hack the Crisis created a template for a rapid, community-driven response to global challenges. It showcased the potential of open innovation and cross-sector collaboration, with government agencies, private companies, and individual citizens working together. The movement also demonstrated the scalability of digital solutions to societal problems, reinforcing the idea that in times of crisis, technology can serve as a critical tool for resilience and recovery.

11. **Hack the Crisis, Sweden**: Hack the Crisis, Sweden, was part of the global Hack the Crisis movement, one of the largest national online hackathons within it. It was specifically organized to find innovative solutions to challenges posed by the COVID-19 pandemic in Sweden. It took place over the course of three days in April 2020 and was initiated by the Swedish government through its innovation agency, Vinnova, and the digitalization agency, DIGG, along with 160 supporting partner organizations, including big tech companies and government agencies. Ann Molin was Head Project Manager, Love Dager was Hackathon Manager, and Carolina Emanuelson was Partner Manager for Hack the Crisis Sweden.

The Hack the Crisis, Sweden, hackathon, with 7,500 participants from 91 countries, aimed to harness the collective skills and creativity of tech-savvy people, entrepreneurs, and other professionals to create solutions that could support society during and after the pandemic. The online hackathon focused on three main areas: saving lives, saving businesses, and saving communities.

Participants were encouraged to develop tools and services that could be rapidly deployed to assist healthcare workers, support businesses in facing economic challenges, and maintain the social fabric of communities during periods of social distancing and beyond. Hack the Crisis, Sweden, was successful in bringing together a large community of problem-solvers and creating practical solutions. The event's agile and community-driven approach allowed for rapid development and implementation of ideas, demonstrating the effectiveness of collaborative innovation in addressing real-world problems in times of crisis.

12. **Pitch for Earth**: This event serves as the grand finale of the Build for Earth acceleration program, an occasion where the teams that have risen to the top through their innovative solutions are given the spotlight once again. Unlike their initial pitches, which may have been more conceptual, this event is the culmination of their hard work and progress—a pivotal platform where they present the evolution and readiness of their solutions.

The teams pitch to a selected panel of investors, companies, and other organizations, each with the potential to catapult these solutions to new heights. The participants are tasked with not just presenting their ideas but demonstrating the tangible strides they've made during the acceleration phase. They must articulate the viability, scalability, and potential impact of their projects with clarity and conviction.

Teams aim to secure funding and partnerships that will provide not just financial backing but also strategic alliances necessary for their initiatives to thrive. They showcase their advancements, underscore the sustainable and innovative aspects of their work, and present a compelling case for investment.

In essence, the Pitch for Earth event is where possibility meets practicality. It's an opportunity for the winning solutions to turn their prototypes into products. It's where the synergy of science, sustainability, and entrepreneurship has the potential to forge a new path for our planet's future, making the dreams of today the realities of tomorrow.

13. **Psychological safety agenda (first session of Build for Earth COP28)**

Welcome and Introduction*

- Greet participants

- Briefly introduce the purpose of the session – Building psychological safety within the team.

- Share the importance of psychological safety for learning, performance, and engagement.

- Highlight that participation from the whole team is preferred in this session, as it is important to include the perspectives of all team members in creating psychological safety.

This sets the agenda and goal for the session, inviting everyone to participate

Icebreaker Activity: Two Truths and a Lie*

- Ask each participant to share two true statements about themselves and one false statement.

- Encourage other team members to guess which statement is the lie.

- Ask team members to expand on their statements by sharing more about themselves.

This exercise helps the team to create an open and personal environment and learn more about each other

Define Psychological Safety*

- Provide a clear definition of psychological safety.

- Emphasize that it's about creating an environment where team members feel safe to take interpersonal risks and express themselves without fear of negative consequences.

This gives an understandable conception of the term Psychological safety and its essence

Share the Importance of Psychological Safety*

- Discuss research and examples that highlight the positive impact of psychological safety on team performance and innovation.

- Share success stories from other teams or organizations that have benefited from a psychologically safe environment.

This gives credibility to the concept of Psychological safety, why it is important for the team and how it relates to specific real world situations

Personal Reflection and Team Discussion Exercise*

- Ask each team member to take a few minutes to reflect on and write down two examples of feeling psychologically safe and unsafe in earlier and/or current teams.

- Encourage team members to share these situations and the emotions and thoughts that were connected to these.

This gives the team members an opportunity to align the concept of psychological safety with their own experiences and practice sharing their own feelings of being in an unsafe team environment

After Action Review, AAR*

Ask all team members to think about (and write down) their answers to the following questions.

- How did we function as a team?

- Did we respect and appreciate each other in this team?

- What can we as members of this team do (specific actions) at the next meeting to make everyone feel even more appreciated and included (contribute to a more psychologically safe environment)?

Let everyone share their answers

This adapted version of an AAR can be used to practice reflection about team behaviors and open up for further learning

Closing*

Express gratitude for the team's participation and commitment to practicing building psychological safety.

Mention the purpose of today's exercises and topics, and summarize key takeaways.

Highlight learning and be a role model when sharing your appreciation for others

14. **World Exhibiton**: World Exhibitions, also known as World Expos or World's Fairs, are large international events designed to showcase the achievements of nations. These exhibitions vary in character and are held in different parts of the world at varying intervals. The concept of the World Expo has evolved since the first Great Exhibition of the Works of Industry of All Nations, held in London in 1851. Since then, these events have become one of the largest and most enduring global mega-events. The most recent one was Expo 2020 in Dubai, UAE held during 6 months between October in 2021 to April 2022 (postponed a year due to the pandemic).

World Expos serve multiple purposes: they are a platform for countries to promote themselves and improve their national image by showcasing innovations, culture, and accomplishments to an international audience. They also provide an opportunity for people to share ideas and solutions on global issues, such as sustainable development, energy conservation, and urban planning. Over the years, World Expos have been responsible for the introduction of numerous technological and architectural innovations, including the telephone, the Eiffel Tower, and the Ferris Wheel.

Expos are organized by the Bureau International des Expositions (BIE), the international organization responsible for overseeing the calendar, the bidding process, and regulations of World Expos. There are two main types of Expos: Registered Expos (formerly known as Universal Expositions), which are larger and occur every five years, offering participants the opportunity to build their own pavilions; and Recognized Expos (formerly known as International or Specialized Expositions), which are smaller, shorter, and occur in the interim years, focusing on a specific theme.

These events are celebrated for their ability to bring together countries, corporations, and international organizations to foster cooperation and cultural exchange, stimulate economic growth, and inspire innovation and progress on a global scale.

Glossary

In *Dream! Hack! Build!*, we dive into the heart of innovation and the world of hackathons. This glossary is your quick reference guide to the key terms and concepts that fuel citizen-driven innovation. Whether you're brainstorming your first project or leading your latest hackathon, these definitions are crafted to clarify the terms we use in this book. As we navigate through *Dream! Hack! Build!*, this section will ensure you're equipped with the knowledge to participate fully and effectively. Embrace it as a tool for empowerment on your journey to make an impact:

1. **Acceleration program**: An acceleration program is a structured support system designed to help start-ups and entrepreneurs rapidly grow and scale their businesses. These programs provide a range of resources such as mentorship, educational workshops, networking opportunities, and often access to capital, typically in exchange for equity in the company.

   Acceleration programs are usually cohort-based, meaning a group of start-ups goes through the program together, and they run for a fixed period, often between three to six months. During this time, participating start-ups work intensively on refining their business models, accelerating product development, and identifying market opportunities.

   Key features of an acceleration program may include:

   - **Mentorship**: Access to industry experts and seasoned entrepreneurs who provide guidance

   - **Funding**: Some programs offer seed funding and the opportunity to pitch to investors for additional capital

   - **Networking**: Connections to a network of peers, potential customers, partners, and investors

   - **Educational components**: Workshops and seminars to cover key areas of business growth, such as marketing, legal issues, and financial management

   - **Demo day**: A culminating event where start-ups present their business to an audience of investors and industry experts

   The goal of an acceleration program is to fast-track a start-up's growth and increase its chances of success by providing the tools, skills, and network necessary to overcome common business challenges.

2. **Brand guidelines**: Brand guidelines, also known as brand standards or style guides, are a set of rules and specifications that outline how a brand presents itself to the world. These guidelines ensure consistency in the use of the brand's elements across all mediums and platforms, which is crucial for building brand recognition and trust. Brand guidelines include a set of rules and regulations with regard to logo usage, color palette, the typography used in company

documents, imagery and photograph style, voice and tone, layout and design principles, and finally core values.

Brand guidelines are essential for maintaining a coherent and consistent brand identity, which helps to make the brand more recognizable and trusted by consumers. They serve as a reference for marketers, designers, partners, and anyone else who works with the brand's assets, ensuring that every interaction customers have with the brand is consistent and aligned with its values and goals.

3.   **APIs**: Short for **Application Programming Interface**, an API is a set of rules, protocols, and tools for building software and applications. It specifies how software components should interact and allows different software applications to communicate with each other. APIs are used to enable the integration between different systems and devices, allowing them to exchange data and functionality easily and securely.

   For example, when you use a mobile app to send a message, check the weather, or view a map, the app uses APIs to communicate with a server over the internet. The server then retrieves the data, processes it as required, and sends it back to your app. This process allows your app to offer features and data from external sources, including social media platforms, weather services, or mapping services, without having to recreate these functionalities from scratch. APIs are fundamental to modern software development, facilitating services such as web services, cloud computing, and the development of web-based applications.

4.   **After Action Review**: The **After Action Review (AAR)** is a debriefing method that can be used by teams to increase learning and thereby the efficiency of the team. It has been shown to increase productivity in teams by up to 25% and can be used in many different formats. It focuses on the performance of the team and not the specific individuals. Using the AAR can be a good way for a team to see if there is a shared view of what they have set out to do during a meeting (purpose and goals), how it was achieved, and what can be done differently the next time. This creates a learning space at the end of each meeting.

5.   **Challenge**: In a hackathon, a challenge refers to a specific problem or theme that participants are asked to address through their team effort. Challenges can range widely in scope and subject matter, from developing new software applications or designing innovative hardware solutions to creating projects that solve social, environmental, or business-related problems. Organizers present these challenges to inspire participants and guide their efforts toward achieving tangible outcomes that address real-world issues. Participants compete or collaborate to develop the most effective, innovative, or creative solution to these challenges, often with the incentive of prizes, recognition, or the potential for the further development and implementation of their ideas.

6.   **Challenge category**: This refers to a group of challenges in a hackathon with the same theme. For example, the *Environment* category might entail challenges regarding the forest, the sea, and agriculture.

7. **Citizen-driven innovation**: Citizen-driven innovation refers to a process where citizens actively participate in the innovation process, contributing ideas, solutions, and actions to address societal, community, or environmental challenges. This approach leverages the collective intelligence, skills, and experiences of the public to co-create innovations that are more inclusive, sustainable, and aligned with the needs and values of the community. Citizen-driven innovation often involves collaboration between citizens, government, NGOs, and private entities, employing tools such as crowdsourcing, participatory design, and open innovation platforms to engage a wide range of stakeholders in the problem-solving process.

8. **Diversity**: Diversity refers to the presence of differences within a given setting. This encompasses variations in race, ethnicity, gender, age, sexual orientation, religion, socioeconomic status, physical abilities, and other attributes through which people identify themselves and others. In a broader context, diversity can also refer to differences in experiences, ideas, knowledge bases, and ways of thinking.

   In a hackathon context, diversity is important because it enriches the hackathon by bringing together a wide range of perspectives, skills, and experiences. This diversity of thought and background fosters innovation, creativity, and problem-solving by challenging conventional approaches and encouraging new ideas. In a hackathon setting, diversity enhances learning by exposing people to a broad spectrum of viewpoints and life experiences, promoting empathy and understanding of differences.

9. **Dream! Hack! Build! Method**: The unique method crafted by the Hack for Earth team to create citizen-driven innovation with hackathons. It revolves around the central idea that the outcome will have a greater real-world impact if many different stakeholders are involved in all the phases of the hackathon, from creating the challenges to participating in the hackathon and making the winning solutions come to life afterward in a customized acceleration program.

10. **Full-range leadership**: The *full-range leadership* model was named by Bass and Aviolo and includes two overarching styles – the transactional and the transformational leader. Examples of transactional leadership styles are Laissez-Fair and Active management by exception. Transactional leadership styles, such as the Contingent Reward style, can be effective, but transformational leadership has been shown to be more successful, leading to higher job satisfaction and better outcomes. A full-range leadership includes both styles, but one is usually dominant over the other.

11. **Graphic profile**: A graphic profile, often synonymous with a visual identity system or brand identity, encompasses the visual elements that represent a company's brand. It's a subset of the broader brand guidelines, focusing specifically on the graphical aspects that convey the brand's identity and values across various media and platforms. The graphic profile typically includes:

    A graphic profile is crucial for ensuring that all visual representations of the brand are consistent, coherent, and aligned with the brand's identity and messaging. This consistency helps to build recognition and trust among the target audience, contributing to a stronger brand presence in the market. It serves as a reference for designers, marketers, and anyone else involved in creating branded materials, ensuring that all visual communications effectively represent the brand.

12. **Hackathon**: A hackathon is an event, typically lasting a few hours up to several days, where people come together to collaborate on software or hardware projects, often with the goal of solving specific problems or developing new ideas. The term "hackathon" comes from combining the words "hack" and "marathon," where hack is used in the sense of creative innovative collaboration, not its alternate meaning related to computer security.

   During a hackathon, participants form teams to work on a project with the goal of creating a functioning software or hardware product by the end of the event. Hackathons often have specific themes or are focused on particular technologies, and they often include competitive elements, with prizes awarded for the best solutions developed during the event.

   Participants are encouraged to be creative and innovative, and hackathons provide a venue for self-expression and technical skills. They are popular in the tech industry but have also been adopted by other sectors (as with Hack for Earth) as a way of quickly generating new ideas and solving problems. Hackathons can be hosted by educational institutions, tech companies, nonprofit organizations, and others, and they serve as a way to foster community and collaboration among developers and other tech enthusiasts.

   The first event explicitly called a "hackathon" was held in June 1999 in Calgary, Alberta, Canada. It was organized by OpenBSD, a group of developers who gathered to develop a cryptographic framework for the OpenBSD operating system in a single weekend. This event set the precedent for the hackathons that followed, combining intense, focused collaboration on software projects with an open, inclusive environment that encouraged innovation and problem-solving.

13. **Impact**: In a hackathon setting, "impact" refers to the significance or effectiveness of the solutions developed during the event in addressing the challenges posed or in meeting the goals set forth by the organizers. It measures how well these solutions can potentially solve real-world problems, improve existing systems, or create value for a specific community, industry, or the broader society.

   Impact is a crucial criterion for judging in hackathons, as it reflects the potential real-world value of the solutions developed. High-impact solutions are those that not only showcase innovative thinking and technical prowess but also are viable and meaningful, with the potential to make a difference in their intended domain. Hackathons often aim to foster solutions that can lead to start-ups.

14. **Jury member**: A jury member in a hackathon is part of the jury responsible for evaluating the solutions developed by participants during the event. Jury members are usually experts or professionals with significant experience and knowledge in the hackathon's focus area, including technology, business, design, and other relevant fields. Their primary role is to assess the submissions based on predefined criteria such as innovation, technical difficulty, usability, impact, and presentation.

   Jury members play a critical role in ensuring that the hackathon's outcomes are evaluated fairly and professionally. Their expertise and judgment help recognize and reward the most promising ideas and solutions, contributing to the overall success and credibility of the event.

15. **Mentor**: In a hackathon, a mentor is an experienced individual who provides guidance, support, and expertise to participants. Mentors are typically professionals with a strong background in the hackathon's focus areas, such as software development, design, business strategy, or specific industry sectors relevant to the hackathon's theme. Their role is to help teams overcome technical and creative challenges, offer insights on project development, and ensure that participants can make the most of the event.

    Mentors contribute as follows:

    - Answering technical questions and helping troubleshoot issues

    - Offering advice on project design, feasibility, and scalability

    - Providing feedback on pitches and presentations

    - Guiding teams on best practices and effective teamwork

    - Sharing their industry experience and knowledge of current trends

    Mentors play a crucial part in enriching the hackathon experience, fostering learning, and encouraging innovation among participants. They help create a supportive environment where novice and experienced participants alike can develop their skills, network with professionals, and potentially turn their ideas into viable solutions or products.

16. **Massive Transformative Purpose (MTP)**: An MTP is a clear and compelling mission statement intended to inspire and motivate individuals and organizations to achieve significant breakthroughs and innovations. It goes beyond conventional goals to encapsulate an aspirational vision for making a substantial positive impact on the world or a particular industry. MTPs are often used by start-ups, tech companies, and forward-thinking organizations to guide their long-term strategy and foster a culture of innovation and purpose-driven work.

17. **Innovation theater**: Innovation theater refers to activities that give the appearance of being innovative and forward-thinking without resulting in any substantive change or real-world impact. This can involve the use of buzzwords, flashy presentations, workshops, hackathons, and the creation of innovation labs that are more for show rather than actually fostering a culture of genuine innovation and implementing changes that lead to new successful products or services. The term is often used critically to describe companies that invest in the image of innovation as a marketing tool, rather than committing to the difficult work of actual innovation.

18. **Partner organization**: A partner organization in a hackathon is a company, institution, or entity that collaborates with the hackathon organizers to support the event, typically through sponsorship, providing resources, or offering expertise. These partners can come from various sectors relevant to the hackathon's theme, including technology companies, educational institutions, government agencies, non-profits, and industry associations. The role and involvement of partner organizations can vary significantly depending on the nature of the hackathon and the level of partnership.

    Partner organizations contribute to a hackathon in several ways:

- *Financial support*: They may provide funding to cover the hackathon's costs, such as venue rental, equipment, catering, and prizes for the winners

- *Technical resources*: Partners can offer software licenses, APIs, datasets, and other technical resources that participants can use to develop their projects

- *Mentorship and expertise*: Employees from partner organizations might serve as mentors, sharing their knowledge and experience with participants to help guide project development

- *Networking opportunities*: By involving industry professionals and organizations, hackathons offer participants valuable networking opportunities that can lead to job offers, internships, or partnerships

- *Challenges*: Partners may present specific challenges for participants to address, aligning with the partner's strategic interests or societal goals

Partner organizations benefit from their involvement in hackathons by gaining access to innovative ideas, identifying talent for recruitment, enhancing their brand visibility among a relevant audience, and contributing to the development of solutions that can address real-world problems. This collaboration enriches the hackathon experience, providing participants with more resources, learning opportunities, and potential pathways for their projects' development and commercialization.

19. **Psychological safety** is a concept originating from the 1960s work of Edgar Schein that was further developed by Professor Amy Edmondson. It is a team concept and the experience of team members that they can communicate openly and be themselves without fear of negative consequences. This atmosphere in a team fosters mutual respect and trust, encouraging members to take interpersonal risks, which lays the foundation for innovation and learning. Research has shown that teams with a high degree of psychological safety are more productive and have more engaged team members.

20. **Seed funding** is an initial type of investment commonly used at the beginning of a start-up's journey. It represents one of the earliest stages of funding, often used to prove a concept, build a prototype, or conduct market research. Seed funding helps entrepreneurs take their ideas from the drawing board and turn them into a working product or service.

This type of funding can come from various sources, including the following:

- *Angel investors*: Wealthy individuals who provide capital for a business start-up, usually in exchange for convertible debt or ownership equity

- *Venture capital firms*: Professional groups that manage funds to invest in companies with high growth potential. At the seed stage, these investments are typically smaller

- *Crowdfunding*: Raising small amounts of money from a large number of people, typically via the internet

- *Friends and family*: Personal connections who offer funding support during the early stages
- *Incubators and accelerators*: Programs designed to support start-ups with funding as well as guidance and resources
- *Government grants*: Non-repayable funds provided by government agencies to support new ventures that align with specific goals or initiatives

Seed funding is crucial as it enables entrepreneurs to take the first steps in building a business. However, it also often involves giving away a portion of the company's equity in exchange for the capital. It's a critical phase in the start-up lifecycle and can set the trajectory for future funding rounds.

21. **Sense of urgency**: A sense of urgency refers to the perception and mindset that an action or set of actions needs to be taken promptly and with a clear focus to address an issue, achieve a goal, or seize an opportunity. It involves recognizing the importance of timing and the potential consequences of delay. A sense of urgency is important for several reasons in business. It plays a crucial role in driving effective and timely actions to achieve goals, respond to challenges, and capitalize on opportunities. Cultivating a sense of urgency is about balancing the need for quick action with the importance of deliberate and strategic decision-making. It's not about inducing stress or panic but rather about fostering a culture or mindset that recognizes the value of time and the impact of timely action on success and growth.

22. **Solo hackers**: Hacker participants in a hackathon who choose to join the hackathon on their own, without a team.

23. **Storytelling** is the art and practice of conveying messages, experiences, or narratives through the use of stories. It is a fundamental human activity used for entertainment, education, cultural preservation, and instilling moral values. Storytelling involves a narrator who shares a story with an audience using elements such as characters, plot, conflict, and settings to engage listeners or readers emotionally and intellectually.

The effectiveness of storytelling lies in its ability to connect with people on a personal level, evoke emotions, and inspire actions or changes in perception. It is a powerful communication tool that has been used across cultures and throughout history to pass down knowledge, traditions, and values from one generation to another.

Storytelling is a vital component in business because it taps into the human tendency to be drawn to narratives. It serves as a powerful tool for building brand identity by conveying a company's ethos, values, and vision in a way that is both relatable and memorable. Through storytelling, businesses can significantly enhance customer engagement, as stories are far more captivating than mere facts and figures. This emotional engagement not only makes marketing and advertising efforts more effective but also simplifies complex information, making it more accessible and memorable.

In the realm of sales, the emotional connection fostered by storytelling can directly influence purchasing behavior, as customers are more inclined to buy from brands with which they feel a connection. Beyond external marketing, storytelling plays a crucial role in internal cohesion and culture building. It allows companies to share their history, celebrate successes, and articulate future goals, thus fostering a sense of belonging and alignment with the company's mission among employees.

Storytelling in business goes beyond mere product or service promotion; it's about crafting a narrative that people want to engage with. It leverages the intrinsic human love for stories to inspire, engage, and drive success in a way that traditional business communication methods cannot match.

24. **Sustainability**: The term sustainability involves ensuring our present actions on Earth don't compromise the ability of future generations to meet their needs. It adopts a holistic approach, integrating environmental preservation, social equity, and economic growth to foster an ecosystem. In this era of globalization, sustainability emphasizes the importance of international collaboration. The interconnected nature of our global economy means actions in one region can impact other areas, necessitating a collective approach to environmental challenges, social injustices, and economic disparities. Global collaboration enables the sharing of innovative solutions, resources, and knowledge across borders, enhancing our ability to implement sustainable practices worldwide. Thus, sustainability aims to achieve a balance where economic development, environmental health, and social well-being are in harmony, securing a prosperous future for all.

25. **Start-up post-mortem**: A term used for reports and analyses from failed start-ups, describing the path and main reasons for the failure. There are several companies that provide large databases of post-mortem reports, including Failory and Autopsy. As most start-ups fail, it is crucial to investigate what factors contributed to their failures and address them in an acceleration program, hopefully increasing the chance of success.

26. **Theory of Change**: The **Theory of Change** (ToC) is commonly used in sustainability and social change, using backward mapping to describe the path that leads to the achievement of long-term goals and their impacts. It can be used both as a process map and for evaluation of progress. Interventions (behaviors) and indicators of outcomes (measurable and observable) show what needs to be done along the way to move forward toward the long-term goal. The ToC model invites stakeholders to participate in defining pathways and outcomes, as well as the inherent assumptions underlying causal pathways and contextual factors.

27. **Transformational leadership**: Transformational leadership is a leadership style that includes leading by being a role model, creating a shared vision for the team that motivates and inspires, challenging and stimulating team members in an innovative environment, and paying attention to the individual needs of the members of a team. This type of leadership fits well together with the aim of creating psychological safety in a team.

Index

‹packt›

Other Books You May Enjoy

If you enjoyed this book, you may be interested in these other books by Packt:

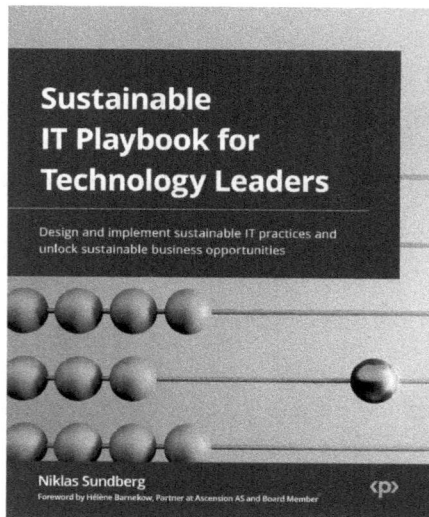

Sustainable IT Playbook for Technology Leaders

Niklas Sundberg

ISBN: 978-1-80323-034-4

- Discover why IT is a major contributor to carbon emissions
- Explore the principles and key methods of sustainable IT practices
- Build a robust, sustainable IT strategy based on proven methods
- Optimize and rationalize your code to consume fewer resources
- Understand your energy consumption patterns
- Apply a circular approach to the IT hardware life cycle
- Establish your sustainable IT baseline
- Inspire and engage employees, customers, and stakeholders

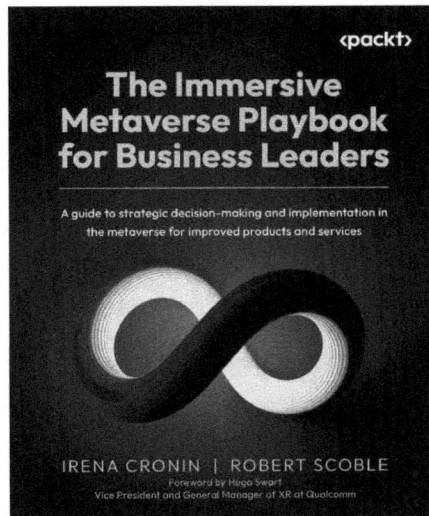

The Immersive Metaverse Playbook for Business Leaders

Irena Cronin, Robert Scoble

ISBN: 978-1-83763-284-8

- Get to grips with the concept of the metaverse, its origin, and its present state
- Understand how AR and VR strategically fit into the metaverse
- Delve into core technologies that power the metaverse
- Dig into use cases that enable finer strategic decision-making
- Understand the benefits and possible dangers of the metaverse
- Plan further ahead by understanding the future of the metaverse

Packt is searching for authors like you

If you're interested in becoming an author for Packt, please visit `authors.packtpub.com` and apply today. We have worked with thousands of developers and tech professionals, just like you, to help them share their insight with the global tech community. You can make a general application, apply for a specific hot topic that we are recruiting an author for, or submit your own idea.

Share Your Thoughts

Now you've finished *Dream! Hack! Build!*, we'd love to hear your thoughts! Scan the QR code below to go straight to the Amazon review page for this book and share your feedback or leave a review on the site that you purchased it from.

https://packt.link/r/1-835-08533-4

Your review is important to us and the tech community and will help us make sure we're delivering excellent quality content.

Download a free PDF copy of this book

Thanks for purchasing this book!

Do you like to read on the go but are unable to carry your print books everywhere?

Is your eBook purchase not compatible with the device of your choice?

Don't worry, now with every Packt book you get a DRM-free PDF version of that book at no cost.

Read anywhere, any place, on any device. Search, copy, and paste code from your favorite technical books directly into your application.

The perks don't stop there, you can get exclusive access to discounts, newsletters, and great free content in your inbox daily

Follow these simple steps to get the benefits:

1. Scan the QR code or visit the link below

https://packt.link/free-ebook/9781835085332

2. Submit your proof of purchase
3. That's it! We'll send your free PDF and other benefits to your email directly

www.ingramcontent.com/pod-product-compliance
Lightning Source LLC
Chambersburg PA
CBHW061807210326
41599CB00034B/6916